Global Libidinal Economy

Global Libidinal Economy

Ilan Kapoor, Gavin Fridell,
Maureen Sioh, and Pieter de Vries

SUNY
PRESS

Cover image courtesy of Anish Kapoor, *Untitled*, 2004. Fiberglass, rubber, aluminum, 128 x 128 x 54 cm. © All rights reserved DACS/ARS, 2022.

Published by State University of New York Press, Albany

For information, contact State University of New York Press, Albany, NY
www.sunypress.edu

Library of Congress Cataloging-in-Publication Data

Names: Kapoor, Ilan, author. | Fridell, Gavin, author. | Sioh, Maureen Kim Lian, 1962– author. | de Vries, Pieter, 1958– author.
Title: Global libidinal economy / Ilan Kapoor, Gavin Fridell, Maureen Sioh, and Pieter de Vries.
Description: Albany : State University of New York Press, [2023] | Includes bibliographical references and index
Identifiers: LCCN 2022041856 | ISBN 9781438493398 (hardcover : alk. paper) | ISBN 9781438493374 (ebook) | ISBN 9781438493381 (pbk. : alk. paper)
Subjects: LCSH: Economic history. | Economics—Psychological aspects.
Classification: LCC HC26 .K37 2023 | DDC 330.019—dc23/eng/20220920
LC record available at https://lccn.loc.gov/2022041856

10 9 8 7 6 5 4 3 2 1

Contents

Acknowledgments

We are most grateful to the two anonymous reviewers for their very positive and helpful feedback. We would also like to thank Michael Rinella and the SUNY Press team for all their efforts. And our immense gratitude, as always, to our families and friends for their love and support.

Ilan Kapoor would like to gratefully acknowledge the support of a SSHRC Insight grant (Social Sciences and Humanities Research Council, Canada), and Gavin Fridell would like to thank the Canada Research Chairs program.

Preface

This book claims that the libidinal—the site of unconscious desire—plays not a supplementary or trivial but a constitutive role in global political economy. For both Freud and Lacan, our emergence as human animals from nature into culture is accompanied by profound loss and alienation (from a mythical sense of wholeness), which we inevitably bring to all our pursuits, be they private or public, material or symbolic, economic or political. Political economy is thereby unavoidably infused with human desire (to recover such wholeness or harmony): consumption, for example, is not simply a way of satisfying a material or biological need but a doomed attempt to soothe our deep sense of loss; and capital is not just a means to material growth and prosperity but, as Marx himself underlined, is invested with "cunning"—what psychoanalysis would call "drive"—that seduces, beguiles, and manipulates in the service of unending "accumulation for accumulation's sake." Thus, in contradistinction to political economy, which assumes a rational subject, libidinal economy is founded on the notion of a desiring subject, which obeys a logic not of equanimity, good sense, and self-interest but unpredictability, profligacy, and indeed irrationality. Hence, by applying a psychoanalytic lens to political economy, our book seeks to uncover the libidinal excesses and antagonisms of global political-economic phenomena.

Our book will show how global libidinal economy differs from the two main approaches to international political economy (IPE)—conventional IPE (classical, neoclassical, neoliberal) and Marxist IPE.[1] The former is predicated on the assumption of an autonomous, rational, self-interested, and advantage-maximizing subject, upon which the goal of a "self-regulating" and "efficient" market, in turn, depends. Here, not only are growth and profit maximization taken for granted, but economic and policy failure are seen as the result of human "error," rectifiable through better policy or intensified efforts to expand or create new market mechanisms. In contrast, Marxist IPE, while also assuming a rational and intelligent subject, takes pains to deobjectify the market, seeing it not as a given or a good but as a sociohistorical construction infused with power inequalities. Here too growth is taken for granted, although failure is now seen at the level not of the individual but of the structure, requiring enlightened collective/state control of capital to better distribute the gains of growth and ensure universal equality.

But libidinal economy suggests that there is more to political economy than meets the eye of either conventional or Marxist IPE. What both miss is the psychoanalytic insight into the obscene unconscious supplement that always already accompanies the global capitalist system and upon which the latter in fact relies. Several examples can be cited here: (a) it is the insatiability of desire that helps explain the relentless drive to accumulate, leading to such irrational phenomena as overconsumption, excessive waste, and environmental destruction—to the point of imperiling not just accumulation but life itself; (b) it is not only the socioeconomic gap between countries but also its accompanying psychic anxieties—the fear of rich countries that "emerging" countries will catch up with, if not overtake, them, and the fear of poorer countries that they will never catch up—that help explain continuing tensions between global North and South today; (c) it is because people tend to be libidinally seduced by capitalism in their pursuit of *jouissance*—they *love* money, iPhones, and corporate media spectacle—that they continue to be invested in it despite knowing better (that is, despite being aware that capitalism implies exploitation, inequality, unevenness, and environmental destruction); (d) it is the sadomasochistic underpinnings of desire that help shed light on the dimensions of humiliation, if not racist enjoyment, involved in structurally adjusting "Third World"[2] countries—auditing them, disciplining them, bringing them to account; and, finally, (e) it is not self-interest but self-sacrifice, notably that of women, which, as Luce Irigaray (1985, 190–91; 1986, 11–12) has argued, enables the nurturing social reproduction that global capitalism depends on yet takes for granted.

Our book expands on these and other examples to make the point that the neglect of the unconscious by IPE has caused it to underestimate not just the irrationality and exuberance of global capitalism but also its durability: capitalism's libidinal seduction of the subject reveals its extraordinary ability to reproduce itself in spite—and because—of crisis. In this sense, we largely agree with Marx's analysis of the crisis-prone nature of capitalism but seek to broaden and radicalize[3] it by focusing on the global libidinal circuits that subtend the ebbs and flows of political economy.

Our book will draw mainly on (post-)Freudian and Lacanian psychoanalysis, including the work of feminist psychoanalytic thinkers (e.g., Teresa Brennan), to make its case for a global libidinal economy. While critical of IPE (especially its classical and neoclassical variants), our intention is not to try and supplant it but to broaden and deepen it (particularly its Marxist variants, whose critique of capitalism we are partial to, although not without disagreements) by heeding its libidinal underpinnings. This is why we take as our main object of analysis the *global capitalist system*. Accordingly, we have elected to structure the book around key IPE categories such as "production," "consumption," "production," "informal economy," "trade," "financialization," "ecology," and "state," while also bringing out significant contemporary themes relating to "gender" and "race." Our overall aim, though, is to unearth not just the political economy mechanisms but also the unconscious libidinal workings of global capitalism as expressed in these categories. The intention here is not to be comprehensive (of either psychoanalysis or GLE) but to analyze what we see as the significant sites of psychoanalytic-economico-political contestation today.

It should be noted, in this regard, that China is the focus of two chapters (trade and the state), indicative of both its growing politico-economic presence in the global market and the accompanying intellectual interest in its role as "emerging" power. What this book adds are the libidinal dynamics at play in such emergence. Also noteworthy is that we illustrate our arguments by drawing on a number of examples and fieldwork-based case studies (e.g., fair/free trade, global value chains, sweatshop labor, land politics, 5G technology, China's Belt and Road Initiative, popular urban governance, communal conservation) focusing on both global South and North (North-South relations; US-China trade and technology politics; political ecology/economy of the Caribbean, Colombia, and Brazil; financialization in the West).

Global Libidinal Economy

International Political Economy
Versus Global Libidinal Economy

If IPE investigates the economic flows and political governance that transcend the nation-state, then global libidinal economy (GLE) analyzes the latter's accompanying unconscious circuits of excess and antagonism. GLE takes the view that, because unconscious desires are unpredictable and profligate, they necessarily disrupt, divert, or deny global economico-political circuits. In this sense, GLE brings attention to the discontinuities and gaps of such circuits—the dirty underside of cross-border decisions about growth or investment in the form of, say, overconsumption or racist humiliation—which conventional IPE tends to ignore or cover up. The goal of this chapter, accordingly, is to compare and contrast (neo)classical and Marxist IPE with GLE by highlighting the importunate role played by the libidinal.[1]

Both classical and neoclassical political economy are premised on *homo economicus*—the figure of the "economic man [*sic*]" who pursues rational and self-interested ends. Classical economist Adam Smith's notion of the self-regulating market assumes (and requires) the prevalence of order and reason for the "invisible hand" of market-organized decision making to take place. According to him, it is the "free" play of rationality and self-interest that brings about the efficiency of the capitalist market as a distributive mechanism. Thus, he famously writes that it is "not from the benevolence of the butcher, the brewer, or the baker that we expect our dinner, but from their regard to their own interests" (1997, 119). In the same vein, early neoclassical economist William Stanley Jevons depicts his theory of political economy as "the mechanics of utility and self-interest" (1970, 90; see also Mill 2004; Locke 2003, 2006; D. Bennett 2011, 10), emphasizing the economic rationality that upholds typical consumer choices. Like Smith, he depicts market actors as independent subjects whose behavior is determined only by market-maximizing calculations. Here, "irrational" market behavior, to the extent that it occurs, is the result not of misguided consumer choices but external market intrusions, principally those of the government. Indeed, neoclassical IPE, just like its classical variant, demands a minimal, "nightwatchman" state, whose role is to provide the necessary conditions (e.g., law and order, private property, and contract protections) for a well-functioning, competitive market. For Jevons and his ilk, it is when governments overstep their nightwatchman role that freedom is constrained, economic rationality suffers, and markets falter.

A similar mind frame is to be found in contemporary variants of neoclassical political economy—rational choice theory, game theory—the former proposing that out of a set of various courses of action available to them, subjects (individuals, corporations) select the one they consider most preferable (Homans 1961; M. Friedman 1963; Coleman 1990), the latter that each subject's choices depend on other subjects' choices, like in a game of strategy (Von Neumann and Morgenstern 1953). Both variants aim to not only describe market behavior but predict it, most often requiring increasingly complex mathematical modeling to factor in anything from prices and savings to elections results and weather patterns. Once again, both hinge on the presence of rational, calculating actors—increasingly within the context of the information economy—the goal being to maximize preferences and profits.

But if rational calculation is privileged in (neo)classical thought, this is not to say that the question of human passions is ignored. Utilitarianism, after all, argues for a "felicific calculus" through which subjects maximize their utility. Jeremy Bentham (1996) suggests that people calculate profit and loss by weighing up pleasure and pain, so that, for example, while the consumption of sugar may be pleasurable, there may be unpleasant health side effects that override one's pleasure. Likewise, in his *Mathematical Psychics* (1967), Francis Edgeworth sees all pleasure as measurable, with the rate of pleasure of a typical commodity decreasing the more of it we consume. But what is noteworthy here is that, while valorizing the psyche, these neoclassical economists subject it to a *calculus*, that is, to reason: rationality trumps passion in the service of the market. Desire is curtailed of its excess and unpredictability in order for *homo economicus* to remain an autonomous, rational, and self-interested market subject. As David Bennett (2011, 12) puts it, this is a "psychologically anorexic model of 'economic man,'" that is, "not so much a colonisation of economics by its traditional other, psychology, as a takeover of psychology by neoclassical economics."

Bennett (1999, 2010) shows in fact how eighteenth- and nineteenth-century Britain, precisely where much of neoclassical political economy was being theorized, witnessed various forms of curtailment of sexual desire. The need to preserve bodily energy, rather than recklessly expend it, became a priority, with masturbation and prostitution emerging as two practices targeted for institutionalized repression. The former, pruriently termed "onanism," was not only discouraged (by the church, medical establishment, etc.) but came to be associated with a growing list of symptoms, including blindness, imbecility, insanity, homosexuality, and death. For its part, prostitution was condemned as not just sinful but also wasteful: those frequenting brothels were seen as nonreproductive fornicators, while prostitutes themselves were associated with profligate "spending" in both the sexual and economic sense—sexually depraved but also conspicuous consumers (as opposed to "savers"). The overarching goal here, according to Bennett, was the subjection of desire to the productivist needs of capitalism, with bodily energies treated as assets to be economized and managed rather than squandered: "While masturbators were censured for wastefully draining their own libido and hence the productive energy needed to build commerce and industry, many Victorian social hygienists focused their anxiety about wasted libidinal expenditure on prostitutes, believing it was mainly they who drained men's seminal fluid and that at the bottom of the slippery slope on which the masturbator embarked was the brothel" (2010, 98).

It is remarkable that more than a century after the Victorian era, under late capitalism, we have moved from the curbing of desire for productivist purposes to its opposite: the embrace of libidinal expenditure for the purposes of mass consumption. This is because, as Todd McGowan explains (2004, 31), the prohibition of enjoyment in favor of productivism has become a limit to recent transformations in global capitalism—the emergence of monopoly capitalism and consumer culture—with the result that, rather than restraining libidinal enjoyment, late capitalism *commands* it (more on this below). Witness, for example, our increasing access to easy and fast credit so we can shop uninhibitedly, or the ubiquity of advertisements that beckon us to indulge our desires (e.g., Coca-Cola's "Enjoy!," Nike's "Just Do It!"). We are encouraged to coddle our libidinal extravagance in order that the late capitalist machine keep churning. So we are all (encouraged to be) masturbators and prostitutes now! No wonder that neoliberal gurus—from Ludwig von Mises (1966) to Milton Friedman (1957)—see "free" consumer choice as the defining feature of market economies. For them, the sovereign consumer is an "agent" capable of leading, if not dictating, economic production. Their overall implication, though, is that, if (neo)classical political economy previously needed to tame our passions in order that we save and labor in the service of production, it now needs us to indulge our passions in order to shop and luxuriate in the service of consumerism. Despite appearances, rationality is still very much in charge here, directing and managing desire to the changing requirements of the market.

Yet, from the perspective of Marxist IPE, it is precisely the dominance of this market rationality that is troubling. For Marx (1887, 311–12; 1993, 650) such rationality perpetuates the liberal myth that the market is benign and "free" (and hence the preferred object of a rational calculus). He argues that neither free markets nor free labor are (or ever have been) the norm. What the "invisible hand" of the market ensures most is the survival of the fittest, with the tendency toward the domination of the few (monopolies, oligopolies) more the rule than the exception. Capital, in this sense, is not simply a set of tangible assets, as (neo)classical IPE appears to think, but a form of disciplinary power. This is no more evident than with regard to labor, which neoclassical IPE appears to mostly ignore in its analysis (Marx 1993, 273–74). Rather than enabling people to freely sell their labor to the highest bidder, private capital coerces them into an exploitative system of wage labor to systematically extract surplus value. Marx draws in part here on classical economist David Ricardo, who, in contrast to Adam Smith, is pessimistic as to the distributive implications of capitalist markets: according to Ricardo (1876, 50–59), the combination of competition and plentiful labor supply under capitalism often implies an "iron law of wages," as a result of which workers' wages tend toward subsistence. Marx agrees, pointing up the resulting socioeconomic inequality and class oppression.

To be sure, unlike (neo)classical IPE, which tends to focus on the micropersonal and subjective (individual freedom, entrepreneurship, etc.), Marxist IPE tends to emphasize the broader macrostructural elements of market capitalism. Foremost, according to this view, is the basic class antagonism and social inequality that inheres between wage laborers and the bourgeoisie (those who own the means of production). In contrast to the neoclassical idea of social harmony produced by the market, Marxist IPE points up the indispensable social inequality on which capitalism is based as a result of historically generated power relations. Here the state is seen as the institutionalization of such unequal power relations, sometimes acting as a tool in the hands of the ruling classes to ensure the status quo, but sometimes also able to play a more remedial and progressive role in class-divided societies (Poulantzas 1975; Miliband 1983; Evans, Rueschemeyer, and Skocpol 1985).

Moreover, unlike neoclassical IPE, which tends to emphasize national economies as self-enclosed orders (i.e., a nation-state world order), Marxist IPE sees market capitalism itself as a globally structuring force so that the capitalist system, driven by the production of surplus value as an "absolute law" (Marx 1970, 436), is a de facto global system. The latter expands spatially at certain historical periods, penetrating new and distant markets everywhere. And because spatial and socioeconomic inequality is integral to capitalism, the globalization of capital necessarily results in uneven development and new forms of disciplinary power (between and among nation-states, the poor and the rich, urban centers and hinterlands, monopoly capital and small entrepreneurs, etc.) (Frank 1967; Wallerstein 2004; Hopkins and Wallerstein 1977; P. Evans 1979; Jenkins 2014; Harvey 2006).

There is no doubt that Marxist IPE as outlined above takes a rationalist view of the world. Like (neo)classical IPE, reason is privileged as a way of investigating our socioeconomic predicament, but unlike (neo)classical IPE, rationality is here seen as a way not of justifying the (capitalist) status quo but of criticizing it and finding a way out. In this regard, Marx was a critic of all forms of obscurantism (including religion) and a firm believer in science and technology, which he thought could also—under the conditions of the collective ownership of the means of production—help in increasing productivity and reducing the drudgery and brutality of labor (Marx and Engels 2003, 1:18; Marx 1992, 389). Moreover, drawing on his reading of Hegel, he interprets human history as a movement toward greater rationality, arguing in favor of a genuinely rational (communist) society in which people could be free (Marx and Engels 2003, 16:474–75; see also Megill 2002, 81ff.).

But this is not to say that Marx ignores human passions or fails to recognize a role for desire in political economy. Alienation, for him, after all, is constitutive of human subjectivity, so that under coercive capitalist conditions, workers are alienated as much from the labor process and products of their labor as from their "species being" (as free, social, and self-realized creators) (Marx 1992, 385–86; Marx and Engels 2003, 3:332–33). Nowhere is such alienation more evident than in what he famously terms "commodity fetishism": "A commodity is therefore a mysterious thing, simply because in it the social character of men's labour appears to them as an objective character stamped upon the product of that labour. . . . There it is a definite social relation between men [*sic*], that assumes, in their eyes, the fantastic form of a relation between things" (1887, 47–48). It is thus because we are seduced by commodities at the level of unconscious desire that, according to him, the social relations between producers are transformed into a relation between things. He does not dwell on this psychoanalytic dimension, putting his faith in the ability of rationality to eventually triumph over social alienation, but it seems clear that he sees the "mysterious" character of desire as a kind of negativity, a rupture, leading to the unthinking and irrational behavior of the market subject. No wonder, then, that Althusser, in his famous essay "On Marx and Freud" (1991, 19ff.), suggests that, despite their differences, one thing Marxism and psychoanalysis share is that they are both antagonistic and conflictual. Marx might champion reason over passion, but like Freud, he sees the subject as split, unstable, out-of-joint, conflicted.

So then if (neo)classical IPE either ignores unconscious desire or tames it to conform to the needs of market capitalism, and Marxist IPE acknowledges it but stops short of developing its antagonistic dimensions, how are we to conceive of a global libidinal economy that incorporates both unconscious desire and this nonconforming, "conflictual" dimension? Psychoanalysis focuses precisely on the question of unconscious desire as a privileged entry point to understanding and engaging with the antagonisms that always already beset us as human animals. For both Freud (1961, 14) and Lacan (1998, 219), our separation from the parent and acculturation into the social world is accompanied by a deep sense of loss (from a mythical sense of unity and wholeness), of which we can never rid ourselves. Our entrance into society *requires* the trauma of castration, which manifests as a never-ending (unconscious) desire to soothe such loss, to recover such imaginary oneness. A psychoanalytic take on political economy thus implies that desire plays not a supplementary or trivial but a constitutive role in economico-political phenomena: "Every political economy is libidinal," writes Lyotard (1993, 111), suggesting that

GLE is founded on a desiring subject and hence that market activities are not simply unavoidably imbued with, but invariably overwhelmed and overtaken by, human desire.

Indeed, what is peculiar about the psychoanalytic view is its decentering of the subject: always punctured by internal conflict and alienation, said subject is seen as inevitably failing to achieve unity, stability, or sovereignty.[2] This is because unconscious desire follows a logic not of predictability and reason but of anxiety, enjoyment, and excess that outwit and destabilize the "knowing subject." But how, exactly? Crucial here is the notion of the "death drive" (or "drive" for short), which Freud discovered in 1920 with the publication of his *Beyond the Pleasure Principle*. He sees the drive not as a human predilection toward aggression and self-annihilation (which is how some, like Marcuse [1955, 51], have interpreted it) but as a predominant social force that manifests as a "compulsion to repeat" (Freud 1961, 38). The subject, according to him, is driven to endlessly repeat the experience of the primordial loss, taking profligate pleasure from such repetition. It is for this reason that Lacan coins the term "enjoyment" (*jouissance*), which he closely associates with drive (1997, 211), aimed at describing not simply the pleasure taken in repetition but the immoderate and excessive lengths the subject may go to in its compulsion to repeat. The death drive, in this sense, refers not to death as an end point, but to the death that occurs within life itself: an eternal undeadness, the "horrible fate of being caught in the endless repetitive cycle of wandering around in guilt and pain," as Žižek puts it (2006, 62). Unable to free itself from the drive's constant needling and excess, the subject is condemned to both suffer enjoyment and enjoy suffering.

The implications of this pleasurable "compulsion to repeat" are far-reaching. It means that the subject acts not necessarily based on what it knows but on what it unconsciously desires and enjoys. The gaps in the subject's knowledge are revealing precisely of a kernel of enjoyment, of which the subject is unaware (and upon which psychoanalysis dwells as a primary object of investigation). Such enjoyment entails that there is a chasm between what the subject knows and what it says and does, but also that the subject may actually desire *not* to know in the expectation of excess and pleasurability. In the same way that the bungee jumper derives thrill not despite but *because* of the danger involved, the subject is moved by the orgasmic experience of recreating the experience of loss, even if it yields to a certain recklessness. For it is indeed the idiotic stupor of enjoyment that makes life worth living, giving it "spice" for all of its foolhardiness.

Yet, organizing life around enjoyment and the avoidance of knowledge inevitably entails self-sabotage. To continually repeat something despite the damage being done, to never learn from one's mistakes because of the pleasure derived from repeating them, is self-destructive. It means acting against one's own self-interest. The death drive thus involves working unconsciously against social betterment, dooming the prospect of progress. Or to turn that around: any progress toward the good implies the contrary antagonistic move to undermine it. The drive, in this sense, is a fundamentally rupturous impulse that obeys an idiotic and irrational logic, which ends up subverting the "normal" flow of things.

We can better glean now why libidinal economy runs counter to (neo)classical IPE. For GLE, the subject is not an autonomous and free agent, as the neoclassicals like to think, but on the contrary, a fundamentally split and alienated subject, often overcome by anxiety and contradiction. Unable to keep a lid on its desires, the subject does *not* necessarily know its interests: its desires obey a logic that runs counter to reason and predictability, often diverting and undermining its intentions, plans, and projects. Libidinal economy thus puts into doubt the "homeostatic model" of market stability and order that supports economic (neo)liberalism. While the latter does take into account human desires, these are gentrified, as underlined earlier—tamed and managed to serve the market. Accordingly, desire is conceptualized in the form of two opposite poles, with the subject seeking pleasure and avoiding pain. Yet it is *by* keeping the two apart that a homeostatic model can be maintained: admitting *jouissance*—taking pleasure in pain and pain in pleasure—would disrupt rationality and stability, since it would entail that market actors actually enjoy making irrational decisions (see chapters 3 and 6).

In other words, what GLE forefronts, and what (neo)classical IPE ignores or disavows, is this "dirty underside" of capitalism. Adam Smith and his peers believe in the "natural" propensity to accumulate, enabling the capitalist to overcome material or technological constraints. What they elide, though, is the prospect that the capitalist might actually enjoy rather than surmount these very constraints. To wit: the unrelenting drive to accumulate, which under late global capitalism especially results in the corporate monopolization or oligopolization of the market, ensuring the demise of small and medium-sized firms and thereby threatening the very rule of "free competition" upon which neoclassical markets are purportedly based (see chapter 2); the corporate obsession with amassing monopoly profits rather than seeking efficient production, which, as Veblen points out (1904, 1965), yields to the deliberate *under*utilization of capital and labor (and hence to unemployment and a growing reserve army of labor and precarious workers, especially in the global South) (see chapters 4 and 6); or perhaps most flagrantly, late capitalist overaccumulation to the point of recklessness and self-annihilation, as witnessed by our current global environmental crisis, which perhaps best illustrates the self-sabotage of the death drive (i.e., unending capitalist accumulation that puts the planet, and our very survival as a species, in grave jeopardy; see chapter 7). To be sure, rather than viewing this planetary crisis as inherent to the system, neoclassical IPE treats it as an "externality" in need of correction through policy intervention (e.g., green technology), all the while failing to grapple with the libidinal investment that propels capitalist (over)accumulation in the first place.

But the recklessness of desire is to be found not just in patterns of accumulation but also in consumption, which stands as the "ultimate driving force of individual advancement" in neoclassical IPE (Gammon and Palan 2006, 102). The problem with neoclassical political economy is that it assumes that, subject to self-interest, consumption remains stable and can be satisfied "rationally" (Pareto 2014, chap. 3). But then it cannot account for such things as unproductive expenditure: what Bataille (1986) characterizes as the self-wasting drive of ecstatic and gratuitous spending, or what Veblen (2006) sees as the "irrational" conspicuous consumption of the wealthy, more interested in showing off their wealth than using it productively.[3] True, as mentioned earlier, in our late capitalist times we have moved away from such a "productivist" ethic toward the incitement of greater consumptive excess: we are now encouraged to "enjoy" conspicuous shopping (see chapters 3 and 6). But now the recklessness lies in how some consumers, by emulating the extravagance of the wealthy and famous, end up endangering their own lives as well as that of their families by overspending (e.g., buying a luxury car at the expense of health insurance, desperately engaging in the drug economy in order to emulate the lifestyles of the rich and famous), or in how overconsumption implies growing waste, garbage, and pollution (most often "dumped" near where indigenous, racialized, and poor remote communities live, especially but not exclusively in the global South). In either case, neoclassical political economy fails to acknowledge or account for the irrationality and damaging socioecological consequences of consumption.[4]

Perhaps the most concerning characteristic of *jouissance* is its sado-masochism, which stems from its recklessness. Indeed, the peculiarity of enjoyment is that it often implicates not just one's own self-destruction but that of others—by reveling in their subordination, suffering, or failings. Here the subject takes cruel enjoyment in dominating others, whether it be in the form of corporate managers or contractors bossing around their (often gendered and racialized) sweatshop workers, the patriarch controlling his household, urban elites dispossessing marginalized communities in favor of the privatization of the commons, aid workers lording it over Third World "recipients," or masculinist international financial institutions "structurally adjusting"—controlling, auditing, disciplining—their debtors (Kapoor 2020, 273–85). Maureen Sioh (2018b) draws attention, for example, to the racist humiliation involved in the Western economic disciplining of Asian economies during the late 1990s Asian Economic Crisis (see chapter 5 and 8), while Dan Bousfield (2018) highlights the racialized hierarchies underpinning Northern European "rational" financial responses to Southern European debt crises. Neoclassical IPE seems only too happy to disavow such inconvenient *irrational* proclivities from its calculus, and as such appears as little other than an ideological justification of the domination and inequalities inherent to the global capitalist system.

As to Marxist IPE, we have already indicated GLE's alignment with it on maintaining the (global) capitalist system as a primary focus of analysis, but especially on the question of antagonism. As McGowan puts it (2013, 7), "Where Freud sees antagonism manifesting itself in the excessive suffering of the individual subject, Marx sees it playing out in class struggle. Despite this difference in focus, they share a belief in the fundamental status of antagonism, which separates them from political thinkers (such as John Stuart Mill and John Rawls) who view the social order as whole, as divided by conflicts but not by a fundamental antagonism." Nonetheless, by inadequately considering the negativity represented by unconscious desire, what Marxist IPE underestimates, ironically, is the "stuckness" and intractability of the material world—the extent to which people become attached to and invested in capitalism, as witnessed not only by their fetishization of consumer goods but also by their libidinal attraction to exploitation and domination of the other (e.g., sweatshop laborers, gendered and racialized groups, aid recipients, Third World debtors, etc.; see chapters 2, 4, 5, and 6). While Marx understood well the power of capital in enforcing inequality and wage slavery, he undervalued the extent to which people can acquiesce to such domination because of their fetishization/enjoyment of the system. Social hierarchy may well be abhorrent, but as much those at the top as on the bottom of the social pyramid can accede to it, as long as there are others below them that they can subordinate or feel superior to (see chapter 5). And commodity fetishism may well obfuscate exploitative social relationships, but even those who are exploited may enjoy, through processes of disavowal, cheap fast food and sweatshop-produced commodities (see chapter 6).

Moreover, while Marx sees antagonism as inherent to capitalism, he does away with it under his ideal collectivized communist regime: once the private appropriation of surplus value has been replaced by the generation of surplus for the common good, he envisions a society without antagonism (Marx and Engels 1970, 51–59). But this is an option that psychoanalysis indubitably repudiates because antagonism is understood as constitutive of our social (and linguistic) structure (McGowan 2013, 9; Žižek 2006, 266–67). To be sure, for GLE antagonism is inherent not just to the capitalist system but to any society, so that even a postcapitalist society would have to contend with the negativity of unconscious desire in all its forms (envy, enjoyment, perversion, drive, etc.). Antagonism means the impossibility of stability, harmony, goodness, or reconciliation. In fact, it is precisely the impossibility of resolution that keeps life (and politics) going, so that without it Marx is at pains to explain how and for what purpose, say, accumulation would continue (what would "drive" it if not some form of enjoyment, with all the latter's attendant perils?) or why envy and domination—generated by new forms of social differentiation (e.g., Communist Party "insiders" vs. "outsiders")—would disappear, as indeed they didn't, as witnessed by the socialist experiments of Soviet Russia, China, Vietnam, North Korea, or Cuba.

Notwithstanding this lacuna, it is important to ask what role antagonism—so central to both Marxist IPE and GLE yet disavowed by (neo) classical political economy—plays in our global capitalist system. The short answer is: the global capitalist system abhors negativity even as it crucially depends on it. That it repudiates antagonism should come as no surprise, since as (neo)classical IPE strongly maintains, the market requires reason, stability, and order to function well (i.e., to ensure unfettered capital accumulation and mobility). As Samo Tomšič writes, "Capitalism is grounded precisely . . . on the foreclosure of negativity. [It] rejects the paradigm of negativity, castration: the symbolic operation that constitutes the subject as split and decentralised" (2015, 163). This is also why, as we have previously stressed, capitalism (and by extension, neoclassical IPE) admits only those human passions that conform with productivism and consumerism: unbridled pleasure and happiness are embraced, while pain is forsaken. It is precisely this disavowal of structural negativity to which Marx draws our attention, underlining how capitalism is founded on the distortion of social antagonisms/class struggle. The ostensibly harmonious, apolitical, and objective nature of neoclassical IPE is thus meant to cover over the rapacious and unstable nature of the system, as we have outlined above. In fact, what neoclassical IPE denies is the very systemic nature of capitalism: systems—capitalist or not—are constructed on the basis of an exclusion, an irreducible negativity, so that what is strategically obscured in neoclassical political economy is "the psychoanalytic insight into the obscene supplement (of violence and repression) that necessarily accompanies every system and upon which the latter implicitly relies" (Daly 2006, 186).

Several examples can be cited to illustrate this: capitalism's fundamental reliance on surplus extraction, exploitation, and socioeconomic inequality, yet its ideological masking of them through the promotion of such ideals as happiness, pleasure, opportunity, and "freedom of choice" (Žižek 1989; see also chapter 3); the recurring cycle of economic booms and busts inherent to the global system (viz. the Third World debt crisis [1980s–1990s], the Asian financial crisis [1997], the global financial crisis [2007–8], etc.), upon which the massive fortunes of banks and financial speculators are made and sometimes lost, yet whose human costs in the form of unemployment, homelessness, or racialized and gendered poverty are rationalized as temporary and solvable (see chapter 6); and the inclusion of only those activities considered "rational" and "efficient" in such key economic measures as GDP, resulting in the exclusion (and taking for granted) of such gendered activities as domestic work, the care economy, and subsistence agriculture (see chapters 2 and 4), upon which social reproduction and growth count (Gibson-Graham 1996).

But to bring out the specifically psychoanalytic dimensions of capitalism's vital reliance on, yet disavowal of, negation, let us consider briefly the role played by desire and drive (further developed and illustrated in chapters 2, 3, and 6). For Lacan, both compulsions stem from our ontological loss as linguistic beings—they are the libidinal supplement to our emergence as subjects, our entry into the sociolinguistic world. But desire targets (putatively lost) objects to try and satisfy the subject's ontological lack, whereas drive targets not objects per se but the unending circulation around them as a recurring enactment of imaginary loss (Lacan 1998, 179). Thus, while the goal of desire is to obtain the object, the goal of drive is (enjoyment in) ceaseless looping and repetitiousness (recalling our earlier discussion of the death drive's compulsion to repeat). Žižek sees the operations of desire and drive so conceived as constitutive of capitalism's expansive movement: "At the immediate level of addressing individuals, capitalism . . . interpellates [us] as consumers, as subjects of desire, soliciting in [us] ever new perverse and excessive desires (for which it offers products to satisfy them). . . . Drive inheres to capitalism at a more fundamental, *systemic* level: drive is that which propels the whole capitalist machinery, it is the impersonal compulsion to engage in the endless circular movement of expanded self-reproduction" (2006, 61; see also Dean 2012). Highlighted here is how capitalism exploits desire in its quest to push consumerism: the desiring subject is encouraged to engage in continuous shopping in search of the "real thing," which always proves elusive. The iPhone or cola drink temporarily gratifies but never quite satisfies. But that is precisely the point: the goal of capitalist accumulation is to ensure consumers keep coming back for more by exploiting their fundamental lack, while at the same time stimulating their desire through the construction of fantasy (i.e., product advertising) and the cheap availability of credit. Meanwhile, at the broader level of capitalist accumulation, it is not desire but drive that is at play. Here, the fundamental compulsion to repeat manifests as the circular drive to "accumulation for accumulation's sake" (Marx 2004, 652). Capitalism feeds off drive's perpetual re-enactment and enjoyment of loss to accumulate more capital, amass more profits, conquer new markets, and create "new" and "better" technologies and products (i.e., product/technological differentiation and obsolescence).

We thus glean how the capitalist system hinges on desire and drive to advance accumulation. The problem, though, is that it either disavows the negative and reckless implications of such unconscious compulsions as discussed above (i.e., socioeconomic exploitation, overconsumption, environmental crisis, sadomasochism, etc.) or it dissuades or represses the negative political possibilities of desire and drive. Indeed, it is revealing that capitalist liberal democracies "tolerate" and increasingly encourage desire in the (positive) form of identity: demands for recognition and civil-political rights (based on sexual, gender, racial, and other identities) are not only acceded—because they pose no real risk to capital accumulation and mobility—but celebrated and commodified (e.g., gay pride, "ethnic chic," green products, etc.) to the extent that they help advance consumerism and the conquest of new markets (Žižek 1997). It is also revealing that psychoanalysis itself is (and has been) minoritized as a discourse, most likely because it is seen as threatening to the system, founded as it is on castration, disequilibrium, and collective alienation, in contradistinction to the broader field of psychology (e.g., behavioral therapy, cognitive psychology, etc.) that appears to thrive in its objective to conform to the demands of the market (reduction of mental "disorders," healing, and reintegration of the individualized subject into society, etc.).

But then how might the negativity of desire and drive be deployed in the service of an antisystemic politics? One route is to orient our desires away from consumerist or productivist enjoyment (which conforms to the capitalist market) toward anti- and postcapitalist alternatives (e.g., social and community economies that put the subaltern first, worker-owned enterprises, transnational regulation of multinationals, a politics of the [intellectual, natural, genetic] commons, antiracist popular education, etc.). Our subsequent chapters will probe the conditions of possibility of such options, but the challenge for the Left will be to find ways of not only constructing and promoting these postcapitalist fantasies but of making them seductive. For, as chapters 3, 4, and 6 will point out, it is fantasy that trains and orients desire, so that the political test then becomes one of building Left fantasies that thrill and attract (Kapoor 2020, 227–30), making them at least as seductive and enjoyable as those constructed by the Right (e.g., through the deployment of nationalism) or indeed the market (e.g., through product advertising). To be sure, with few exceptions, the Left has been much less successful than the Right in deploying social passions for political purposes; psychoanalysis offers a way of doing so that harnesses the critical-negative dimensions of the unconscious.

The other, more radical,[5] political route is the one offered by drive: drawing on Žižek, Kapoor (2015b, 75–76; 2020, 88–90, 229–30) makes the case for a politics that inhabits the drive as a way breaking out of our capitalist liberal democratic stronghold. The relentlessness and intensity of the drive is what can enable the revolutionary subject (individuals, movements, coalitions, radical states, and parties) to stubbornly stick to its objective of antisystemic change, without compromising its desire (de Vries 2007), such as the liberal Left has been wont to do in the form of reformist and welfare politics that leaves the system mostly intact (see chapter 7). The view here is that it is not postcapitalist alternatives that the Left lacks—there are many, as mentioned above—but the commitment, organization, and drive to intransigently struggle toward them through thick and thin, that is, through a self-sacrificing enjoyment for a more just (if still fraught) future. As McGowan proclaims, "It is by abandoning the terrain of the good and adopting the death drive as its guiding principle that emancipatory politics can pose a genuine alternative to the dominance of global capitalism rather than incidentally creating new avenues for its expansion and development. The death drive is the revolutionary contribution that psychoanalysis makes to political thought" (2013, 21). The big catch of course is also understanding the intractability of loss, so that the revolutionary struggle would not be for some ideal society or ultimate future enjoyment; a postcapitalist order, as underlined earlier, would still depend on desire and drive, accompanied by all the messy politics and struggles that accompany them.

GLE and Dialectical Materialism

The approach to global libidinal economy we advocate here is decidedly a dialectical materialist one. What counts, according to this approach, is not simply matter (our physical and material conditions), seen as first principle or ultimate substance from which all else emerges, but rather *the split or cut in matter* that enables subjectivity. As Žižek states, "Subjectivity emerges when substance cannot achieve full identity with itself, when substance is in itself 'barred,' traversed by an immanent impossibility or antagonism" (2014, 49). Such a position is consistent with modern science (e.g., quantum mechanics, wave theory), which points to the dematerialization of matter, the impossibility of apprehending it without the intervention of an observer. This is to say that the solidity and unity of material reality is always already shot through with a negativity, so that from such immanent self-blockage emerges the (split) subject. Our material world, in this sense, is always both necessary and contingent; it exists independent of us, but only becomes so at "the very moment of its discursive creation." It is not materially constituted by us, but neither is it independent of us: "Reality's own inherent negativity/contradiction appears as part of this reality precisely in the form of the subject" (Zupančič 2017, 82, 121; Žižek 2012, 707–8). So while everything may be subjectively mediated, this does not imply the subject comes first: matter is primary without being a first principle (which is why we are dealing here not with idealism but with dialectical *materialism*), but meaningless, unrepresentable, without its self-alienation. If anything is primal, then, it is neither substance nor subject but antagonism: Žižek gets at this with his Hegelian coinage of the term "absolute recoil" (2014)—the recoil that reveals the very object from which it recoils (Hamza 2016, 167). Matter "becomes" matter only retrospectively, as a consequence of its internal rupture and only *after* the intervention of subjectivity/representation.

We can now better understand why psychoanalysis makes the question of negation so central to its concern—to bring out the alienation that is constitutive of our lives, with the subject as the very name of the antagonism that makes reality incomplete. Psychoanalysis is, in this sense, not just a parochial discipline investigating the human psyche but a profoundly philosophical discourse centered on the formation and structure of the subject. This means, first, that instead of being considered as only one among many other objects, the subject is viewed as a privileged object of study that illuminates the fracture "at work in the very existence of objects as objects. It refers to the way in which the impasse/contradiction of reality in which different objects appear exists within this same reality. . . . The (Lacanian) subject is not simply the one who thinks, it is also and above all what makes certain contradictions accessible to thought" (Zupančič 2017, 122).

And this means, second, that psychoanalysis is deeply materialist, in the sense of unearthing the ontological negation that infiltrates all matter. As Alenka Zupančič formulates it, "This is what makes psychoanalysis a materialist theory (and practice): it starts by thinking a problem/difficulty/contradiction, not by trying to think the world such as it is independently of the subject" (2017, 123). It is this feature that distinguishes the psychoanalytic approach to political economy from certain (but not all) Marxist variants of dialectical materialism. Marx's well-known assertion that it is "social existence that determines . . . consciousness" (1970, 21), for example, is often interpreted as a deterministic theory of history based on the materiality of production (i.e., the "base-superstructure" model, which sees consciousness/culture as an epiphenomenon of the material base). It is such determinism that sparked a rethinking of Marxism in the early twentieth century by the likes of Lukács, Gramsci, and the Frankfurt school, who turned to culture and politics to redress what they saw as the economism of dialectical/historical materialism.[6]

For psychoanalysis, the unconscious (or what Lacan denotes as the "Real") is that which testifies to the presence of the contingency of matter/necessity, the cut through which meaning is both created and threatened;

it is the notional term for what must go wrong in reality for an idea to emerge in the first place. The negativity of the unconscious, in this sense, is not an external obstruction but that which must infiltrate any object or thought for it to manifest as a positivity, albeit an always discontinuous and fractured one. The subject, of course, is the very embodiment of such negativity and discontinuity, so that at the level of subjectivity, the unconscious is revealing of both the subject's lack (its alienation from its imaginary primordial wholeness with Matter) and excess (its surplus enjoyment in recreating its primordial loss). It is such lack and excess that make life destabilizing yet also colorful and pungent. As Žižek states, "Humans are not simply alive, they are possessed by the strange drive to enjoy life in excess, passionately attached to a surplus which sticks out and derails the ordinary run of things" (2006, 62).

Global libidinal economy presupposes, therefore, not just the discursivity of the economico-political but the very fracturing of the latter as revealed through unconscious desire. Or to put it the other way around, the incompletion and excess of the capitalist political economy reveals the space of unconscious desire. So it is neither that the unconscious comes first and the goal is to see how capitalism incorporates it, nor that political economy comes first and the goal is to analyze its production of desire; instead, what GLE claims is that capitalism is always already fissured by the unconscious—unconscious desires are immanent within it—so that, as Samo Tomšič maintains, today's unconscious "is nothing other than the capitalist unconscious, the intertwining of unconscious satisfaction with the structure and the logic of the [late] capitalist mode of production" (Tomšič 2015, 108–9; see also 79, 131). The structure of subjectivity today mirrors the structure of capitalist political economy.

It is for this precise reason that GLE takes such phenomena as patriarchy and racism deadly seriously (as chapters 2, 5, 6, and 8 illustrate): these are treated not as epiphenomenal but as integral to the workings of contemporary capitalism. They are constitutive of the (unconscious) reckless proclivity toward domination and inequality that capitalism fundamentally depends on, as underlined earlier. Such a proclivity stretches back to the very rise of capitalism/colonialism, as several analysts have pointed out (Quijano 2000; Robinson 2000; Lugones 2016; Wilderson et al. 2017; Bhattacharyya 2018), when the gender and racial categorization and inferiorization of the colonized other was needed for control of labor and the slave trade. Patriarchal and racial domination is what, accordingly, helped (and continues to help) address the socioeconomic antagonisms of capitalism. This is why dealing with gender and racial discrimination as a problem of "tolerance," as liberal political economy tends to do, misleads and miscarries; if such discrimination is constitutive of the system, as we claim, it requires not just political recognition and the granting of civil rights (which leave the fundamentals of the system intact) but changing the coordinates of the system itself to unravel the domination and exploitation on which it is founded.

Note here as well that it is the negativity at the core of GLE that makes it intrinsically political: as Jacques Rancière (1999) suggests, the political is that which challenges and ruptures the status quo. The castration-as-negativity that psychoanalysis spotlights is therefore to be seen as the site of an unsettling politics, aimed at disrupting the very *homo economicus* that neoclassical IPE justifies as a system of reason and good order. Like Marxist IPE, GLE points to the inherently political nature of the global capitalist system, founded as it is on logics of antagonism and exclusion. Žižek appropriates the term "class struggle" (2011, 198) to bring out such logics. For him the term refers not to a positive identity (e.g., working-class, bourgeoisie), as Marxists tend to believe, but rather the opposite: it is a signifier of negativity that reveals the traumatic deficiencies of the system. Class struggle, in effect, designates, what Rancière (1999, 9–11; Žižek 1997, 50) calls the "part of no-part"—the system's outcasts, destitutes, and pariahs—those whom it depends on but relegates to the margins (e.g., slum dwellers, sweatshop workers, migrants, gendered and racialized subalterns, the precariat, indigenous communities, the disabled, etc.; in short, the "reserve army" of labor whose composition forever changes as new systemic antagonisms arise). It is they who disclose the truth of the system—its systematic exploitation and exclusions. Class struggle thus functions as the unconscious of the global capitalist order, serving as marker of its basic failures and impossibility (see chapter 4).

Finally, there is the question of the state: we believe it to be a significant political subject/actor, with the material and discursive power to affect political economy. Several chapters (4, 6, and 7) point up the neoliberal state's role in aiding and abetting capitalist accumulation in much of the world. But chapters 5 and 8 specifically showcase the Chinese state as an emerging superpower on the world stage, strategically directing the country's domestic and foreign economic relationships (in trade, investment, and technological development). Yet by focusing on the libidinal, we see the Chinese state as split (i.e., as any agentic subject would be from a libidinal perspective): its economic calculus is accompanied by a notable psychoanalytic dynamic aimed at responding to its erstwhile subordination and racial humiliation in the global order. Psychic anxiety, in this sense, is integral to China's global dealings, even or perhaps especially when it presents itself as a an outwardly coherent actor.

But the state-as-split-subject is also to be gleaned in GLE's view of it as the site of a key social deadlock—class antagonism. This is in keeping with the notion that the social is ruptured by socioeconomic differences/contradictions, so that the state emerges in particular historical conjunctures as the political authority to address said contradictions, most often (but not always) serving the interests of the most powerful social classes/groups. The state thereby maintains the system, and as Marx has argued, under bourgeois capitalism, it has effectively become a tool for class domination (Marx and Engels 1970, 15). This is all the more true in the age of the globalization of capital, when the nation-state form facilitates rather than regulates the mobility of capital: unable to adequately manage socioeconomic flows under and above the state, the nation-state has essentially turned a blind eye to the antagonisms produced, in particular by transnational corporate activity (inequality, unevenness, environmental destruction, increasing enclosure of the commons, etc.; see chapters 2, 4, and 5–8). GLE thus underscores the (neoliberalized) state as a mechanism for reproducing and covering over, rather than addressing, the antagonisms of the global capitalist order, most often abrogating its social welfare role in favor of facilitating endless accumulation to the benefit of sociopolitical elites and at the expense of the subaltern and laboring classes (China is no exception here; see chapter 5).

What GLE offers as alternative is a view of the state that, rather than reconciling social antagonisms, aims at embodying them: by identifying first with those who are excluded from the system—the part of no-part—who stand as symptom of class antagonisms. It is because the part of no-part have no stake in the system that, when the state identifies with their demands for equality-freedom (*égaliberté*), it is acting in the interests of all (Žižek 2008, 379, 427; Kapoor and Zalloua 2022, 165–68, 177–84), as when catering to the health needs of the marginalized implies attending to universal interests (no one is excluded from the health system), or when state land reform in favor of indigenous communities begins to put the most downtrodden on a more equal footing socioeconomically with others. Thus, rather than aiming at eliminating alienation (the ultimate

Marxist fantasy, as stressed earlier), the state would become a techno-cratic apparatus that imposes on us all the conditions under which all humans and nonhumans, especially the Excluded, can thrive (albeit never without struggle or antagonism). In our current times of the COVID-19 pandemic, for example, such a view of the state is exactly what some (including the World Health Organization) say is pressingly required—relying on both science and effective global collaboration/coordination to ensure that everyone, not just the privileged, has equal access to vaccines and health care, because without such universal access the virus mutates and spreads, meaning no one—and certainly no country—is safe.

Conclusion

We have argued for a global libidinal economy that, in contrast to the market tendency to reduce the subject to a positive, unified, and hence commodifiable identity, views it instead as the embodiment of instability, if not irrationality, anxiety, and disorder. This is because the libidinal is the site of the recklessly desiring subject that is often overcome by excess to the point of self-sabotage and abandon. It is this recklessness that makes GLE dialectically materialist: desire's excess is what forever troubles our material reality, so that the latter is always punctured by a gap (i.e., the unconscious). It is also this recklessness that helps explain such global capitalist ills as social exploitation and domination, overconsumption, and the drive to endless accumulation, which threatens not just accumulation but the planet itself. And yet it is also such recklessness and relentlessness that, we suggest, can equally enable the subject to break out of the choke hold of global capitalism.

In what follows, we flesh out the above arguments in the context of what we see as key contemporary categories of IPE: production (chapter 2), consumption (chapter 3), informal economy (chapter 4), trade (chapter 5), financialization (chapter 6), ecology (chapter 7), and the state (chapter 8). We readily embrace Marxist IPE's claim that capital is the main struc-turing force globally today, but our purpose is to investigate and highlight the libidinal dimensions of such a structuring force in and through these categories, paying attention to them in the context of both the global South and North. Typically, "race" and "gender" do not fit the standard roster of IPE categories, but we explicitly include them as cross-cutting themes in several chapters, our point being to dialectically inflect main-stream IPE with critical broader questions of culture and power: such neglect in (much but not all) standard IPE, in our view, is revealing precisely of a disavowal of key axes of domination and exploitation.

2

Production

The Drive toward Capitalist Globalization

The global economy is marked by an unprecedented level of economic integration, characterized by the expansion of trade and investment, and the pervasiveness of international production and supply networks managed by transnational corporations (TNCs). The largest of these TNCs are bigger, in economic terms, than many nation-states and dominate globalized production through their control of financial, technical, managerial, branding, and market information and access. They frequently deploy the idea of "free trade" to push for economic policies that are better understood as involving "deep integration"—the creation of new institutional frameworks to reduce or download corporate risk, harmonize rules and regulations, and ensure that cross-border production networks operate in the interests of corporate profitability (WTO 2011; Baldwin and Lopez-Gonzalez 2015; Roman and Velasco Arregui 2015). The complexity of globalized production has given rise to growing interest in global value chains (GVCs) and similar frameworks in IPE that explore how value flows across chains and how corporations and nations do or should behave to gain greater access to that value. These approaches have been criticized for offering overly linear, neutral, and ahistorical approaches that obscure relations of exploitation and inequality that underpin chains and their dynamic growth (Taylor 2011; Bernstein and Campling 2006; Fine 2013; Havice and Campling 2013, 2612; Starosta 2010; Fridell 2019). In this chapter, while agreeing with the root insights offered by critics, we extend the discussion to explore why GVC thinking remains so popular despite foundational criticisms that often expose their "doublethink" (Selwyn 2017, 4). Intense devotion to GVCs persists, in part, due to their connection to powerful libidinal drives, which endures not only despite the contradictions in globalized production but because of them and the central antagonisms they offer. Understood in this way, "the paltry pleasure that can be garnered from securing material gains and a peaceful existence" (Kingsbury and Pile 2014, 31) is outmatched by the numerous possibilities for pleasure GVCs offer through the failures, repetitions, challenges, rituals, and routines embedded within them.

In the first part of the chapter, we explore GVC analysis and what "drive" adds to the discussion through attention to human passions, in particular lack, failure, and excessive enjoyment (*jouissance*). This is followed by a global libidinal economy (GLE) analysis of drive as applied to two case studies: the new and growing concern among TNCs, wealthy states, and international institutions around gender and GVCs, and the shifting dynamics between GVC inclusion and exclusion in the Eastern Caribbean. In the end, we reflect on how the libidinal drive toward accumulation is inseparable from traditional materialist concerns of critical IPE, offering us lessons for rethinking GVCs and political economy more generally.

The Political Economy of Global Value Chains

The most common IPE approaches for investigating globalized production are a range of works building on global commodity chain (CCC), global value chain (GVC), or global production network (GPN) frameworks. Between and within these bodies of work are debates around the possibilities for successful "upgrading"; the overly linear nature of "chains" versus "networks"; a propensity to minimize the significance of local relations of gender, class, and race at multiple sites of production; a tendency to downplay the importance of the state and other social actors; and the effectiveness of often inflexible typologies to capture the complex social relationships embedded in production, distribution, and consumption (Bair 2009; Daviron and Ponte 2005; Ponte and Sturgeon 2014, 219; Gereffi, Humphrey, and Sturgeon 2005; Bair and Werner 2011; McGrath 2018; Bush et al. 2014). Despite differences, there is growing convergence around what Bush et al. (2014, 3) call "one distinct GCC/

GVC/GPN 'family'." For this chapter, we will adopt the terminology of "GVC," both for convenience and for its emphasis on how surplus "value" is extracted from human labor along the chain (Sturgeon 2009; in the next chapter, we will see the imporance of connecting surplus value to "surplus *jouissance*" [see Böhm and Batta 2010]).

What the members of this family share is an approach for analyzing market integration that speaks of a "chain" or "network" as a heuristic tool, without firm boundaries, challenging the assumptions in neoclassical trade theory that economic agents are independent firms, connected by isolated market transactions. Instead, transactions take place across chains that are informally coordinated by "lead firms" that govern institutional frameworks through their economies of scale and control over market access, marketing budgets, and the "normative work" required to determine quality and moral conventions. Far from a world of neutral economic transactions, GVCs are driven by power and political economy, with the value produced along each node in a chain—whether from small-scale coffee farmers or women textile workers—flowing unevenly into the hands of lead firms, headquartered predominantly in the North (Bair 2009; Daviron and Ponte 2005; Ponte and Sturgeon 2014, 219; Gereffi and Korzeniewicz 1994).

Despite recognition that chain approaches can be "descriptively accurate" (Starosta 2010, 440), they have come under persistent criticism, in particular by Marxist thinkers who argue they suggest a relatively smooth, unilateral flow of value from sites of production to sites of consumption, as opposed to "the actually existing dynamics of a world economy characterized by unevenness, planes of economic inequality, and racialized, politicized, and gendered structures of domination" (Havice and Campling 2013, 2612). In placing emphasis on exchange along the chain, GVC approaches neglect capitalist social relations of production in specific contexts that give rise to the chain in the first place, driving competition, profit maxmization, accumulation, and increasing labor productivity (Taylor 2011; Bernstein and Campling 2006; Fine 2013; Havice and Campling 2013, 2612; Starosta 2010; Fridell 2019). The result is a bias toward the possibilities of upgrading (as opposed to subordination for weaker economies), market inclusion (as opposed to exclusion), and economic growth (as opposed to labor exploitation) (Bair and Werner 2011; McGrath 2018; Selwyn 2017; Suwandi 2019; Fridell 2022). Without attention to the specific imperatives of global capitalism, observes

Ben Fine (2013, 232), a great deal of GVC work fails "to examine what defines and determines the chains themselves with this generally taken as self-evident by virtue of case studies" (see also Starosta 2010).

These critiques are expanded in recent work by Benjamin Selwyn (2017, 2016), who points out that GVC thinking naturalizes the existing order, delegitimizes alternatives, and takes as given that "development" involves economic upgrading under the leadership of TNCs. Obscured are the ways that GVCs *reproduce* poverty and inequality, as lead firms download risk onto global suppliers and "preside, at a distance, over heightened labour-exploitation" (Selwyn 2016, 13). Selwyn calls for relabeling GVCs "Global Poverty Chains (GPCs)" and shifting research toward the activities of laboring classes as they struggle to build alternatives and gain a greater share of the uneven pie. Along similar lines, Intan Suwandi (2019, 21) has criticized GVC thinking for hiding imperialism and labor exploitation "behind the veil of globalized production." She proposes a focus on "labour-value commodity chains" rooted in monopoly capitalism, unequal exchange, and an unequal global hierarchy of wages. In this context, Southern manufacturing giants—China, India, and Indonesia—combine low wages with high productivity, resulting in the hyperexploitation of Southern workers and "the extraction (or drain) of surplus from the poor countries by the rich countries and/or their corporations" (Suwandi 2019, 16; see also chapter 6).

These works provide formidable challenges to the growing trend within GVC thinking of downplaying or ignoring ideology, power, and politics, to construct ever more technical and apolitical analysis and typologies (Fine 2013; Bair and Werner 2011; McGrath 2018; Fridell 2022). What remains to be unpacked, however, is why GVC thinking remains so popular despite its shortcomings and foundational weaknesses. To Selwyn (2017) and Suwandi (2019), exploitation and a relational conception of wealth/poverty are cloaked by the dominant, commonsense ideology of capitalists and Western states, who use their material and political power to dominate the discourse of GVCs in international organizations, governments, and NGOs. Power and knowledge can never be separated, giving hegemonic institutions substantial sway in defining the boundaries of "legitimate" discussion and debate, as Gramscian and Foucauldian thinkers have long observed (Peet 2018; Hannah, Scott, and Trommer 2016; Goldman 2006). At the same time, there is something deeper still behind the obstinate popularity of GVCs; a "drive" toward accumulation that persists not only despite the contradictions in globalized production but because of them.

Adding "Drive" to the GVC Debate

The Marxist critique of GVCs draws attention to how "economic growth" is specifically capitalist growth, where the accumulation of wealth among corporations and rich nations involves extracting surplus value from multitudes of laboring classes. Unprecedented wealth is created alongside inequality, uneven economic development, and climate chaos. Despite contradictions, globalized production continues more or less unabated, with temporary blockages along the way, driven not only by Northern-based TNCs but increasingly by TNCs based in rising powers in the global South, such as China, India, and Brazil. What "drives" this relentless accumulation?

Standard accounts of GVC expansion point to the material benefits that emerge from jobs, new technology, mass consumption, irrigation systems, dams, schools, paved roads, and so on (World Bank 2020; WTO 2017, 2018; Sachs 2005). These benefits, however, are distributed unevenly and experienced in highly differentiated ways, depending on where one is located in the social hierarchies that underpin global capitalism. For those at or near the top of the chain, awash in material goods, capitalist accumulation goes well beyond immediate needs, pointing to the centrality of human desire and "the multiple nuggets of enjoyment inherent in the accumulation drive" (Kapoor 2020, 87). As Selwyn (2017) and Suwandi (2019) have observed, it is here that we can locate the dominant thinking around GVCs, which tends to be elitist, "capital-centered," and imperialist, and heavily influenced by Western TNCs, policy makers, academics, think tanks, and politicians, as well as Western-dominated international institutions such as the World Bank, the IMF, and the WTO. It is these hegemonic institutions that we focus on in this chapter, as they are central to the "global" drive behind GVC expansion, and its ideological and material biases in favor of Western interests.

At the same time, while the human drive has increasingly become an accumulation drive under global capitalism (described below), this drive is experienced in varied ways throughout the world. For instance, Pieter de Vries (2007, 25–27) has argued that the potential benefits of GVC integration in the global South should not be underestimated or dismissed as reflecting "fake" or "naïve" desire on the part of millions of people. Instead, this reflects often unfulfilled desires that expose the "gap" between the promises of (Western) experts and "depressing reality." Sustaining the capacity to desire the benefits of GVCs, despite failures and contradictions, is not strictly material but fantasmatic and imaginative, with people refusing to "compromise on their desire for development" and instead "demanding the 'real' thing" (40).

Along different lines, rapid economic growth in Asian economies, in particular China, has had a major impact on reducing global inequality, with significant material and libidinal implications for global politics (Hung 2016). Maureen Sioh (2014b, 2014a) has observed that economic success in GVCs often reflects emerging powers' impulse to demonstrate "full human status" ("naturally" enjoyed by Western powers) and stave off anxieties around "future humiliation as a legacy of collective past humiliations" from colonial powers (Sioh 2014a, 284). A deep sense of lack can be (temporarily) overcome when Southern TNCs demonstrate tenacious global competitiveness against established Western TNCs. This also leads to anxiety over GVC success, experienced by both traditional economic leaders and emerging challengers. Sioh argues that postcolonial subjects may experience failure in the global economy as a failure to live up to the Western Other's "racialized hierarchy of competence" (290). At the same time, White Westerners may experience trauma at the economic success of racialized, non-Western Others as a loss of racial, national, and class status and as humiliation (Sioh 2018b).

Despite differences, a central pivot around how success is measured hinges on the "drive" of global capitalism. As chapter 1 has noted, in Lacanian terms, both drive and desire are related to *jouissance* and to each other. Each represents different outcomes of the deeply held sense of lack, or traumatic loss, that emerges as humans enter the symbolic order, moving from nature into culture. "Our initiation into language," states Kapoor (2020, 77), "thus introduces a fundamental absence (of a mythical sense of plentitude) that forever haunts us." To fill this sense of lack, desire targets a lost, and ultimately elusive, object. Its role in capital accumulation is most often assigned to the realm of consumption (discussed in chapters 3 and 6), where desiring subjects "engage in endless shopping, moving from one commodity to the next, forever searching for the 'real thing,' which always proves elusive" (79).

Drive, in contrast, targets not an object of desire, which represents a final "goal," but rather the "aim" itself, the route or way to the goal. Drive emerges, argues Žižek (2020, 438), "when the failure of desire to reach its satisfaction is reflected upon itself and becomes itself the source of satisfaction." *Jouissance* is attained not by the object but by missing and encircling it: trying, failing, and trying again in a cycle of repeated failure.

Pleasure emerges from the perverse enjoyment of endless circulation and excess. Consequently, "Desire's quest for enjoyment can never be attained (no object satisfies), whereas drive's search is always satisfied (in reenacting loss)" (Kapoor 2020, 78; see also 87). Satisfaction, however, can itself become a trap as people end up ensnared, through unconscious libidinal attachments, in an inescapable cycle of accumulation and capitalist expansion, leading to irrational enjoyments, even to the point of threatening the basis of capitalist growth through unchecked climate change.

GVC expansion reflects how, under capitalism, human drive becomes an accumulation drive, unleashing a cycle of endless expansion that reproduces the circuit of capital globally. The limitations and contradictions of capital are overcome, temporarily, through a perpetual process of seeking and creating new markets, sources of cheap labor, raw materials, and commons that can be stolen and privatized through accumulation by dispossession, as elaborated by David Harvey (2003). The libidinal drive embedded in this process occurs not at the individual level but through common language and social rituals. At the symbolic level, people experience drive as an unconscious and quasi-impersonal compulsion to accumulate. While individuals enjoy (and suffer) through the process of accumulation, an impersonal, collective *jouissance* takes over, overwhelmed by the drive to accumulate for accumulation's sake, and to "enjoy for capital's sake" (Kapoor 2020, 86–87). Capital, as Kapoor (87) observes, "serves as master signifier, a sacred object or rallying term—like God, Nation, Democracy—that people identify with and enjoy without really knowing what it implies." More than the material goods in themselves, people are seduced by Capital, its rituals, routines, beliefs, and bureaucratic procedures, libidinally drawn to "its seemingly limitless and thrilling circuits, repetitions, and challenges" (87).

Applying this insight to GVCs, three themes stand out. First, a GLE perspective places emphasis on the enjoyment drawn from the "routines, repetitions, and dictates of doing business" (Kapoor 2020, 86). Drive is about more than the accumulation of surplus value in solely material terms; it is about the libidinal pleasures involved in the process itself—the "aim," the endless repetition involved in encircling the object/goal itself, missing, and then trying again. Through GVCs, *jouissance* can be satisfied through building chains, managing them, disciplining a global labor force, creating elaborate organizational and marketing structures, lobbying for government policies that facilitate globalized production and accumulation, raising investment funds and selling shares, and identifying weaknesses in chain governance and targeting them for "solutions."

Second, the failures in GVCs that are the focus of a great deal of research and attention—whether labor exploitation and environmental degradation or more technical concerns around barriers to the smooth flow of goods—are not side issues or externalities to GVCs but central components of the drive embedded within them. The libidinal kick draws its greatest enjoyment from failure, which encourages new efforts to overcome, resolve, repeat, and try harder, ultimately imbuing the rituals and procedures around keeping capital circulating with meaning. The discovery and (temporary) overcoming of obstructions to GVC expansion represents "the unconscious reenactment of loss [which] has no limits, to the point of excess" (Kapoor 2020, 81).

This leads to the final interrelated theme of excess—central to both *jouissance* (as excessive enjoyment) and failure (overcome, temporarily, through excess). Surplus enjoyment is in fact required to define, retroactively, what the "normal" state of things is that needs to be overcome (Žižek 2020, 141). GVCs are replete with excess, whether in the form of the rich funneling their wealth into ostentatious displays of wealth (or "conspicuous consumption" in Veblen's (1953) terms); workers and farmers striving for excess through new forms of mass consumption, infrastructure development, or technological innovations to meet their " 'impossible' desire for development" (de Vries 2007, 29); or attempts by capitalist managers and government bureaucrats to manage GVC impacts. In the latter case, pleasure can be derived not from negative impacts themselves but from ritualistic devotion to Capital, while remaining "unaware, inattentive, or callously unconcerned about the consequences" (Kapoor 2020, 87). This can be seen with the many Western economists who claim devotion to liberal human rights while simultaneously offering unwavering defense of "sweatshop" labor and its necessity for capital accumulation (Krugman, Obstfeld, and Melitz 2018, 37–39; Sachs 2005; Bhagwati 2002).

Contradictions such as these form an unconscious "central antagonism" around which the GVC fantasy is built, entailing not only an account of what *is* happening but, as Žižek (2020, 382) observes, an account of "what could have happened (but didn't)"; that is, defining both the limits of what *is* and offering "illusory" hope around what should yet *be*. What is disavowed is not only the immediate negative effects of GVCs—which are often the focus of analysis—but also the attractive possibilities for libidinal pleasures through the failures, repetitions, challenges, rituals, and routines embedded within them. This is further explored in two examples below.

Gender, Labor, and GVCs

A main issue of concern around GVCs has been the central role of women workers in global export industries (apparel, electronics, horticulture, tourism, and call centers). For free market advocates, this is a cause for celebration, offering women paid employment with higher wages than those available in domestic sectors. They acknowledge that these jobs often reproduce gendered inequalities (women are generally paid less, treated worse, and experience poorer working conditions than men) but see the latter as a reflection not on the nature of GVCs but on their inefficient functioning (Bamber and Staritz 2016, 17; WTO 2017; Staritz and Guilherme Reis 2013; World Bank 2020). Such views have been criticized by feminist and Marxist researchers for celebrating as "liberating" or "empowering" the "recomposition of gender subordination" under new circumstances—from the patriarchal household to the patriarchal factory (Gunawardana 2017; Hickel 2014). Women are not only paid less than men, but their wages are well below a living wage. They experience frequent sexual harassment and gender-based violence, an increased overall burden combining unpaid reproductive labor with waged work, an unequal distribution of income within the household (with women's wages often increasing the income of men), and the disproportionate impact of neoliberal reforms, leading to cuts to public spending and social services (İzdeş Terkoğlu et al. 2017; UNDP 2012, 182–204; Elson 2009; Akram-Lodhi 2018; Gunawardana 2017; Hickel 2014; Selwyn, Musiolek, and Ijarja 2020). Gendered exploitation and inequality is not an oversight to the functioning of GVCs but rather key to the competitive advantages sought by corporations and national economies (İzdeş Terkoğlu et al. 2017).

Widespread recognition of the gendered inequalities in GVCs has only given further impetus to the expansionist drive behind them, with concern for gender moving to the fore of corporate social responsibility (CSR) and state trade policy. Governments have adopted gender-inclusive trade policies, while negotiating nearly eighty women or gender-related components into bilateral or multilateral trade agreements (World Bank 2020). The latter generally entail loose language and lack of meaningful enforcement, although they have opened political space for public deliberation around gender inequalities. At the same time, Roberto Bissio (2017) has observed that outward support for gender-inclusiveness can serve as a "Trojan horse," perpetuating free trade without regard for its negative impacts on women—such as cuts to public spending, increasing costs for medicine, and the general feminization of low-paid precarious work (Bissio 2017; Macdonald and Ibrahim 2019). Terms such as "intersectionality" have become adopted in narrow, instrumental ways as "buzzwords" devoid of their original, more substantive meaning (Parisi 2020; Tiessen 2019). The goal of gender equality is subordinated to economic growth, while women's empowerment becomes adopted to promote trade liberalization: any new or old trade barrier, as Bissio (2017) asserts, can potentially "be claimed to be a barrier to women's participation." In this way, evidence of gendered inequality within GVCs has become marshaled as proof of the necessity for further GVC growth (Hickel 2014; Selwyn 2016).

While building on these critiques, we must unpack their embedded unconscious desires, which we claim lead to a reproduction of the problem despite awareness of inherent ideological contradictions and inconsistencies. Three issues stand out. First, there is a paternalistic and colonial dynamic at play here, upholding a sense of Western mastery and superiority, in the face of the mounting economic (and moral) success of rising powers (Sioh 2014a, 284). The bulk of GVC research is Western-dominated and, as such, is often constructed around a fantasy of Western mastery aimed at "an attempt to preserve privilege by dominating the Other (the Third World, the subaltern) through the fantasy of sameness" (Kapoor 2020, 128). This fantasy is built upon a mythologized Western, capitalist society—of wealth, democracy, rationality, freedom—contrasted through a stereotyped non-Western Other, seen as traditional, irrational, uncomplicated, underdeveloped, static, emotional, and unpredictable. Westerners draw on this fantasy to strengthen their own self-worth, while projecting anxieties and failures onto the Other, denigrating and denying difference. The non-Western Other is "inferior" to the West and farther behind but ultimately on the same trajectory. States Kapoor (129), "In this way, the Other is recognized (inclusion), but only in some distant past that culminates in the West's own present (exclusion)."

Concern for gender equality in GVCs can become a source of libidinal pleasure, allowing Westerners to "revel in pride" about their superiority over the Other (reflected in Western commitment to economic growth *and* gender rights), denying fears over the rise of the South, while projecting anxieties over their own failures, complicities, and contradictions onto the Other (Sioh 2018b). Through disavowal, relations of (socioeconomic and racial) dominance between Western and non-Western nations are replaced symbolically with an economic narrative wherein economic growth (of the West) becomes synonymous with high moral standing.

Western experts insist on the economic necessity of intensified exploitation of women's labor (to become like the West), while simultaneously
condemning non-Western actors for the repressive politics required to
do it: "a form of moral outsourcing, if you will" (Sioh 2014b, 1164–65).
Beyond disavowal, however, Westerners place themselves in the position
of superiority, chastising and teaching the Other. As Hickel observes, such
a process "casts blame for underdevelopment on local forms of person-
hood and kinship, which it judges from the standpoint of Western ontology" (Hickel 2014, 1366). Western denial over its centrality to the process
of gender-based exploitation in GVCs simultaneously becomes a source
of pleasure, affirming the fantasy of Western mastery and superiority.

Second, through growing concern about gender and GVCs, exploitation within value chains becomes something not to be covered up but
exposed as a new, constitutive antagonism that opens up fresh avenues
for action. The growing popularity of GVC thinking has brought with it a
gradual depoliticization and dehistoricization of GVC theories. This is also
apparent in the foundational work on gender and GVCs, which originally
focused on criticizing the limitations, injustices, and gender-blindness
embedded in GVCs (Tallontire et al. 2005; Barrientos, Dolan, and Tallontire 2003; Lyon 2010). However, much of the newer work that is celebrated
and advanced by Western governments, international institutions, and
corporations has instead drawn out the pleasures in this discovery, shifting
the discussion from exploitation and trauma to the creative pursuit of
new projects and initiatives to overcome failure or lack. As Kapoor has
observed, "The more capitalism misses its mark, the more drive enjoys"
(2020, 86). The capitalist drive continually threatens capitalist development itself (through overaccumulation, overexploitation of resources,
financial crashes, etc.), which can then be overcome through new rounds
of accumulation (see chapter 6). Along similar lines, the exploitation and
denigration of women's labor, once recognized, becomes a new source of
enjoyment for a new round of accumulation—this time, with "inclusive
growth" at its core (Bamber and Staritz 2016; Shepherd 2016).

Concern for gender rights has thus become central to the rituals and
activities of the same institutions that dominate GVCs and their uneven
gendered impacts. Corporations have adopted the view, advanced by
economists Penny Bamber and Cornelia Staritz (2016, 2), that we need
to "harness the potential for GVCs to contribute to both economic and
social goals, including gender equality." The evidence that corporations
have done this, though, is not good. In many cases, gender inequality

has been "a source of export competitiveness," due to corporate sourcing policies, demands for low-cost products, and use of flexible, seasonable labor (7). Recognition that GVCs may in fact "reinforce gender issues" reveals how much more remains to be done—corporations now need to "reverse" their current production and sourcing policies to become leaders in gender equality (iv, 18). From this stem numerous opportunities to elaborate new gender policies, develop gender-specific analysis, expand metrics and indicators, and promote training and awareness raising aimed at overcoming the "*failing* to understand and address" the exploitation of women workers (7; emphasis added).

Overcoming gender inequality has also become central to the rhetoric of global trade policy, with organizations like the World Bank and the WTO positioning themselves as leaders in gender equality through events, reports, and workshops. A 2020 report copublished by the World Bank and the WTO asserts that trade improves the lives of women, through cheaper goods, employment, and higher wages—which, globally, can be (a fairly modest) 2.5 percentage points higher in exporting firms (World Bank 2020, 40). At the same time, the Bank and WTO recognize that women's gains have been unexceptional compared to what they could be, that women remain considerably more economically vulnerable than men—especially given the gendered impacts of COVID-19—and that "about 80 percent of women still occupy low- to medium-skill roles" in the global economy (World Bank 2020, 28). The solution here is intensifying trade liberalization, combined with the somewhat contradictory goal of new efforts to "*overcome* the challenges of trade" (14; emphasis added). A whole new set of opportunities now exist to creatively address gender inequality, for example by improving women's access to education, financial resources, digital technologies, and information; promoting policies aimed at improved capital and labor markets, macroeconomic stability, and effective governance; and/or demonstrating the "political will and commitment to sustain gender diversity and equality in the economy" (14). In this way, exposing the gendered weaknesses of GVC integration does not block the pursuit of *jouissance* but becomes its source—an inadequate "normal" that needs to be enjoyably *overcome* by filling its lack with new efforts (Žižek 2020, 141; Wilson 2014).

Finally, libidinal pleasure is expressed through gender and GVC thinking not only through the nuggets of enjoyment in overcoming gendered exploitation but also through callous, reckless *indifference to it*. As Kapoor has argued, there is an "impersonal type of sadomasochism" in the drive to accumulate, where pleasure is derived from an unwavering and unconscious devotion to Capital itself, as master signifier or sacred object. In this sense, irrational or nonsymbolizable libidinal drives are satisfied through identification and enjoyment with Capital "without really knowing what it implies" (Kapoor 2020, 87; Böhm and Batta 2010). The accumulation drive lies at the heart of gendered exploitation (low wages, poor working conditions, etc.), while simultaneously providing a constitutive antagonism that feeds the drive. Perhaps the most pervasive form of enjoyment comes from the capitalists, state officials, politicians, and policy makers who "on the whole . . . are primarily enjoying and following capital's drive to accumulate, no matter (or despite) its socioenvironmental impacts" (Kapoor 2020, 87). Perpetually recognizing gender inequities, while not doing much about it because of the unrelenting demands of Capital, reveals one's secret devotion and dedication to Capital itself.

This aspect of the drive is reflected in the fact that, despite recognition of gendered injustices in GVCs by powerful corporations, states, and international financial institutions, these same organizations are not interested in effective global policies around living wages, decent work, unionization, free health care or childcare, or any number of ideas that would significantly improve the lives of women (Hickel 2014). What better way to address the gendered wage gap, for instance, than for a corporation to pay workers and subcontractors much better (especially in relation to the massive payouts to corporate executives and shareholders)? Here we are told this cannot be done given the reliance on low-paid women's labor for a country's or company's competitive advantage. Expressed concern for women rings hollow compared to the role it plays as a fantasy upon which to demonstrate quasimechanical devotion to Capital. Western proponents of GVCs are thereby constructed as superior both "morally" (given their concern for women) and "rationally" (given their recognition that they cannot do much about it, because of the unquestionable demands of Capital) (Sioh 2014b).

The impersonal drive to accumulate is also evident in the fact that most concern around gender extends only as far as the boundaries of GVCs themselves. Feminists have criticized trade and gender initiatives because they place issues that are not directly related to economic growth on the back burner, if they are recognized at all (Parisi 2020; Tiessen 2019). This includes a long list of urgent challenges around reproductive rights, gender-based violence, time poverty, supporting the care economy, gender equality in peace building, or the harassment, discrimination, and violence faced by LGBTQ+ people globally. The mainstream gender and GVC agenda appears to be concerned with these issues only if and when they infringe on production, with solutions invariably aimed at creating autonomous "market citizens" as ideal workers and consumers for Capital (Parisi 2020; Tiessen 2019). The effect is not only to neglect the social impacts of gender inequality but also to reproduce, rather than disrupt, the view that gender inequities matter when they matter to Capital. The stated concern for gender equality is then nothing but an opportunity to demonstrate one's true devotion to the accumulation drive—a "compulsion to enjoy for capital's sake" regardless of gender injustices.

GVCs and Exclusion

The majority of GVC research, both mainstream and critical, focuses on integration and inclusion, debating the best ways for countries to enhance integration and promote economic and social upgrading. The result, as Jennifer Bair and Marion Werner (2011, 989) have observed, is an "inclusionary bias," which "tends to downplay, if not ignore, the fact that changing geographies of global production reflect moments of inclusion *and* exclusion" (see also McGrath 2018; Fridell 2022). Exclusions are recognized but disavowed as exceptions to how GVCs should or will operate. Thus, the World Bank and WTO report mentioned earlier acknowledges the negative impact COVID-19 has had on women (millions of whom have suffered job and income losses), while adding that postpandemic governments need to adopt policies that "generate long-term gender-inclusive growth" so "that trade can *continue* to benefit women" (World Bank 2020, 2–3; emphasis added).

Along similar lines, Caribbean economies, and the challenges they have faced in the neoliberal era around GVC inclusion and exclusion, provide a powerful example of how failure can be read as success (for the drive). Indeed, Caribbean economies have been integrated into the global economy for hundreds of years on highly uneven terms, through a violent process of conquest, slavery, and colonialism (C. A. Green 2007; Thomas 1974; Levitt and Best 1975). In the post–World War Two era, many nations gained political independence while simultaneously intensifying integration into GVCs through preferential access to the European market for bananas, sugar, rum, rice, and other exports. In the 1990s, spurred by trade disputes at the WTO and the new era of "free trade," these arrangements were abandoned or rendered ineffective, with disastrous impacts for many (particularly smaller) economies. For instance, such countries as Saint Vincent and the Grenadines (SVG), Saint Lucia, and Dominica had come to rely on bananas for 50 percent of their export earnings and one-third of employment. But post-1990s, they were devastated by a massive drop in exports, sparking unemployment and bankruptcy for thousands of farmers, with TNCs shifting their supply chains to low-cost competitors in Latin America and Africa (Fridell 2022; C. A. Green 2007; Myers 2004).

Many Caribbean nations have, as a result, experienced increasing exclusion from GVCs over the past thirty years, giving rise to efforts to disavow, overcome, and exceptionalize this failing (Fridell 2022). Most notably, in 2008, EU members and fifteen Caribbean states signed an Economic Partnership Agreement (EPA) to replace declining preferences with a new "free trade" agreement. Many Caribbean governments reluctantly signed the EPA under intense pressure from the EU, recognizing that it offered little benefit to most Caribbean nations, which already had duty-free access to the EU for core exports (Fridell 2022; Sanders 2011; Brewster, Girvan, and Lewis 2008). As many predicted, the years following this signing have produced disappointing economic results. Most Caribbean countries (except for the considerably larger Dominican Republic) have experienced deteriorating macroeconomic indicators, worsening debt-to-GDP ratios, declining public revenue from tariffs, limited new investment, and little change to poverty and human development indicators. The value of merchandise exports from CARIFORUM states to the EU dropped by one-third from 2008 to 2013, with particularly poor results for small islands states: SVG, Saint Kitts and Nevis, Dominica, and Saint Lucia saw declines of around 75 percent (Singh et al. 2014, 79). In some countries, such as SVG and Saint Lucia, the illicit cannabis industry, aimed primarily at local and regional markets, has emerged as a major source of replacement income for rural growers (Edmonds 2020).

Despite these failings, evidence of economic exclusion has not met with reflection on the limitations of market integration (the *goal* of drive) but rather become a rallying point for trying again (the *aim* of drive). As with the case of gender and GVCs, three main issues stand out in this regard. First, the discourse around the EPA is replete with disavowal in a manner that asserts a paternalistic and colonial vision of Western mastery and superiority. Disavowing the centuries-long colonial relationship between the regions, the EPA sees as its main objective the promotion of "gradual integration of the CARIFORUM States into the world economy" (EPA 2008, article 1.c). Drawing on the fantasy of sameness, the EU positions itself as the superior and prosperous region charged with leading the inferior and otherwise static Caribbean (still awaiting integration) into Europe's present. The EU has even chastised the Caribbean for attempting to cling to the preferences of a bygone era. Instead, it prefers to celebrate how the "EPA *creates a more equal partnership*," where "Each Region opens its market to the other, and reaps the benefits" (European Commission 2018, 3). Caribbean countries have reportedly "*enjoyed* preferential access to the EU" for too long; "Now, both sides have obligations as well as rights—as in any free trade agreement" (3; emphasis added).

The use of free trade in this way has an unmistakable colonial thrust, constructing a fantasy of Western harmony, in contrast to the retrograde thinking of non-White Others (Wilson 2014). The latter cling to paternalism and discriminatory trade, afraid of a genuine partnership of equals. "Preferential" treatment takes the place of "tradition" or "local" knowledge in customary colonial discourse, serving as "stand-ins for the primitive and inferior customs, beliefs, and practices of the (racially marked) Other" (Kapoor 2020, 248–49). Critiques of the EPA from Caribbean experts are denigrated as backward, irrational, and even submissive. Despite hundreds of years of distorted trade benefiting colonial empires, Caribbean "partners" are told that it is time to move on. Caribbean states have putatively "enjoyed" their "one-way" relationship for too long, costing the EU "dearly," so it is now time to embrace new thinking around reciprocity (European Commission 2018, 3; Humphrey 2011, vii; Borrell 1994, 1). Through this process, Caribbean economic subordination is reaffirmed, while free trade ideology promotes and obscures "the (not so) guilty pleasure of dominating the Other" (Kapoor 2020, 240).

Secondly, the failing of the EPA to promote GVC integration has only further intensified the accumulation drive, sparking a new set of creative projects, as economists, policy makers, and international institutions spend hundreds of millions of dollars on trade-related technical, institutional, economic, private sector, and "cultural" mediations (European Commission 2018, 3) to address the lacuna and insert in its place the "fantasy of a harmonious market society" (Wilson 2014, 8–9). From 2008 to 2020, the EU provided around US$1 billion in official development assistance to support EPA adjustment in CARIFORUM states (Humphrey 2011; G. Green 2015; Singh et al. 2014; European Commission 2018). The result has been the construction of countless programs aimed at "enhance[d] political buy-in" and "continued awareness-raising" of the benefits of GVC integration through stakeholder forums, institutional capacity building, monitoring and evaluation, training, and technical support (G. Green 2015, 6; Singh et al. 2014, 15). Through these programs, GVC experts are reportedly trying to overcome the "apparent reluctance" on the part of Caribbean government and private sector actors "to exploit market access opportunities" (Humphrey 2011, ix–x). Here, the opportunities for unconscious repetitive pleasures are revealingly conveyed by Errol Humphrey, consultant on EPA implementation to the Ministry of Foreign Affairs and Foreign Trade in Barbados, when he points to the many "political, communication-related, philosophical, cultural, institutional, financial, technical, capacity-related *and more*" challenges opened up by EPA (5; emphasis added).

Interestingly, even the relative shortcomings of aid itself have given further impetus to the drive to overcome them. Despite the EU giving hundreds of millions of dollars in trade-related aid to the Caribbean, to many the total amount is insufficient compared to the estimated costs of EPA adjustment (Humphrey 2011; G. Green 2015; Singh et al. 2014; European Commission 2018). The EPA was designed to be unique as a trade agreement, recognizing within the text that "development cooperation" was required between the unequal partners, that joint institutions would be created for regular dialogue around implementation, and that the EU was committed to development aid to support a range of technical and capacity-building efforts (EPA 2008, articles 7 and 8, 227–232). In practice, the joint institutions have developed slowly with little meaningful dialogue and with EU aid seen as "a major disappointment" (Humphrey 2011, viii; G. Green 2015; Singh et al. 2014). By one estimate, EU development aid to the Caribbean from 2008 to 2013 of $508.67 million covered only 43 percent of the "total cost of EPA related adjustments" (G. Green 2015, 5). As a result, EPA defenders have continued to call on the EU to fill in the Caribbean's "resource deficit" (or lack) (5). Others, like Humphrey, have focused more on the Caribbean actors for failing to be "proactive." Instead, Humphrey argues, "Caribbean political leaders and their representatives in Brussels must seize every opportunity to remind EU countries of their unfulfilled [Aid-for-Trade] commitments and maintain constant pressure for them to deliver" (2011, 37). Caribbean officials are now called upon to ensure the commitments from powerful European partners; they must *seize every opportunity* to overcome the gap between promise and practice.

Finally, the libidinal pleasure of the drive is expressed through callous indifference to the impacts of GVCs, in favor of unwavering devotion to Capital. The end of preferential trade is seen as inevitable, while the solution to the problems it has caused is further GVC integration (whether it works or not). Ritualistic dedication to this belief, despite the near collapse of several Caribbean economies, is a form of enjoyment itself, rooted in identification with Capital's drive to accumulate. Outward concern for the dangers and failings of Caribbean economies once again belies latent desire to demonstrate devotion to Capital. Indeed, trade economists, while acknowledging a few shortcomings of GVC integration, appear to barely contain their disdain for GVC critics by characterizing them as "foolish," "silly," "emotional," and even "mad" (Krugman, Obstfeld, and Melitz 2018, 37; Broude 2018, 25, 28; Hirsh 2019).

Conclusion: What Drives GVCs?

While critical IPE scholars effectively demonstrate how GVCs are rooted in, and systematically reproduce, exploitation, inequality, and exclusion for the sake of capitalist accumulation, GLE further problematizes these trends, unpacking their persistence despite, and often *because* of, their failings and shortcomings. The libidinal underpinnings of the drive toward GVC integration are inseparable from both the materialist and epistemological/institutional concerns of political economy: under capitalism, drive becomes inseparable from accumulation drive, while the material, knowledge/power, and indeed moral status of those working within and around GVCs (from capitalists, state managers, and workers to GVC researchers in international institutions or academia) are invested in the success of globalized production, profits, growth, and income (de Vries 2007; Sioh 2014a). This puts us in a difficult bind when challenging the drive of GVCs on several fronts.

First, IPE scholars often point to how hegemonic capitalist ideology hides and naturalizes the exploitation inherent in GVCs through its assumptions and exclusions (Suwandi 2019; Ben Selwyn 2017; Fine 2013; Starosta 2010). What is often downplayed, though, is how much people across the chain (capitalists, but also workers, advocates, consumers, economists, and government officials) uphold GVC thinking, whether in academic or popular forums, for similar reasons. As an ideological fantasy,

GVC thinking hides "in plain view" (Kapoor 2014, 1128) our emotional connection to globalized production, as well as the traumas, gaps, and contradictions many prefer to disavow. This is intensified by the fact, as Richard Peet (2018, 264) observes, that "many people combine the roles of perpetrator and victim" within global capitalism.

Second, while critical political economy exposes the shortcomings behind the opportunities offered by GVC expansion (jobs, income, consumption, economic growth), frequently overlooked are the numerous nonmaterial opportunities that a GLE perspective forefronts, including those that may be self-destructive. GVCs offer abundant libidinal pleasures through the endless repetition and failure of the aim of the drive, upon which are constructed deep emotional bonds to routines, rituals, repetitions, beliefs, and bureaucratic processes that are themselves sources of great pleasure. The powerful appeal of GVCs lies not solely in their material offerings but also in their connection to unconscious drives, offering us a fantasy of temporary fullness overcoming lack, through identification with Capital. In seeking to confront and denaturalize GVC assumptions, these libidinal pleasures need to be centrally integrated into IPE to unpack and confront the obstinate support GVC integration so often receives.

Finally, while the ideological critique offered by IPE scholars often exposes the weaknesses and traumas of GVC integration, the politics around it remains a great challenge because, in many instances, rather than block the pursuit of *jouissance*, the failings themselves become a source of enjoyment, serving as a constitutive antagonism that must be (enjoyably) overcome (Žižek 2020, 141; Wilson 2014; de Vries 2007). The challenge here is not only that institutions of power, such as the World Bank and the WTO, gentrify failings to reenergize hegemonic discourse (arguing that global capitalism is the *solution* and not the *cause*) but rather that they depend on powerful disavowed unconscious drives, taking refuge in a ritualistic devotion to Capital. Such seductive powers need to be brought to the center of critical analysis, as proposed by a GLE approach. Otherwise, we run the risk of what Žižek terms "fetishistic disavowal"— recognizing the limits of GVCs but reproducing, extending, and enjoying them anyway—a theme that we pick up in the next chapter (Žižek 1989). It is libidinal devotion to GVCs, as an expression of the accumulation drive, that remains among the greatest barriers to contesting and subverting their enduring appeal.

3

Consumption

Desire and Commodity Fetishism

Marketing research that explores consumer behavior has grown exponentially over the past fifty years to meet the ever-expanding needs of capital to grow markets and create new ones (Dawson 2003). In their 2011 article in the *Journal of Brand Management*, marketing consultants and researchers Neale Martin and Kyle Morich criticize the vast majority of this work for being based on the misguided assumption that "consumers are rational agents making conscious decisions about the branded products and services they purchase and use" (2011, 1). This view is derived from standard economic theory and the idea of *homo economicus*, which posits that individuals are driven by rational self-interest, carefully balancing economic choices to attain the greatest amount of personal satisfaction (Martin and Morich 2011; İzdeş Terkoğlu et al. 2017; Hudson and Hudson 2021). According to Martin and Morich, most of the research built on this assumption has been a waste of time, with new product introductions failing at a rate of around 80–85 percent. The reason, they argue, is that marketing research has neglected "that the majority, if not all, of human behavior either begins as an unconscious process or occurs completely outside of conscious awareness" (2011, 1, 13).

While the growing attention paid to the unconscious in marketing marks an important turn, in this chapter we will argue that, despite claims to be offering something "radically different" (Ariely 2009, 80), the new marketing approaches replicate many of the failings of old ones by offering a superficial reading of consumer desire that neglects its broader collective material and libidinal underpinnings. More effective at unpacking the motivations behind modern patterns of mass consumption has been the work of political economists who have explored these patterns' evolving, uneven, and historically specific dynamics under global capitalism. Much of this work, however, has either celebrated or critiqued consumerism, while neglecting the significance of the unconscious desires that make people, as desiring subjects, so devoted and addicted to endless consumption in the first place. We take up this issue through a GLE reading of Marx's essential concept of "commodity fetishism," arguing that predominant political economy interpretations ignore or downplay the significance of the fetish itself, which is not a distraction or distortion of consumption but one of its primary objectives.

In the first part of the chapter, we unpack behavioral marketing and political economy approaches to consumption and contrast them to a GLE approach, which seeks to challenge and subvert the hard distinction offered by "productivists" between the substance (material) and appearance (libidinal) of a commodity. This is followed by an analysis of Fairtrade, a leading example of ethical consumerism, and the ways in which it conforms and concedes to commodity fetishism, as well as offering some new directions for potentially seductive alternatives—in particular, ones that emphasize Southern producer experiences and relations between organizations, as opposed to consumerist fantasies of superiority and beneficence (Lyon 2006; Naylor 2018; Melo Maya and Pittoello 2021).[1] We argue that identifying and challenging commodity fetishism requires careful attention to the fetish itself, which is constitutive of the sociolinguistic order. Rather than seeing the fetish as obscuring only the relationship between producers and consumers, the GLE approach emphasizes how the fetish also crucially obscures the unconscious desires, pleasures, and traumas that people project onto it. The fetish, in this sense, is not a barrier to enjoyment but a core component of it. This requires efforts not to overcome fetishism itself but to traverse the symbolic fantasies transferred to the commodity as the elusive *objet a* of desire.

Consumption and Unconscious Desire

Dominant economic theories of consumerism, building off foundational thinkers such as Adam Smith and Jeremy Bentham, have long been constructed around the view that consumers are rational "utility" maximizers (see chapter 1). "Utility" is understood, in Benthamite terms, as pleasure (and avoidance of pain), with consumers making the choices that allow them as individuals to maximize the utility/pleasure of their economic decisions based on their own self-determination. Limits to rational action are acknowledged, with consumer behavior understood as "bounded" by existing knowledge, imperfect information, cultural conditions, imperfectly competitive markets, and the limits of cognitive capacities (Martin and Morich 2011; İzdeş Terkoğlu et al. 2017; Hudson and Hudson 2021). Ultimately, however, proponents of rational utility claim it offers, at the aggregate level, the most predictive models possible. But this view has faced a growing challenge from behavioral economists and psychologists who assert that consumers are ultimately "emotional, myopic, and easily confused and distracted" (Ariely 2009, 84). On this basis, Martin and Morich critique the use of marketing surveys, focus groups, and laboratory tests in favor of their own model, which seeks to probe people's unconscious behaviors as they respond to stimuli, triggering automatic processes (behavioral mimicry, trait and stereotype activation, nonconscious goal pursuit) that affect consumption choices. The measure of success is not "customer satisfaction," which has proven elusive to measure and difficult to predict, but rather "customer reinforcement," which, if done well, increases "the chances of habit formation around their brand" (2011, 18–19).

Behavioral models are said to offer "an integrated, holistic view of the consumer" that transcends the "flawed assumption of ever-conscious decision making" in standard economics and marketing (Martin and Morich 2011, 4,12). At the same time, many of the core assumptions behind standard approaches are maintained, especially as they relate to desire and pleasure. First, while asserting that true satisfaction is difficult to measure and does not provide a sound basis for predicting future behavior, it is simultaneously assumed that increased consumption *is* the road to attain it. The result is somewhat contradictory reasoning: consumer satisfaction cannot be determined but *can* be fulfilled. Better marketing models could "provide endless opportunities to create the *perfect* products and services and deliver billions of dollars in annual revenue" (6; emphasis added). Consumers may not be rational, but consumerism is. The unconscious consumer is, ultimately, not far removed from the conscious one—each aspires to have their straightforward goals met by purchasing goods and services on the market, only now they are considered less in touch with what they *really* want. Consumer desires can be satisfied through the right marketing approach, guiding people away from fleeting and capricious desires, toward what they "truly" ought to want. Thus, Martin and Morich state, "The only measure of satisfaction that seems to predict repurchase is 'delight,' a mercurial measure at best. If delight results from *exceeding expectations*, consumers likely revise their expectations in light of this feedback, making the future chance of failing to meet expectations more and more certain. But because 'delight' influences repurchase positively, many companies have [used] 'delighting customers' as part of their advertising, not realizing that elevating customer expectation makes delight that much more difficult to achieve" (4). Here, Martin and Morich recognize the importance of "delight," while simultaneously disavowing it as too "mercurial" (unpredictable, volatile, emotional) to base a sound advertising strategy on. What if, however, consumers are driven by the desire for products that *exceed expectations*, leaving both themselves and marketers in an inherently unresolvable, repetitive, and unpredictable bind? This is an issue to which we will return.

Second, akin to standard economics, the new behavioral theories are not interested in questions of power and political economy. Instead, they construct their position on the basis of methodological individualism, taking atomized individuals as the foundation of society, with social and cultural institutions of concern only insofar as they serve as stimuli that nudge consumers in one direction or another (Milonakis and Fine 2009). This disregards an extensive political economy literature exploring consumption as a collective movement rooted in the historically specific conditions of global capitalism. The latter works have examined the environmentally destructive, socially unequal, and gender-blind basis of the dominant modes of consumption, which obscure the significance of household consumption and nonmarket domains of care and reproduction; neglect the power of capital to drive market consumption through deskilling individuals and spending billions on advertising; and ignore the consequences of endless consumption on the sustainability of the planet (Fine, Heasman, and Wright 1996; Dawson 2003; İzdeş Terkoğlu et al. 2017; Soper 2020; Hudson and Hudson 2021). The injustices and inequalities associated with consumption are mostly overlooked by behavioralists, who, it must stressed, often carry out research in partnership with corporate capital, conveniently discounting the idea that there are any contradictions between the goals of corporate profitability and making "their customers happier" (Ariely 2009, 80; Martin and Morich 2011).

In the political economy literature, the lines between the pleasures and pains of consumption are far less clear. Marxist thinkers Ian Hudson and Mark Hudson, in their recent book *Consumption* (2021), offer a useful review of the literature, breaking it into three groups. The first group, "consumerists," focus their analysis on the ways in which individual consumerism is part of a wider consumer culture, central to how people define their identities, status, values, and attitudes (Stolle and Micheletti 2013; Boström, Micheletti, and Oosterveer 2019). While some view the desire for consumption as going back thousands of years, and others depict a distinct shift under capitalism to a mass consumer society beginning in the 1600s, there is general agreement that people aspire for consumption beyond basic material needs; they tend to be "savvy" consumers pursuing consumption "with genuine meaning, as people quest for affiliation, recognition and purpose" (Soper 2020; Hudson and Hudson 2021, 17). Along these lines, Roberta Sassatelli (2015) has criticized the focus on individual, self-interested utility maximizers among both the defenders and critics of consumerism. Instead, she argues that people also aspire for "responsible" consumer utility, deploying creativity, slow consumption skills, and relationship building to shape the "capacity to aspire and to imagine a better future" and seek out "both collective goods (environmental concerns, equality, democracy) and private happiness (in terms of critical, creative fulfillment as opposed to acquisition and spending power)" (483, 489).

In contrast to the consumerists are the "productivists," the camp in which Hudson and Hudson (2021) locate their own work. For them, the driving force behind the unprecedented scale and pace of mass consumption in the modern era has not been consumer demand but changes in production. Modern consumption is conditioned by the historical emergence of capitalism, where worker exploitation and class conflict drive the production of surplus value: firms must compete for markets, resources, and new investments; and goods and services are produced at a constantly escalating rate, as commodities that *must* be sold on the market for capitalists to realize their profits. While commodities must have some value for consumers, the process is determined by the needs of capital, which, according to Hudson and Hudson, spends billions on advertising to "manipulate" human desires, create new "needs," generate innovation of dubious benefit, and encourage consumption to fill the "void in people's lives created by the current system of production" (Hudson and Hudson

2021, 16). Whereas behavioral economists view corporate marketing as a societal good, giving people what they want, productivists see it as an alienating and oppressive situation, one in which "people's wants and needs do not originate with themselves" (15).

Both consumerists and productivists offer distinct perspectives on desire and consumerism. But whereas consumerists are correct to point to the deeply held symbolic and social values embedded in desiring commodities, they fail to explore desire itself (i.e., its elusive and conflictive character), leaving us locked in perpetual cycles of pleasure and pain (Carveth 2018). Under capitalism, this unattainable desire is linked to endless shopping, which, as Hudson and Hudson (2021, 42) observe, can result in a situation that "keeps us happy, but in chains nonetheless." Yet the productivist position often downplays the role of desires in consumption, seeing these as nothing but an object of manipulation by capital. As we will see in the section below, productivists often criticize consumers for being drawn to a commodity's "fetishistic," magical, or mysterious qualities, deceived into ignoring the labor and the labor exploitation embedded in it. The challenge that emerges, however, is that it is precisely the fetishistic qualities of a commodity, seeking to fill a deeply held "void," that we are so often drawn toward (Böhm and Batta 2010; Kapoor 2020).

Finally, there is a third group, whom Hudson and Hudson call the "fence-sitters." This camp seeks a multicausal approach, viewing both consumption and production as spheres containing agency and domination (Hudson and Hudson 2021, 18–20). They point in particular to the work of Ben Fine, who has developed a system of provision (SOP) approach. A SOP is defined as a "chain that unites particular systems of production with particular systems of consumption, focusing on the dynamics of the different actors (producers, distributors, retailers as well as consumers)" (Bayliss, Fine, and Robertson 2013, 11). Both production and consumption take place within the context of capitalism, but also within different "material cultures" at diverse sites of production/consumption. Individual consumption is driven neither by rational self-interest nor misguided false needs but by collective norms that meet human desires yet are contradictory and chaotic. Consumers here are not passive but "reflexive," within the limits imposed by varying SOPs (Fine 2013, 226). From this approach, numerous insights have emerged, including emphasizing that individuals are both producers and consumers, that the state plays a major role in reproducing patterns of consumption and production, and that moral values are embedded in all forms of consumption (not just those deemed "ethical") (Fine, Heasman, and Wright 1996; Bayliss, Fine, and Robertson 2013; Fine 2013; Brooks 2015).

Most significantly for the argument here, in subverting the productivist/consumerist or material/cultural divides (which Hudson and Hudson critique as "fence-sitting"), the SOP approach parallels what we seek to do with the GLE framework by rejecting a clear divide between material and libidinal agency. This divide is explicit or implicit in much of the productivist work, which often relegates consumption to the realm of the cultural, emotional, and irrational, while assigning production and capital to the realm of the rational and material. Such a perspective, as Teresa Brennan (1993) has argued, creates an artificial distinction between production and consumption. In fact, production under capitalism *is* consumption—entailing an ever-faster extraction of the world's resources at a rate beyond the ability of nature to reproduce itself (118–65). In this chapter, we emphasize the material and libidinal as dialectically imbricated in both production and consumption, which includes the SOP emphasis on the reflexive, chaotic, and contradictory but sees these specifically as a function of unconscious desire.

Rethinking Commodity Fetishism

A significant entry point for distinguishing the GLE approach to desire and consumption from other approaches is to engage with Marx's notion of "commodity fetishism" (Marx 1978, 319–29). Capital accumulation drives unprecedented production, capable of meeting fundamental material needs (in highly unequal and uneven ways), while simultaneously pushing consumption beyond any seemingly rational hierarchy based on the "relative intensity of needs" (Mandel 1986, 14–15; Soper 2020). Desiring subjects, both rich and poor, become hooked to the goal of endless consumption, regardless of its longer-term social, health, or environmental impacts, locked in "a default assumption that wants and desires are best satisfied through commodity consumption and that choice over commodities is a fundamental aspect of freedom" (Hudson and Hudson 2021, 42).

To many productivists, commodity fetishism obscures the relationship between substance and appearance in a commodity. Atomized, alienated, individualized consumers shop in a manner that hides the actual labor that has gone into the commodity—it appears not as something that has been transformed from nature through human labor but as an abstract, "natural" commodity in its own right. At the same time, commodities play a fetishistic role, imbued with magical or mysterious qualities that we desire (i.e., to improve our social status) (Elson 1988; McNally 1993; Guthman 2002; Fridell 2007a; Hudson and Hudson 2021). In this way, as Hudson and Hudson assert, consumers are perpetually alienated from the products they consume, compelled to meet their desires through consumption, "rather than through other means," without genuine knowledge "about the labor and parts of nature that are embodied in it" (2021, 44).

A GLE approach to commodity fetishism, in contrast, places far more emphasis on the fetish itself, not as a distraction or distortion to the goal of consumerism but as one of its primary, albeit ever-elusive, goals (see also chapter 6). Here the hard distinction offered by the productivists between the substance (material) and the appearance (libidinal) of a commodity is dissolved. Drawing on Žižek's reading of Lacan and Marx, Böhm and Batta (2010) advance a conception of commodity fetishism that roots its economic structure within the relational structure of the subject's linguistic world: "There is always a constitutive lack at the heart of both the subject and the symbolic order, which Lacan calls the Other" (356). While productivists view alienation as emerging from capitalist social relations, for Lacanians, the subject is always alienated (from both itself and the Other) due to a constitutive lack (the Real). Desire thus emerges out of the impossible, fleeting task of seeking to fill this lack with a (mythical) lost object. Fetishism arises when the anxieties around lack are transferred "to a symbolic system, or what Lacan calls the Name-of-the-Father. What contemporary consumer capitalism has arguably achieved is that it has provided a symbolic system onto which the subject's constitutive anxieties (lack) can be transferred, creating a set of fantasies for people to believe in. Nike and its global brand appeal is at the heart of this relationship" (354). The commodity, from this vantage, assumes the role of *objet a*, summarized by Žižek (2020, 39) as "an 'imagined' (fantasmatic, virtual) object which never positively existed in reality—it emerges through its loss, it is directly created as a fossil." No sooner is desire met by the elusive commodity than the impossibility of being satisfied is revealed, leading to redoubled efforts to try and satisfy desire. Under capitalism, as Böhm and Batta (2010) maintain, the process of commodification is fueled not only by the creation of surplus value, which inhibits pleasure through worker exploitation and discipline, but surplus *jouissance*, aimed forever at filling the constitutive lack. Capital recognizes and measures surplus *jouissance* to an unprecedented degree. Through commodities, it offers countless fantasies, "which is precisely what gets us out of bed in the morning" (355). These fantasies cannot satisfy the demands of *jouissance*, and once highly seductive commodities quickly become stale and unfulfilling. Consequently, "pretty quickly Nike's consumers realize that the fantasy they have been promised does not provide full enjoyment. Lack is introduced, which Nike, of course, will try to fill again with a new product" (355).

Understanding the fetish in this way shifts it from being a veil or mask that hides a commodity's true form to its character as an object of desire. The subject's "needs" are always symbolically mediated, that is, activated and directed by the construction of fantasy (through advertising). Consumers, in this sense, buy not the physical object but the mythology (marketing, branding) surrounding it; they strive to fill their inherent constitutive lack through the fantasy of shopping. Commodity fetishism, Böhm and Batta (2010, 356) assert, provides "an image or linguistic system that enables the individual to identify with, and enjoy, the Other [capital]." Yet, despite never quite being satisfied with the product consumed, and despite growing awareness of the social and ecological ills that underpin globalized production, "millions of consumers still flock to NikeTown and other shopping temples to buy expensive branded products" (346). We thus continue to shop, even if we know about the ills of consumption.

Two fundamental issues can be drawn from the above. First, in depicting fetishism as a mask that obscures the relationship between appearance and substance, productivists reproduce the notion of an ideal future (fully transparent) society in which "we can enjoy directly" without the need of the fetish as a substitute for our anxieties and lack. A GLE perspective, in contrast, emphasizes the constitutive character of the fetish and the inherent alienation of the subject. According to this view, we cannot overcome alienation, so that, as chapter 1 emphasized, even a postcapitalist society will be blighted by fetishism of one kind or another.

Second, it is essential to recognize that the fetish serves as both an object of pleasure and a substitute for traumatic loss. As Kapoor states,

> The fetish is not just a pleasurable and magical object, it is also one that enables the subject to (unconsciously) deny the harshness of reality. As a substitute for fundamental trauma, the fetish is a site of disavowal, allowing the subject to better

master her world by ridding it of lack and difference. Additionally, by behaving single-mindedly toward the fetish object as if it possesses a sublime quality, the fetishist forecloses other possible worthy objects or sociopolitical goals. Mastery, disavowal, and foreclosure thus become the hallmarks of fetishism. (2020, 123–24)

It is not the commodity, on its own, that is so often desired, but its fetishistic qualities, which act as a mechanism for repressing or disavowing the traumatic Real. This means that, rather than being *duped* by the commodity form, people are instead *seduced* by its fetishistic qualities. As a result, despite possessing knowledge or awareness about a commodity and how it is produced, we are often still drawn into buying it, enthralled by its magical qualities (Böhm and Batta 2010). The productivists view tends to ascribe to the Marxist idea of "false consciousness," which problematically distinguishes a "true" from a "false" reality, as a result of which some (i.e., the vanguard) know while others (the masses) are misled ("duped"). GLE averts the mistake of claiming any neutral or objective ground from which truth and falsehood can be distinguished. Instead, not only does it maintain that all subjects are ideologically interpellated but, more importantly, that the subject can continue to commit the same mistakes despite knowing. Which is to say that knowledge is not enough: all of us—even the so-called vanguard—can be seduced at the level of the unconscious, even if we are critically conscious.

Commodification, Decommodification, and Recommodification in Fairtrade

Let us illustrate by focusing on fair trade. Over the past forty years there has been a steady rise in a range of socially responsible, sustainable, and ethical consumerist projects aimed at major markets in the global North and South, driven by an array of private governance initiatives led by transnational corporations (TNCs), industry associations, multistakeholder forums (e.g., the Forest Stewardship Council, the Roundtable on Sustainable Palm Oil), NGO collaborations, and third-party, voluntary certification systems (e.g., Fairtrade International, Rainforest Alliance, the Better Cotton Initiative) (Auld 2014; Raynolds and Bennett 2015; Boström, Micheletti, and Oosterveer 2019). While seldom explicitly stated, these initiatives often have as one of their main implicit goals overcoming the barriers of commodity fetishism. Combining an official commitment to social and ecological objectives with transparency and "consumer awareness," the initiatives offer to bridge the "distance" between producers and consumers—bringing them together to expose and address common concerns through a process mediated by the market (Princen, Maniates, and Conca 2002; Lyon 2006). Generally speaking, most have had limited, poor, or modest impacts for workers and small farmers, although they vary depending on the communities and projects in question. While selectively showcasing positive activities, TNCs have simultaneously demanded intensified production and extraction, and lower costs and prices, leading to downward pressure on wages and working conditions, with the responsibility for addressing social and ecological harms passed down the chain to dependent suppliers and farmers (De Neve 2009; Nelson and Martin 2013; Cramer et al. 2014; LeBaron and Lister 2015; Oya et al. 2017; Suwandi 2019; LeBaron and Lister 2020).

But does ethical consumerism provide a model for surmounting the "gap" between producers and consumers? The question has most frequently been explored by those researching Fairtrade certification, perceived as a best practices example of ethical consumption. While there is no space here to examine the history of Fairtrade certification (See Fridell 2007b; Anderson 2015; E. Bennett 2020; Reed 2021), Fairtrade is often depicted as a best practice example because of the centrality of social justice activists to its operation; its independent, third-party verification; its relatively higher standards (including minimum floor prices, democratic rules for coops and unions, and social premiums to fund community-driven projects); and the relatively greater involvement of producer voices in the governance system, emerging from a long and ongoing struggle by Southern Fairtrade groups (E. Bennett 2018; Hudson and Hudson 2021).[2] While recognizing limits to Fairtrade's overall size and impact, many have argued it represents a challenge to commodity fetishism, exposing the conditions under which goods are produced (challenging their commoditization into goods that appear to have a life of their own) and affirming noneconomic values of fairness and solidarity (confronting the atomized, alienated decision making of individual consumers, concerned with their own utility) (Simpson and Rapone 2000; Elson 2002; Raynolds 2002; Lyon 2006; Hudson, Hudson, and Fridell 2013). To Hudson and Hudson, the ability of Fairtrade to realize these goals has been obstructed by corporate marketing, imperfect information, and competitive markets, which distort its ethical and political goals. Fairtrade does, however, have the potential to overcome these barriers, providing a tool for "training consumers to think about the social and environmental implications of their consumption—to refuse to see commodities as they appear" (Hudson and Hudson 2021, 142).

Critics of this view have argued that projects such as Fairtrade can actually intensify commodification, drawing further into the liberal-colonial fantasies around the imagined mastery and "beneficence" of sovereign Northern consumers, far removed from the realities of actual producers (Maniates 2001; Fridell 2007a; Goodman 2010; Kapoor 2013; Fridell 2014). To Gramscian thinker Juan Ignacio Staricco (2017), the idea that Fairtrade is even based on a "subaltern-consumer nexus" is itself a hegemonic construct that obscures the power of global trade and capital, which have set rigid boundaries on Fairtrade from the start, serving to strengthen and reaffirm, rather than challenge, existing power hierarchies. The complexity of the debate, and the extent to which Fairtrade can be understood to confront or concede to commodification, is captured by Laura Raynolds and Nicholas Greenfield, who suggest a perpetual process of "decommodification and simultaneous recommodification of a growing array of fair trade products" (2015, 31; see also Naylor 2018).

What does a psychoanalytic lens add to this debate? From a GLE perspective, the core of commodity fetishism is to obscure not only producer-consumer relations but also the desire embedded in the fetish itself (as well as the anxiety that comes with perpetually seeking and failing to fill one's sense of lack through the fantasized commodity, or *objet a*). While it is true that consumers are seldom aware of the specific conditions under which a product is created, the general conditions are increasingly widely known in the world of the Internet and social media; it is difficult to imagine that the "average" consumer does not have the sense that a five-dollar shirt could well have been, and very likely was, produced under sweatshop conditions (Böhm and Batta 2010; Brooks 2015). While the magic of the fetish involves offering us a tool to disavow the conditions of production, this is only one aspect of its wider appeal as a fantasy. For instance, pleasure from the commodity can emerge not strictly from denying the unequal and exploitative conditions of globalized production but *because* of them. The quest for excessive, unconscious gratification to (temporarily) overcome a sense of generalized lack necessarily requires a "normal" to exceed or transgress (Žižek 2020). In global terms, the excessive consumption of the working or middle-class "First World" consumer can be defined only against those who do not have access to the same goods or services, or the leisure time to enjoy them. In this sense, the class, racialized, national, or gendered inequalities of globalized production play a central role in defining the pleasures of excessive (over) consumption. This occurs not because these inequalities are hidden in the commodity but because they are recognized (unconsciously) within them, making the commodity an object of excess, reserved for a privileged group of consumers.

In addition, while much of the debate around commodification/decommodification in Fairtrade assumes as the ultimate goal a society of full transparency and direct, unmediated enjoyment, such a goal ignores the constitutive nature of fetishism: as Böhm and Batta assert (2010, 351), "The fantasy that fetishism describes is at the heart of what we call 'the subject' as such." A commodity without fetishism would be much less desirable. It is precisely capital's ability to draw on surplus *jouissance* by linking commodities to fetishism that creates such powerful, libidinal investments in it. This poses challenges for the productivist vision of confronting commodity fetishism, which, as Hudson and Hudson (2021, 143) maintain, relies "on consumers actually accepting the duty-bound and depressing version of consumption rather than the fun-filled one." The outcome would appear to be a cycle of perpetual disappointment, hoping for the emergence of responsible, calculating, rational, and duty-bound consumers, all of which downplays the significance of people's desire for pleasure, excess, and fantasy. The challenge becomes not one of confronting pleasure with a "depressing" alternative but rather the (admittedly difficult) task of developing enjoyable confrontations with commodification where people are "seduced at the level of the passions" and not intellect (Kapoor 2015a, 1624).

Finally, building on previous observations, it is essential to recognize that the pleasure the fetishized object brings masks not only conditions of production but also the fetishist's own sense of lack. Fairtrade thus brings with it the emotional content of any fetishized commodity and is a site of many unconscious mechanisms, serving simultaneously as an object of displaced fantasies of mastery and authority (in particular, the exaggerated power of the Northern consumer); a personal source of (ethical, fair, sustainable) comfort and encouragement against trauma and lack; and a form of disavowal, recognizing the exploitation embedded within global supply chains while simultaneously upholding global supply chains as symbols of modernity, growth, and progress (Fridell 2014; Sioh 2014b; Selwyn

2016; Staricco 2017; Fridell and Walker 2019). Perhaps most notable is the notion of *foreclosure* that, as Kapoor has argued, entails "narrowly fixating on an object, by reducing and simplifying the world in order to better master it." In this way, the fetish "excludes difference, foreclosing anything that cannot be assimilated into it" (2020, 125). Very often, this includes foreclosing the messiness and unpredictability of politics, which disturbs the magical fantasy offered by the fetishized object. Thus, the vision of a straightforward chain connecting a (Northern, wealthy, White) consumer with a (Southern, poor, racialized) producer can easily be disturbed if one considers the many antagonisms, conflicts, and struggles operating around actual value chains (West 2012; Fine 2013; Brooks 2015; Naylor 2018). Sipping a cup of ethical coffee at a Starbucks not only represents a limited form of engagement but, depending on how intense the emotional connection is, also forecloses other (more "political") possibilities for action and understanding—for example, unionization, worker ownership and management, strict regulation of TNCs, and so on. The fetishized commodity offers a fantasy of mastery that can persist only with such forms of dissent excluded in advance.

Indeed, Fairtrade has long debated whether it is a stepping stone to other forms of political action or a foreclosure of them (Fridell 2007b; Stolle and Micheletti 2013; Anderson 2015; Raynolds and Bennett 2015; Staricco 2017; Hudson and Hudson 2021). There is likely no simple answer to this question, as Fairtrade represents a broad social movement with complex and competing dynamics, involving hundreds of thousands of producers and supporters. In the 1990s and 2000s, it was widely perceived (by major Fairtrade organizations and powerful institutions such as the World Bank) as offering an alternative to wider political action—be this regulation on prices and labor standards or more radical proposals for a redistribution of wealth and power globally (Fridell 2007b; Jaffee 2007). Today, many Fairtrade groups have recognized the limits of viewing Fairtrade as predominantly a consumer-driven movement seeking to overcome such limits. One way they have done this is by making trade justice advocacy more central to their agenda, that is, working within existing Fairtrade organizations by creating new advocacy initiatives to push governments on a range of issues, including human rights due diligence, modern slavery legislation, global living wages, tax avoidance and evasion, ethical public procurement, and active competition policies to curb uneven power in global supply chains.[3] This disturbs the foreclosure of Fairtrade as consumerism, introducing messy and uncertain political activity into the image of the ideal fair trade "supporter," while seeking to direct the quest for *jouissance* into trade advocacy.

Another important shift in Fairtrade has been driven by Southern producer groups themselves pushing to have greater autonomy and governance of Fairtrade standards. After several years of mobilization, for example, Fairtrade International changed its governance structure in 2012 so that producers have equal votes on the board to those of Northern certification bodies. Likewise, Southern producers created their own label in 2005, the Small Producers' Symbol (SPP), which has higher standards than traditional Fairtrade, including higher minimum prices and greater purchasing commitments from importers, and is managed by small farmers, workers, and the artisans themselves (Melo Maya and Pittoello 2021; Pruijn 2021; Reed 2021). This has been combined with calls to reframe the Fairtrade experience around producers as they seek to build community economies based on dignity and respect, recognizing the asymmetries built into the world trading system. Lindsey Naylor (2018) has observed that during her fieldwork with Fairtrade producers in Chiapas (Mexico), farmers made "almost no mention of coffee consumers (those 'ethically-minded' purchasers of coffee)," instead focusing on the long-term relationships being built between farmer cooperatives and roasters (Naylor 2018, 1038; see also Lyon 2006). It was these interdependencies that were central to "the messiness and unevenness of building livable worlds" for producer communities (Naylor 2018, 1041). This struggle to reframe Fairtrade more centrally around the goals, activities, and visions of producers challenges the centrality of the consumer and consumerist fantasies (of colonial superiority, omnipotence, and beneficence), potentially opening new doors for politically passionate engagement around reimagining Fairtrade.

Conclusion: Fetishistic Disavowal and Commodity Fantasy

The above demonstrates efforts to dampen or avoid the limits of commodity fetishism by directing desire away from the commodity itself and toward social activity that symbolizes Fairtrade in a different way. A major challenge that will remain, though, is the powerful pull of commodity fetishism itself, and whether new initiatives can compete with the passion embedded in the Fairtrade commodity as an object of pleasure and substitute for lack. Trade justice advocacy, for instance, in seeking to expose the inequalities in global trade and advance difficult and complex political responses, can run counter to the pleasures of Fairtrade commodity fetishism, which includes disavowal of these very inequalities and foreclosure around a magical object that is simpler, freed of trauma and conflict (Goodman 2010). Fairtrade alternatives will need to be similarly seductive, providing fetishistic objects for channeling enduring libidinal drives (Böhm and Batta 2010; Kapoor 2020).

Speaking more generally, the pull of fetishism offers many barriers to confronting the inequalities inherent in global capital, simultaneously providing seductive images. Žižek (1989) in particular points to "fetishistic disavowal," through which we recognize something is wrong, and assume a certain ironic distance from it, yet enjoy it anyway—the magical quality of the object is too tempting to resist. In this sense, despite moving ever closer to climate breakdown, despite pervasive high-level dialogue on the need to pressingly address it, we continue to consume and emit carbon at unprecedented rates. This includes looking for ever more environmentally friendly products to soothe the traumas of our overconsuming behavior. The result is a circuitous loop—pursuing the ever-elusive *objet a* that would magically cure our anxieties and antagonisms. According to Kate Soper (2020, 164), ultimately, this never-ending cycle can be broken only with an "alternative hedonism" that shifts "some of the discourse away from the looming horrors towards the pleasures of living and consuming differently."

Such a move would require a politics of "traversing the fantasy," critiquing not solely the material underpinnings of production, exchange, and sale of the commodity but also the deep libidinal desires that the fetish obfuscates (Žižek 2015). The goal, as Kapoor has suggested, is "to identify, and come to terms with, the unconscious process at play in ideological fetishism—the kernel of enjoyment that makes us choose the fetish despite knowing better" (2014; 2020, 142). This necessitates a very different approach to understanding commodity fetishism than that of the productivists. Rather than seeing the fetish as only obscuring the relationship between producers and consumers, the GLE approach emphasizes how the fetish also obscures the unconscious desires, pleasures, and traumas that people project onto it (see chapter 6). Rather than depicting the fetish as a barrier to direct or "false" enjoyment, the GLE approach understands the fetish as a core component *of* enjoyment. The fetish offers a symbolic fantasy, through which subjects exorcise their constitutive anxieties—their never-ending pursuit of *jouissance*. It is only by demystifying the relationship between the commodity and the irrepressible fetish that we can begin to recognize and address the distinct, destructive, and repetitive cycle of *commodity* fetishism.

4

Informal Economy

The Unconscious of Global Capitalism

Let's start with such a common assertion as the informal economy of Peru is estimated to be "between 35% to 60% of GDP" (Machado 2014). The statement reveals that the division between the formal, as a legitimate and known realm, and the informal, as an unregulated and hence unknown realm outside of the purview of the state, is utterly artificial. Which is a way of saying that there are many unknowns about the economy of Peru, let alone the ways in which "informal" slum-based sweatshops in the country may play a crucial role in supporting processes of capital accumulation. So then what function do concepts such as "informal economy" play in political economy? What is it that such a notion evokes that makes it resistant to precise definition? Our wager is that psychoanalysis is particularly adept at approaching the evocative, imaginary, and undefined qualities of informality. But rather than bemoaning or ignoring the lack of clarity of the concept, we will argue that it is precisely its opaqueness as an empty signifier that makes it attractive. The informal sector is in this sense an empty signifier that both reveals and hides the instability of the global libidinal economy. Our point of departure, as underlined in chapter 1, is that the economy is itself splintered, divided from within, and this fissure stands for the impossibility—the antagonism-as-Real—at the center of capitalism. Or, to put it differently, capitalist economic life is always incomplete, inconsistent—non-all.

But the trope of informality is more than an element of a discourse because it refers to a fantasmatic object that produces an eerie kind of fascination. So an additional question this chapter sets out to answer is: What is this object or "Thing" that we name "informal sector" that causes both fear and mystery? And how does it relate to GLE? By way of illustration, let us compare the concept of the informal with another signifier used to evoke the negative: the inhuman. The latter does not designate a realm outside of the human as, say, the animal world. Tellingly, such oppositional determination does not exist for the animal (i.e., the notion of the "in-animal" makes no sense). The inhuman is not, then, the opposite of the human; rather, it evokes what is potentially more human than the human: its hidden, repressed truth—in short, its unconscious.

Our contention is that "the informal" thus speaks to the shadowy, illegal, unregulated, and libidinal sides of the global economy—a realm of exploitation and corruption, as in the case of child labor in slum-located sweatshops, or, for that matter, Colombia's, Mexico's, or the United States' drugs economy. But the concept can also refer to the creative, improvised qualities of an economy invisible to the bureaucratic gaze. So the informal, just like the inhuman, refers both to an excess (of libidinal energy) and a lack (of bureaucratic form) in the global economy. The informal and inhuman are supplementary signifiers aimed at dealing with the excess or lack of that to which they are opposed (the "organized" economy and the stable subject). In Lacanian terms, they are objects that give body to excess or lack, which Lacan calls *objet petit a*, the object cause of desire. Our argument here is that this elusive object operates both as a lure and a veil. It signals an absence by putting a "Thing" in its place to disguise lack (at the center of capitalism). Hence, the impossibility of approaching the *objet petit a* directly; it can be approached only sideways, in an anamorphic way.

The Birth of the Informal

If we were to claim that the concept of the informal economy is an invention, some would read it as a postmodern provocation aimed at destabilizing commonsense ideas about economics, development, and the global South. Others may read it as an iteration of the poststructuralist trope of history, with knowledge as the arbitrary outcome of a will to power (Escobar 1995). In the case of the informal sector, however, it is important to point out that it was introduced as a planning conceptual device at an International Development Studies conference at Sussex in 1971 by anthropologist Keith Hart, who wanted to address common anxieties in development circles about the fear of mass unemployment in the global South.[1] The story itself is fascinating: Hart (2008), a young PhD student in Accra, had seen the opportunity to supplement his meager fellowship by engaging in smuggling activities in the city's harbor. To his surprise, he discovered that such unregistered, often illegal, activities were a thriving segment of the urban economy. In his ethnographic portrayal of the informal sector, he showed that migrant slum dwellers without formal jobs were not idling around, as many presumed. As he put it,

> I would ask questions that just didn't make sense to my informants, for example concerning household budgets. How much do you spend on food a week? Households were in any case often unbounded and transient. Assuming that someone had a regular wage (which many didn't), it was pitifully small; the wage-earner might live it up for a day or two and then was broke, relying on credit and help from family and friends or not eating at all. A married man might use his wage to buy a sack of rice and pay the rent, knowing that he would have to hustle outside work until the next paycheck. In the street economy people were moving everything from marijuana to refrigerators in deals marked more by flux than stable income. (2008, vii)

Hart reported his findings at conference on urban unemployment in Africa, which became a key input for a series of conferences organized by the International Labor Organization (Hart 1973). An important issue for international development organizations such as the ILO at the time was whether the modern economy would be able to respond to the demand for employment of urban migrants. If there existed a segment of the economy that was productive but hidden, then it would be possible to argue that the path from the traditional to the modern economy could be facilitated by supporting "informal" activities. The next step was giving a name to this field of activity and theorizing its relation with the modern economy. As Hart put it, "The ILO did want to coin a concept and that is what it has subsequently become, a keyword helping to organize a segment of the academic and policy-making bureaucracy" (2008, ix). This, in short, led to the invention of the term "informal sector."

Hart was not saying that the informal sector was the answer to the threat of unemployment (although this was often how he was interpreted).

What he was saying was that those who could not be absorbed in the capitalist economy were surviving in precarious ways, and were doing so in a manner intricately tied to the legal economy. He saw the term he invented as a means of pulling the discussion away from the then dominant paradigm of the dual economy and "acknowledging the value of drawing attention to activities that had been invisible to the bureaucratic gaze" (2008, xx). As he stated,

> Most economists saw the idea in quantitative terms as a sector of small-scale, low-productivity, low-income activities without benefit of advanced machines; whereas I stressed the reliability of income streams, the presence or absence of bureaucratic form. . . . The idea of an "informal economy" . . . came out of the lives of Third World city-dwellers, lack of money makes them about as conventionally poor as it is possible to be. . . . I did not identify the informal economy with a place or a class or even whole persons. Everyone in Accra, but especially in the slum where I lived, tried to combine the two sources of income. Informal opportunities ranged from market gardening and brewing through every kind of trade to gambling, theft and political corruption. My analysis had its roots in what people generate out of the circumstances of their everyday lives. (xx)

In short, it was the absence of a regular income stream that made urban slum dwellers especially vulnerable. This in contrast to peasants who count on self-produced, noncommoditized goods. Hart was also very clear to highlight that the modernity-tradition/formality-informality binary is, in his view, an interlinked pair, so that the informal cannot be thought without the formal, and vice versa, as much in the global South as in the North.

Five decades later, the notion of the informal economy has become a key topic in academic thinking about precarity and the global economy, and the idea that it was invented sounds counterintuitive to most. But what analysts (e.g., Ledeneva 2018) often fail to acknowledge is that it was a conceptual invention meant to deal with the anxieties caused by the inability of the economy to provide enough labor opportunities for urban migrants. Its function was to exorcise the ghostly fear of unemployment.

As is so often the case, the "invention" was appropriated by academic and policy circles in unexpected ways, leading to theories about the resilience, ingenuity, and surviving capacities of the poor (e.g., Bromley 2018; Portes 1996). Analysts thereby imagined the informal sector as having a logic of its own, as functional to the modern economy, or even protocapitalist (e.g., de Soto 1989). This, however, was not Hart's aim, as he was thinking about creative ways of combining the survival skills of the poor with the merits of bureaucracy so as to render possible forms of policy and planning that would be able to avert the specter of mass unemployment. As he put it, "The question was therefore: how are 'we' (the bureaucracy and its academic advisors) going to provide the people with the jobs, health, housing etc. that they need? And what will happen if we don't? The specter of urban riots and even revolution raised its head. Some advocated forcibly returning the urban mob to peasant agriculture where they would be likely to do less damage" (Hart 2008, xvii). His concern, of course, was the same as that of Marx, who coined the term "industrial reserve army" to capture a putative frightening political potentiality. Implied here is a preoccupation about surplus populations that could not be absorbed by capitalist economy. Hart's invention thus had a double provenance: a belief in the potentialities of development planning to ward off the threat of unemployment, and a fear of revolution. He was wary of romanticizing the informal economy as a site of democracy against the bureaucracy and market. And his aim was to theorize the dialectic of the formal and the informal so as to harness "the complementary potential of bureaucracy and informality" (xxx). He was, in effect, intervening in a longstanding debate about the importance of reformist regulatory frameworks for dealing with the labor question, very much in the social democratic tradition of Polanyi.

Hart could not have predicted the popularity of the notion he coined; nor that informality would be fetishized as an independent realm with a logic of its own, delinked from the formal state, the latter being reshaped as the true obstacle for development. In this vein, Hernando de Soto (1989, 2000) argues, for example, that the poor are so because they are not able to register their assets, their access to credit being impaired. Accordingly, the poor are seen as the victims of a predatory state bureaucracy that accrues benefits from taxes imposed on the registration of property rights. Such an argument underlines that the cheap and effective distribution of property rights will enable the poor to capitalize on their assets and hence compete with the corporate sector, thus forging a popular capitalism. No consideration is given to the fact that the poor may prefer not to register their properties or may refrain from finding much reason to register changes in property rights (from land sale or inheritance) thus attesting to the strength of nonstate normative frameworks.

Currently, in the latest reiteration of the concept, multinational corporations, inspired by philanthropic organizations such as the Gates Foundation, have stopped blaming the state bureaucracy, resorting instead to corporate social responsibility schemes paired to private-public arrangements. Expanding de Soto's "entrepreneurialism of the poor," capital here is refashioned as creative, flaunting its capacity to reach the bottom of the pyramid through financial technologies (ranging from microcredit to debit cards). The financialization of poverty ("poverty capital"), in this line of thought, enables the informal economy to pair the advantages of reciprocity relations (social capital) with the financial knowledge of multinational corporations. Two types of capital thereby encounter each other: social capital (entrepreneurialism of the poor) and knowledge capital (metrics about the need and use of money, or the repayment capacity of the poor). This is what Roy (2010) calls "poverty capital"; it replaces the antagonism between bureaucratic form and informal improvisation with a friendly encounter between neoliberal financial capital and a presumed creativity of the informal poor.

But before concluding this discussion, let us briefly outline a few key differences between Hart's "invention" of informal economy and Arturo Escobar's poststructuralist argument (1999a) about the "invention" of development. Both aim at highlighting the power of an apparatus of government. However, Escobar's analysis concerns an expansion of governmentality to the most remote areas of the Third World, focusing on the subjugation of people to a new regime of truth. Hart's analysis, however, tells us more about the anxieties of development theorists and practitioners, providing development planning with an afterlife by proposing that there is a realm of economic activity that eludes the gaze of the development apparatus.

To put it in epistemological terms, the difference corresponds to two different types of encounters: in Escobar's case, that of people in the global South and the development apparatus, and the ways in which the former's world is being corrupted by the latter's epistemic violence; in Hart's case, that of the state and an ambiguous and negative informality, with the latter as a source of anxiety, fascination, and fear. It is this second encounter that we wish to pursue from a psychoanalytic point of view, highlighting informality's enigmatic and luring qualities.

Implications

The following implications ensue. First, contrary to what poststructuralists such as Escobar argue, the discourse of informality has little to tell us about actually existing urban economies in the global South. To be sure, there are a number of fine studies that investigate the origins and characteristics of informal economies (Quijano 1970; Geertz 1978; Long and Roberts 1978; G. Smith 1989). Many of these are part of the discussion about transitions from precapitalist to modern market economies (e.g., the notion of petty commodity production as a transitional moment in the movement toward capitalism; see de Janvry 1981). Yet, by the end of the 1970s, with the onset of neoliberal globalization, it became clear that such transitions had already taken place, so there was no outside to capitalism (Hardt and Negri 2000). In fact, the nightmare of the coexistence of capitalism with a global reserve army of labor became increasingly true, as evidenced by growing precarious labor, inner city "ghettos"/favelas, child labor, and slavery.

However, what most of this literature tends to gloss over is the very question of disavowal in the construction of informality: the uncomfortable truths about the gendered and racialized violence upon which the organized capitalist economy crucially depends, or the inability of planning to deal with the surplus enjoyment of financial speculation and exploitation (see chapter 6). Ferguson (1990) famously points out, for example, the World Bank's insistence about Lesotho being an agricultural country, ignoring that the rural economy there in fact relies on migration to South Africa's mines (i.e., precarious migrant labor is key to both Lesotho's and South Africa's capitalist economies). This amounts to a form of deliberate neglect of what does not fit the World Bank's neoliberal view of the world—a disavowal of the fears, anxieties, and inconvenient truths about the antagonisms of capitalism (Kapoor 2014). The task of GLE is precisely to investigate the "return of the repressed" (i.e., the symptomal messages of the Real)—what informality tells us about the disconnection between the discourse of development institutions and the actual functioning of (libidinal) capitalist economies.

Second, the notable pitfall is to attribute to informality any ontological status, whether in a positivist or poststructuralist sense: our claim, in line with Hart's argument, is that it is not a well-defined sector, nor does it generate a subject; rather it is an imaginative figment, a myth, a fiction. It does not really tell us much about the Other (the "Third World" or the subaltern); rather it tells us more about the anxieties of those deploying it (Breman 2013). The informal is the discourse of those who represent state and market institutions—planners, entrepreneurs, economists, development theorists. In Lacanese, the informal is a signifier representing one subject (the poor, the precarious) to another signifier (the development industrial complex). We are in the realm of what Lacan calls the "discourse of the university" (2006), rooted in modern institutions of higher learning and symptomatic of the fears and anxieties about the contradictions and crisis-proneness of the global capitalist economy.

Third, approaching the empty signifier of informality from the formal viewpoint of enunciation raises the epistemological question about the difficulty of approaching GLE directly, and consequently the advantages of looking at it sideways—that is, from the perspective of that which is labeled irrational or libidinal, and hence "extimate"[2] to how it can or should function (i.e., impossible to define, manage, or control). We are asking here what is the fascination, the fantasy, that draws the expert and academic to the informal? We suggest there is enjoyment here (by the typically white Western "expert") that goes beyond the mere pleasure of viewing the spectacle of informality—the voyeuristic, sadomasochistic *jouissance* derived from precarity and casualization: from hollowing out the state, cutting social services, converting people to entrepreneurs of the self, and so forth. This, in short, is the fascination with the death drive that animates late modern capitalism, exemplified, for example, by the enjoyment of self-sacrifice that characterizes Donald Trump's or Narendra Modi's politics (sacrifice to make one's country "great again," no matter if it resorts to falsities or demeans and destroys one's so-called adversaries/ enemies).

The point not to be lost is that this is the perspective of a privileged subject who knows they are "safe" yet is fascinated by the precarious and supernumerary Other. It is the insider's view of the outsider lacking the advantages of a stable income. To be sure, while the study of informality does not (and by our reckoning, cannot) capture informality, it nonetheless provides academics, policymakers, and planners with an object-cause of anxiety: it enables frenetic activity, as manifested in the writing of scores of academic papers, policy documents, and project proposals, while secretly never wanting to alter the unequal relationship between protected insiders and precarious outsiders. Such frenzied busy-ness/business is a sure sign of the privileged subject not wanting for anything to change (like the obsessional neurotic who talks all the time in order to avoid the analyst's questions).

To understand this better, the Lacanian difference between the eye and the gaze is important. The eye is the viewpoint of the subject, while the gaze is the object looking back, generating a mix of anxiety and fascination. It is what Robert Pfaller (2012) calls interpassivity, obsessive activity whose function is to hide that nothing must change. The frenzy serves to assuage the guilt that the voyeuristic look on the precarious brings about. Lacan theorized the gaze as the partial object of the scopic drive, the gaze of the Other that produces fear and anxiety, exorcised only by the "rational" discourse of the university by projecting imagined qualities on the Other. While the eye views the object directly, the gaze can be apprehended only in an anamorphic way. Thus, Lacan affirms that "not only is the picture in my eye, but I am also in the picture" (1997, 63), his point being that the picture can be accessed only by attending to the "weird," extimate object that gives body to the subject's "out of jointedness"—the object cause of desire/drive. Hence the idea of the "scopic drive" as a voyeuristic *jouissance* generated by the mixture of guilt, fascination, and disavowal that the "suffering" Other instills in the affluent viewer.

In the study of participatory planning in Recife that we present in the last part of this chapter, we show that the obsession with the need to cleanse the city from *palafitas* (stilt houses) that proliferate in front of wealthy neighborhoods and First World shopping malls constitutes the partial object looking back on the viewer—the stain in the eye or the bone in the throat that spoils the pleasure of living in a potentially "world-class city."

The Informal-Formal Dialectic: Slum Upgrading in Recife

Before focusing on the Recife case study, a brief theoretical note: as implied above, Hart (2008) provides a useful (Hegelian) theoretical framework for analyzing the relationship between the formal and the informal as an interlinked pair. According to him, the *division* between formal rule and its informal application produces *content* that always deviates from the designs of lawmakers and policymakers. The contradiction between design and reality provides mala fide actors opportunities to subvert the intent of the Law in creative, but also sometimes corrupt and violent, ways (e.g., drug trade, land grabbing, etc.). This, in short, is the *negation* of the intent of formal rules. It leads to the creation of a normative framework in the shadow of the Law; a *residue* or excess in the form of implicit rules, as a result of which communities deal with the threats of illegality and violence. Such subversion, in turn, impels the state to create new formal rules. So Hart's prescription is to make the bureaucracy receptive to disruption from below, which is to say, open to a kind of legal pluralism.

Hart abides by a social democratic program that avoids the tendency to see either the state bureaucracy as the enemy of people's creativity or the informal as the source of legal insecurity that hinders foreign investment in Southern economies. In what follows, we draw on his conceptual device but depart from his reformist intent by introducing Lacanian concepts to highlight the inconsistent and non-all character of the capitalist economy. Accordingly, we conceive the relationship between the formal and the informal as one of impossibility, following Lacan's dictum that "there is no sexual relationship" (see Zupančič 2017). This compels us to start with the "residue" (i.e., informality) as an element that cannot be included in the dominant order—the bone in the throat that spoils the fantasy of the relation between organized and unorganized economy, rendering both incomplete, or non-all. The dominant order deals with such impossibility by constructing an ideological fantasy (neoliberal development) aimed at covering over antagonisms, yet it is never able to completely cloak them, opening up possibilities for disruption.

In what follows, we deploy this revised Hegelian-Lacanian framework to analyze the rise and decay of a participatory slum governance system in Recife, based largely on field research carried out from 2010 to 2018 (Nuijten, Koster, and de Vries 2012; de Vries 2016a, 2016b). We start with a short characterization of informality in Recife before analyzing the trajectory of the city's governance system.

The Establishment of Dual Governance in Recife

Recife is known as the city of slums, where most of the poor live. Slums in Brazil are officially defined as "subnormal" informal settlements with little tenure security, lacking basic services such as sanitation, water, energy, and access to public transport. In Recife, slums, or favelas, as they are derogatively called, can be big and small (*favelinhas*). Big favelas are located in the city's center but also on the river basin and the coastline. Even in upper-class neighborhoods *favelinhas* can be found beside apartment towers. They comprise 30 percent of the built territory and 60 percent of the population of the city (da Silva and de Vries 2022). Nowhere within a radius of one kilometer of the city do slums fail to appear. A typical picture of Recife is that of stilt houses located in the rear of a "world-class" shopping mall, or on a canal in one of the upper-class neighborhoods.

The ubiquity of favelas/*favelinhas* in Recife is the result of a swath of massive land occupations since the end of the 1970s, organized by a popular movement under the protection of the Justice and Peace Commission, an entity founded by the Catholic Church comprising leftist activists and academics inspired by liberation theology. During the Brazilian dictatorship (1964–85), urban development policies in Recife aimed at relocating informal settlements to areas outside of the city, using the recurrence of floods in "precarious areas" as a justification for the forced displacement of "vulnerable populations." In the mid-1970s, the floods were exceptionally intense, so under the leadership of the Justice and Peace Commission, slum dwellers set off to occupy unused private and public land rather than letting themselves be displaced.

This popular movement exposed the existence of a category of people whose belonging to the city could no more be denied by the dominant powers: what Rancière denominates as "the part of no-part"—those who are present but not represented (see chapter 1 and Read 2007). In our terms, this is the residue/excess, the poor living in "subnormal" conditions such as stilt houses. For the first time in the history of Recife, the poor became an acknowledged political actor after their popular mobilization, demanding the right to be heard and participate in the governance of the city. Bolstered by the irruption of the no-part, a series of progressive municipal governments established alliances with the popular movement in order to formalize the existence of this "residue." The result was the creation of a participatory slum governance system, the Plano de Regularização das Zonas Especiais de Interesse Social (PREZEIS), which ascertains the right of the poor to live and work in the city.

The PREZEIS law was promulgated in 1987. It is unique in that, in disputes over tenure, it prioritizes the rights of informal occupants and tenants over property owners, based on the principle that "all who live here belong here." It also has at its disposition a fund for slum-improvement projects aimed at making the slum a viable place to live—an important difference from slum-upgrading projects, which aim to integrate the slum into the city (a topic we will return to). Decisions regarding tenure regulation and infrastructural improvements are made according to rules of a participatory democracy in designated commissions of urbanization and legalization (COMULs) aimed at ensuring the largest possible consensus after lengthy deliberative procedures. Decisions regarding tenure regulation and infrastructural improvements take place in collaboration with technicians of the municipality and civil society advisors (members of specialized NGOs funded by the PREZEIS fund). Accordingly, the effectiveness of the PREZEIS system is measured by the levels of participation in meetings and the quality of decision making as the outcome of a process of collaboration with bureaucrats and other experts. Slum dwellers elect delegates at COMUL meetings for a citywide slum-governance structure, called the PREZEIS forum. This in contradiction to representative electoral democracy, where citizens elect representatives who compete for votes following a market logic, something that in Recife's slums (and elsewhere in Brazil) amounts to vote buying.

The establishment of a participatory democracy based on rules of direct participation, alongside a representative democracy operating according to a patron-client logic of electoral competition, in effect amounted to the creation of a dual power system in Recife. The effectiveness of the participatory system relied on its capacity to rein in electoral patron-client politics by improving direct participation and the creation of a popular democratic consciousness (a revolutionary subjectivity), hence expanding the quality of democracy, or as de Sousa Santos (2005) calls it "the democratization of democracy." In Lacanian terms, the PREZEIS participatory democratic system was part of a struggle for a new kind of rule, for a new "master signifier," standing for the sovereignty of the popular movement. This is an openly antihegemonic discourse, and yet, as we discuss next, it is one that relies on the local state bureaucracy, which stands in an equivocal position vis-à-vis the popular movement.

Indeed, at the intersection of the participatory and representative democracy is the bureaucracy, composed of municipal technicians, planners, and policymakers, who are accountable both to elected politicians (the councilors and the mayor) and to the participatory process (the COMULs and the PREZEIS forum). For our purposes, it is important to highlight the central role the bureaucracy plays in the deployment of the *division* between the formal and the informal as an organizational conceptual instrument. Thus, the distinction between a participatory system for the poor in informal settlements and a representative system run by politicians led the bureaucracy in Recife to establish a *division* between the *formal city* and the *informal city* as a conceptual device for mapping their fears and anxieties on those areas of the city that are beyond their control (de Vries 2016).

This division is utterly artificial, as attested by the existence of formal rules and obligations in the participatory system in the "informal city" and the pressure by construction capital to expand the formal city through corrupt "informal" practices, what Roy (2005) calls the "informalized production of space." Yet, within the bureaucratic discourse, this division operates as follows: the formal city benefits from a governance structure consisting of areas where registered citizens are ensured good services, whereas the informal city is made up of "precarious areas," which are vulnerable to environmental hazards and largely inaccessible to governmental services, including low levels of taxation and population registration. Accordingly, the distinction between the formal and informal city has become a shorthand for talking about the problems of governing a city with a majority of the population living under "subnormal" circumstances, lacking the social capital to conduct themselves as "proper" citizens. Furthermore, given the establishment of the PREZEIS participatory governance system, it is not possible anymore to evict the poor from areas considered to be strategic for the growth of the city. In Lacanian terms, this construction of informality as a governance problem is an example of the discourse of the university (i.e., a rational discourse that projects state bureaucratic designs onto the part of no-part).

The issue we turn to next is how this new articulation of the informal and the formal in Recife gives rise to a new content: how the poor construct a popular economy.

RECIFE'S POPULAR ECONOMY: EMERGENT OUTCOME
OF THE INFORMAL-FORMAL DIALECTIC

Hart's description of the "informal economy" is very apt for describing the popular economy in Recife. Contrary to binary representations of the informal as the Other of the formal, here we set out to show that the popular economy is a compromise formation emerging from the contradiction between the existence of a participatory system (grounded in the right to work and live in the city) and the expansionary needs of capital. We also argue that governmental attempts to overcome the informal-formal split leads to the creation of a new residue.

Indeed, the poor may well be unemployed, but they do work ("informally"), as we stressed earlier. In actual fact, the strategic location of slums in the inner city has spawned a thriving popular economy comprising different levels of employment security, such as work for governmental institutions, registered and unregistered businesses, and self-employment in trade, transport, small-scale manufacture, retail shops and street food, and domestic and construction work. Obtaining formal employment with a fixed contract is a boon for most families in the popular economy. Hence the importance of hierarchical relations of dependence, instrumental for gaining access to such work opportunities but thereby reinforcing entrenched patron-client relations. Recife's economy is a typical case of neoliberal informalization driven by processes of subcontracting and flexibilization. The availability of abundant and cheap labor near the harbor and the city center ensures the reproduction of a popular economy combining "informal" precarious employment in sweatshops with a diversity of self-employment activities.

A case in point is the cultural economy around big events, such as Carnival. The city's Carnival is promoted as a multicultural, democratic, and inclusive event, in contrast with that of other cities in Brazil (Rio de Janeiro, Salvador de Bahia) where Carnival has become highly segregated. In Recife, it is both a popular "fest" and a source of income for the poor who are involved in the making of fantasy dresses, the sale of food and beverages, and so on. The history of Carnival in Recife, as a popular and democratic celebration, is strongly tied to the history of strong popular movements and collective resistance against efforts by capital and the state to privatize public space. Carnival is thus a symbolic performance about the Right to the City of the poor (da Silva and de Vries 2022).

The media and dominant classes respond to the ubiquitous presence of the poor by producing images of the popular economy as "dangerous," "promiscuous," and "criminal." Hence the pressure on the state to control the urban poor, especially those living off illicit, often criminal and promiscuous, activities (e.g., prostitution, drug trade) in areas with relatively little state presence. One way to govern the poor is by creating "inclusive" urban reform programs aimed at incorporating "informal settlements" within the city grid, thus expanding the formal city. As a rule, these urban reform programs are presented as "participatory" slum-upgrading projects, often giving slum dwellers compensation in the case of evictions (in the form of housing or money), provided they have proper registration documents as residents, which most lack. The result is that many who belong to the slum are not included in "participatory" slum-upgrading projects. Or to put it differently, many who are present are not represented in such projects.

"Participatory" slum upgrading in Recife differs from the participatory slum governance system in that it is funded and designed under the supervision of international financial institutions, such as the World Bank, in close cooperation with the federal, state, and municipal governments, using the modality of public-private partnerships. They are planned at a citywide level using the technical discourse of "urban reform," justified by the importance of protecting "vulnerable" communities from floods and landslides. Hence their categorization as products of strategic planning, in contrast to the participatory planning of the PREZEIS slum governance system. Problems concerning poverty and unemployment are, as a rule, not tackled by these projects, as they are seen as being beyond their remit (i.e., a matter of market, not state, initiatives).

The participatory democratic system, in contrast, operates according to the precept that "everyone who lives here belongs," without demanding any formal documents, thereby defending residents from the excesses and control of the bureaucratic gaze. Furthermore, the prioritization of belonging over inclusion in the participatory system goes together with formal rules of participation aimed at protecting slum communities from the predatory drive of real estate capital to appropriate slum territory through "informal means" (i.e., bribing PREZEIS delegates, civil servants, and politicians).

The result has been the emergence of a popular economy as the determinate *content* of informality—precarious (self)-employment within the formal rules of a participatory system aimed at defending the right of the poor to live and work in the city. It would be wrong, therefore, to view the popular economy as a "natural" economy outside, or as an alternative to, the capitalist economy (e.g., a postcapitalist economy). The popular economy is both highly integrated with the global economy *and* an obstacle to the expansion of urban capital. It cannot be stressed enough that its viability relies on the formal rules of a participatory democracy that defends the poor from the predatory pressures of real estate capital.

Ironically, the moment that reformist political forces set out to overcome the contradictions between capital and the poor to create an "inclusive" World Class City, the reproduction of the popular economy was threatened, triggering a new moment in the informal-formal dialectic and giving rise to a new residue/excess. This is what we turn to now.

RECIFE WITHOUT PALAFITAS: DECAY OF THE
PARTICIPATORY SYSTEM

The PREZEIS participatory slum-governance system was part of a political
project aimed at the expansion of popular sovereignty in Recife, as against
the demands of capital to expand in strategically located slum areas in
the inner city. The PREZEIS managed to survive and even expand from
1987 until 2000, in spite of the opposition of rightist administrations.
But ironically, the PREZEIS was neglected by the leftist Partido de Tra-
balhadores (Worker's Party; PT) that governed the city from 2001 to 2013.
At both the municipal and federal levels, the PT in power shed its radical
promises and embarked on a reformist path aimed at conciliating the
interests of the working classes and the elite. It promoted a vision of the
"inclusive city," benefiting from a booming economy and large infrastructural projects (expansion of the port, large road construction programs)
and openly using its political control over the Participatory Budgeting
program for electoral purposes. The PT hegemony, however, was rattled
when the administration was accused of receiving large kickbacks from
a building consortium in return for a license to start a huge construction
project in the former dock areas of the city.

Symptomatic of this postpolitical approach was a new program,
Recife sem Palafitas (Recife without Stilts), aimed at beautifying the city
by cleansing it of stilt houses, especially in strategic locations. The PT
used its political influence in inner city slums to gain the support of
slum community leaders, under the expectation that slum upgrading,
together with beautification through the Recife sem Palafitas program,
would increase the value of property. This PT betrayal of the demand
for the right to live in the city provided real estate corporations with the
opportunity to gain access to lands by bribing COMUL delegates so as
to change slum boundaries.

The stilt houses operated as both a lure and a veil—the object-cause
of the drive to beautify the city and a disguised betrayal of the principles
of the popular movement. In Lacanian terms, this was a hysteric reaction
to the state's inability to counter the drive of capital. The result was the rise
of a new class of intermediaries, brokers, and community leaders, drawing
on their knowledge of local politics to gain the financial support of their
new masters: it inaugurated the beginning of the decay of the PREZEIS
slum governance system and the conversion of participatory democracy
into an electoral market. Eventually, the turn of a leftist administration

espousing reformist and pro-poor policies toward a neoliberal modernist aesthetic weakened the ability of the Left in Recife to counter accusations of corruption, leading to the demonization of the participatory system as complicit with electoral corruption.

Remarkably, as a reaction to corporate appropriation of slum land by illegal means, community leaders started once again organizing occupations of unused public land, partaking in "the informalized production of space." The result was the expansion of new *favelinhas*, often in the form of stilt houses (*palafitas*). This, in short, is the production of a new "residue," an indivisible remainder or excess, standing for the inherent antagonisms of the city. The stilt houses of the no-part reappeared like the return of the repressed—that which cannot be totally eviscerated and always comes back in the form of ghostly "nightmares."

Conclusion

This chapter has argued that the informal sector is an invention driven by the fear of the "dangerous classes"—the mob, lumpenproletariat, reserve army, part of no-part. It differs from other (scientific) inventions in that it produces forms of knowledge whose aim it is to leave untouched the basic parameters of global capitalism. As an empty signifier—a container concept—the trope of the informal economy is an appropriate example of the deployment of what Lacan denominates as the discourse of the university as vehicle for stabilizing and gentrifying the excesses of capitalism. But we also argued that these discourses are reactions to an emancipatory and anticapitalist discourse, that of the analyst, which in the case of Recife stands for the discourse of a popular movement that questions and destabilizes the bureaucratic subject, forcing it to react, either by trying to cover over inherent social antagonisms or by reluctantly accepting popular mobilization.

We have drawn on, and radicalized, Keith Hart's dialectical theorization of the relationship between the formal and the informal to argue that representations of informality as the realm of freedom against the "tyranny of the state bureaucracy" are complicit with neoliberal projects of globalization. Disputing Hart's social democratic reformist attempt to reconcile the informal with the formal, we have argued that this is a relationship marked by a constitutive impossibility that is the very hallmark of a GLE approach: libidinal economy thrives in times of crisis as a way of dealing with inherent instability and inconsistency. The result is the creation of a category that does not fit: Hart's "residue" or Rancière's "part of no-part." This, in short, is the name of a category that stands for the inherent antagonism of the social order, located at the edge of the void (Badiou 2007). The residue-as-excess-as-unconscious that GLE alerts us to is what subverts the universal intent of the Law (the inscription of formal rules in the symbolic register) from within, pointing to the political antagonism (i.e., "class struggle" in the Žižekian sense; see chapter 1). For Fanon (1963) the name of this residue is the postcolonial Third World subject, an unintended but necessary outcome of imperial design, or in class terms, the lumpenproletariat who have nothing to lose but their chains. In the Recife case study we presented here, the residue is another name for the *palafitas*, the stilt houses that cannot be included in the city—a stain in the eyes of the wealthy and the powerful who see only the devaluation of their investments, provoking feelings of fear and revulsion.

We presented the case study of participatory slum governance in Recife, created by an alliance between a popular movement and leftist activists, to argue that the institutionalization of such an emancipatory form, as a counterpoint to the informality of wealth and power, is central to the defense of the right of the poor to work in the city. Formal rules were pivotal for the creation of this system, ensuring the Right to the City of those who are seen by the elite as unfit to live in it—the residue. The mobilization of the urban poor, living under the permanent threat of eviction and excluded from the urban project of creating an elite World Class City, was central to the construction of the participatory democratic system. This system coexisted with representative democracy, creating a marked division between the informal, competitive, and patron-client logic of electoral democracy and the formal rules required for the implementation of the Right to the City by participatory democracy. As long as the two systems were kept apart, the emancipatory thrust of the slum governance system was sustained. Their tense separation exemplified a certain uneasy agonism, as a result of which the emancipatory formal thrust of the PREZEIS participatory slum governance system stood precariously alongside the desire of the elite to incorporate the slums within the "formal city," commoditizing space for the sake of capital accumulation. Such an agonistic relationship rendered possible a new *content*, linking the informal creativity of the poor with the formal rules aimed at defending their right to live and work in the city.

However, with the ascendancy of the reformist Left (under the leadership of the PT), intent on conciliating the demands of the elites and the popular movement, the participatory democratic thrust of the slum governance system was diluted. This was enabled by the deliberate politico-epistemological division of the city between a formal and informal city, each area targeted by planning interventions: strategic planning for the formal city aimed at making it attractive to corporate investments, and "participatory" planning for the informal city aimed at controlling the urban poor through urban slum-upgrading projects. Such a move meant the negation of the dialectic between the formal and the informal, disavowing the missing socioeconomic ground of the city by attempting to overcome its antagonisms. Ultimately, the drive of the market aimed at controlling the urban poor for the sake of the commoditization of urban space trumped the desire for the Right of the City of the popular movements. But this in turn meant the return of the Real/unconscious, the residue in the shape of the proliferation of stilt houses, evidence of the impossibility of capitalism to cover over or eliminate its inherent inequalities, exploitation, and domination.

To the extent that the informal sector is not a definable sector, it is always present yet "extimate" to the capitalist order. There is, then, no question of romanticizing it as a revolutionary subject (in the form of Recife's vibrant favelas, or the creativity of slum dwellers, for example), but rather seeing it as an amorphous presence/absence, inherent to the very creation of the formal capitalist economy, and one that always troubles, destabilizes, and threatens the latter. The favelas are, in this sense, the spectral and unwieldy shadow constitutive of formality's alleged "order." Their unwieldiness *may* have revolutionary potential, but this needs to be organized and directed by a political subject, with no guarantees (in the way that Recife's popular sector succeeded in achieving temporarily, ironically failing under a Left reformist regime). The unconscious, in this sense, provides the ingredients for radical acts but needs to be channeled and coordinated to have political impact, successful or not. Yet, what a GLE approach underlines is that, regardless of whether such rupturous potential is politically sublimated, it always remains immanent, lurking in shadows—a bone in the throat of any system, capitalist or not.

This has far-reaching implications for our current global economy: instead of being a thing of the past, the informal sector has swelled rather than shrunk, with the ILO (2022, 80–83) estimating current temporary employment to be as high as 28 percent worldwide (as a percentage of the employed population) and steadily rising. Most employment casualization and precarity affects women, primarily in the rural sector. But increasingly, it has been the service and technology-related "platform" sectors that are relying on the "gig economy" (i.e., temporary, contract, low-skilled, and on-call employment), especially postpandemic. The result has been not only falling wages and rising global income inequality (see chapter 6) but also climbing social unrest (e.g., *Gilets jaunes*, Podemos, Occupy, "freedom convoys," peasant/small farmer revolts in India and China, fuel and food riots in North and sub-Saharan Africa, etc.) at unprecedented levels. Indeed, Ortiz et al. (2022) estimate that protest movements have tripled around the world in the last fifteen years. All of this is revealing, then, not just of global capitalism's increasing reliance on a reserve army of labor (the part of no-part) but also of the real/Real "threat" that informality poses to the system.

Trade

Emotional Labor and Psychological "Bowing" in the US-China Trade War

Might—whether military or technological—does decide geopolitical reality. Morality is a platform for victims to complain and victors to preach.

—Andrew Sheng (2021)

The need for economic growth in a developing country has few if any economic springs. It arises from a desire to assume full human status by taking part in an industrial civilization, participation which alone enables a nation or an individual to compel others to treat it as an equal.

—Chalmers Johnson (1982, 25)

A *Dictionary of Economics* (Black, Hashimzade, and Myles 2013) defines a trade war as a situation where countries seek to damage each other's trade using tariffs, quota restrictions, bans on imports, or even subsidizing or providing credit to other rivals of the trading country. To query the definition of "trade war" on Investopedia.com, for example, brings up the US-China trade war, as if it has come to define all trade wars. Indeed, this war is significant. First, because it involves the two biggest economies in the world. Second, because it represents the latest evolution in trade wars, with the trade war morphing into a tech war. Where previous trade wars were fought over goods produced, this one is fought over intangibles—knowledge that has *yet to be produced*, such as the constantly evolving 5G technology. Technology is seen as key to the construction of the Internet of Things, which, in turn, is central to the creation of "smart cities"—our projected future physical and psychological environment. And third, the US-China trade war underscores how economic behavior is replete with moral judgment and assumptions around who has the power to define what morality means. To mention "trade war" in any discussion today immediately conjures up the specter of an underhanded, authoritarian, human rights-violating China in a struggle over the survival of democracy and civilization with the United States (Peters 2020). This coding is evident in the framing of the US-China rivalry as being one of moral enforcement over foreign cheaters, at least when it comes to intellectual property rights. Saskia Sassen (2008, 241–42) notes that the focus on IPR is not a historical one but rather the result of corporations' recent recognition of the significance of technology in driving profits. Since the United States' identity as a superpower is so intrinsically tied to its technological supremacy, any challenge on that front becomes not just a political-economic one but a status challenge. The urgency in resolving trade tensions lies in its potential to become a flashpoint for a new Cold War (Allison 2017b).

So what do we really mean when we talk about *this* trade war? While it always seems implicit that what is being fought over is very little about the trade in commodities, there seems to be an *omertà* around its discussion in the West. Any discussion of the US-China trade war is coupled with an unverbalized parallel conversation about Mars rovers, artificial intelligence (AI), and all the cultural coding that technological supremacy and the economic success signify. The trade war has become a veiled reference for who controls our future material environment. And the pathway to constructing that environment is dependent on economic and technological primacy, the two indicators of a contemporary hegemonic identity.

In this chapter, we argue that the vitriolic discourse surrounding the trade-war-as-tech-war is unsurprising if we understand the "war" as a container for anxieties about national identity in political economy and geopolitics. We argue that the trade negotiations can be analyzed as a struggle, on the part of China, against the emotional accommodation of the submissive-dominant dynamic imposed upon it in international relations. In that sense, the practical significance of the trade war is the potential for the tensions around ostensibly economic issues to drift into conflict over technology, because its protagonists see the battle over technology as a battle for psychic survival. As a result, what this chapter contributes, perhaps to a greater extent than the other chapters in this book, is a focus on the intricate and micropsychoanalytic processes at play in GLE, as emergent in the recent US-China trade negotiations/war.[1] Our approach traces the anxiety threaded throughout the dry economic and legal texts to highlight the links between the legacies of trauma and policy decisions. Here, post-Freudian psychoanalytic theory (Heinz Kohut, Arlie Hochschild) is particularly insightful in helping us understand the interpersonal psychoanalytic dynamics immanent to global politico-economic hierarchy.

Note that our attempt to understand China's perspective does not imply approval of its politics. As we underline in chapters 1 and 8, countries can be both perpetrators and victims, and lost in the US-China focus are the numerous global South countries that have to contend with both. But a psychoanalytic approach is less about passing moral judgements and more about understanding the logic underpinning policy/politics, a logic that may be emotionally judicious but isn't necessarily intellectually rational for either China or the United States. The excessive reaction by the protagonists, which goes beyond what is profitable (Hass and Denmark 2020), is an indicator of the narcissistic rage present in negotiations. This is precisely the indicator that a psychoanalytic framework may be a more fruitful approach to analyzing the intractability of the trade negotiations, as opposed to more conventional business and international relations models.

Theorizing the Dynamics of the US-China Trade War

The most common approach to analyzing the US-China trade war has focused on determining who is likely to lose more economically (Lau 2019, 2020b; Qin 2019; Nicita 2019; Liu 2020, Hass and Denmark 2020). In conventional trade models, the impact of tariffs is to raise the prices of imports, thus reducing their demand. Tariffs can also divert trade to other countries as importers seek to avoid them (Nicita 2019, 4). In both situations, the targeted country loses economically, but the country imposing the tariffs also loses if it cannot find an appropriate replacement supplier. From an international relations perspective, the significance of the US-China trade war is its potential to transform into a new Cold War, commonly framed as the "Thucydides' Trap" after Allison's (2017a) monograph on US-China power rivalry. For Allison (2017b), the key question is whether China and the United States can escape the trap. Although he concludes that war is not inevitable, the idea has taken off, receiving over eighty thousand references on a Google search.

Among the scholarly community, there has been criticism that Thucydides' Trap frames the US-China rivalry through a Western-centric lens. Peters (2020) argues that the framing ignores that China might not view geopolitics in such binary terms. Similarly, Benjamin Green (2020) criticizes the approach for ignoring the possibility of a multipolar world, as opposed to the zero-sum, winner-takes-all approach that Western analysts, especially Americans, favor (see also Arrighi 2009). And Mou (2020) argues that, historically, China has preferred the option of diplomacy rather than outright confrontation. Allison (2017b, 3), quoting Samuel Huntington, notes that America is a "missionary nation," which seeks to impose its values on others. Mirroring this, the mainstream American position tends to depict China as similarly seeking to impose its ideology on others through its own economic ascendance (see chapter 8). Allison (3–4) argues, however, that China is strategically pragmatic without needing the ideological conversion of others. But perhaps his most interesting insight is his caution that the protagonists at the center of the rivalry *must*, above all, avoid humiliating each other. This intriguing claim leads us to a different framing of the trade war as proxy for superpower rivalry—that establishing a global order is achieved through controlling a global hegemonic identity.

We derive the definition of a global hegemonic identity from Morrell and Swart's (2004, 92) definition of hegemonic masculinity. Given colonialism's equation of "race" with inferiority, hegemonic masculinity in globalization is equated with a *mastery* of economy and technology. The World Bank still divides the world into more and less "developed," using the distinguishing factor of economic performance, which, not accidentally, generally corresponds to global racial difference (90). However, Connell and Wood (2005, 47–48) argue that we are seeing a new pattern of hegemonic masculinity emerging through the economic, political, and cultural shifts labeled as "globalization." As traditional models of masculinity take the form of financial power (352), those who control the technology that enables financial transactions become the standard bearers of new hegemonic identity (see chapter 6). Accordingly, contemporary hegemonic masculinity takes the form of technological and economic success as a compound indicator of superiority and entitlement. Our new "warriors" are economically powerful individuals who have achieved that status first as technological "heroes" (Elon Musk, Jeff Bezos, Mark Zuckerberg, Bill Gates). Technological tools such as 5G technology become important symbols in hegemonic performance in the shape of AI, smart cities, and the seemingly magical multiplication of virtual wealth from blockchains and cryptocurrency. They are important because if race and gender are markers of intellectual difference, the attainment of intellectual superiority implies becoming more like the "master" through lactification and remasculinization. Performance and identity are linked in trade negotiations, deployed as they are to achieve desired outcomes on the international and domestic stages (Kim and Margalit 2021). Democratic elections and trade negotiations set the stage, as we shall see, for the scripting of a hegemonic identity.

Although there are few, if any, psychoanalytic studies of trade wars, taking a psychoanalytic approach to studying trade war negotiations as manifestations of anxious masculinities is not as farfetched as it might first appear. Allison (2017b) and mainstream Asian experts on China such as Julia Qin (2019), Lawrence Lau (2020a), and Carrie Shang and Wei Shen (2021) have referenced psychological categories such as "emotion," "anxiety," "shame," and "existential threat" in their work, which suggests that the biggest danger to an inaccurate analysis of the trade war is to discount these dimensions. Using their comments as a starting point, we argue that because the prestige of a group's identity is so closely associated with its economic status, a change in its global technological standing is experienced as narcissistic injury. Indeed we engage with the concepts of narcissistic injury and rage developed by Heinz Kohut (1973) to analyze antagonistic trade negotiations.

Kohut's conceptualization of Freudian narcissism is relational. When he deploys the term "selfobject," he uses it to mean any narcissistic experience in which the other is in the service of the self, with the construction of self as an intrinsic part of an individual's sense of psychic coherence. He sees (1973, 628, 637–38) a selfobject as providing essential support for the vulnerable self through an "approving mirroring response," which becomes the basis of self-esteem. But he argues (477, 628, 756) that if the grandiose self, defined as the "exhibitionistic" self demanding of attention, has not experienced the transformation of the narcissistic investment into a healthy self-esteem and is deprived of an "approving mirroring response" from the selfobject, it will experience a narcissistic injury and respond with extreme rage. It should be noted that if the self requires a mirroring response from the selfobjects, Kohut's conceptualization suggests that the selfobjects, in their idealizing role, contain within them the *power* to confer or withhold approval. Sioh (2018b) has applied the self/selfobject framework to analyzing the Western response to the 1997–98 Asian financial crisis. In this chapter, we apply the same concepts to the United States and China, respectively.

Kohut (1973, 644) goes on to propose that the extreme defensive response of narcissistic rage is activated when confronted with the recalcitrant selfobject because it is not considered an autonomous source. Instead, recalcitrance is perceived as a "flaw" in the narcissist's "reality," which the narcissistically vulnerable self expects to control. Thus, the selfobject's independence is experienced as offensive. This, we claim, is the crux of the United States' reaction to China's economic and now technological success. Since the narcissist must exert absolute control over its environment and obtain unconditional approval for its self-esteem, it must "grind down" the opponent who threatens to outshine it. Accordingly, the United States perceives China's success as a narcissistic injury: the latter's desire to create its own technology and exert its independence from the United States provokes anxieties. Additionally, China promotes its rapid economic growth as a function of its own politico-economic model ("communist/authoritarian capitalism"), destroying the sense of unconditional approval of the Western model ("capitalist liberal democracy"). Following Kohut (1973, 644), China is now a "flaw in a narcissistically perceived reality" of the United States. And the trade war highlights the evolving dynamic between the United States as grandiose self and China as recalcitrant selfobject, as witnessed by the latter's "emotional labor" expended in the trade negotiations.

The term "emotional labor" comes to us from Arlie Hochschild (2012, 7), who defines it as "the management of feeling to create a publicly observable facial and bodily display." Emotional labor can be sold for a wage and therefore has exchange value. Hochschild suggests (9) that the public face of an emotional interpersonal system involves three discourses—labor, emotion, and display. She uses the term "transmutation" (19) to convey the translation of private behaviors into systematic public acts (e.g., showing gratitude or constraining anger) that become an accepted part of a work performance. We use transmutation, then, in the context of how emotional interpersonal relations are institutionally mobilized at the scale of international trade negotiations. We redefine payment not as wages between employer and employee but as revenue from commodities worth billions of dollars, or dignity forfeited to preserve that economic power. And we argue that imposing or accommodating rules and behavioral transgression in trade talks tell us a story about the social hierarchies that structure trade negotiations. But rather than focus on individual facial and bodily display as Hochschild does, we focus on the language of the negotiators, among whom are politicians whose public utterances constitute the broader negotiating strategy.

"Feeling rules" set out what is owed in gestures of exchange between people according to a "mental ledger" based on social hierarchies (Hochschild 2012, 76, 78). Subjects act on these rules by "bow[ing] to each other not only from the waist but from the heart," a practice Hochschild calls "psychological bowing" (76). To bow psychologically employs emotional labor, in that the subject pays another with a *plausible* display of *appropriate* feeling of what is presumed owed according to a social hierarchy (81). In fact, what we think of as intrinsic to feeling has already been shaped socially and put to civic use (18). For Kohut, "psychological bowing" would be the appropriate mirroring response between the self and selfobject. Since what is considered appropriate is a function of social hierarchy, the status of the subject determines the degree of bowing and the extent of the emotional labor expended on giving a plausible performance (Hochschild 2012, 84–85). An example of a low-status group bowing psychologically would be the subject's resignation to humiliation, whereas giving a plausible performance would entail the subject *appearing* to accept that the humiliation is justified. Tellingly, deference, praise, or admiration are seen as "normal" behaviors for servants, women, or anyone with a "lower" status (84).

Conversely, an implausible performance or inappropriate emotion may be interpreted as nonpayment according to the "feeling rules" of social hierarchy (Hochschild 2012, 83). Emotional accommodation in the form of accepting someone else's entitlement is thus a major act of psychological bowing. Similarly, disavowal of humiliation by the selfobject is also an important act of psychological bowing and hence a trigger for narcissistic rage from the "grandiose" self when the selfobject refuses to disavow mistreatment. And in contrast to private life, where the appropriate degree of bowing can be negotiated, the relative fixity of rules in public life makes it harder to negotiate and concede without losing face. So the

US-China trade war highlights the evolving dynamic between the former's grandiose self and China's recalcitrant selfobject through the changing degrees of emotional labor expended in the negotiations.

Introjection and Projection

Psychological bowing is a phenomenon that creates a sense of disempowerment in the victim by wearing down the psyche through repeated experience. It is a slow drip that destroys the victim's sense of agency through the experience of disrespect and the constant emotional labor of accommodation to those in power. Rycroft (1987, 187–88) defines psychic trauma as an unexpected experience which a subject is unable to resist and assimilate. It need not feature physical wounds but will still produce long-lasting effects in the form of anxiety and defensive behavior. Herman (2015, 33) amplifies that definition to incorporate the common denominators of feeling "intense fear, helplessness, loss of control and the threat of annihilation." But Freud's (1959, 65) original conceptualization of trauma suggested that it was constituted by two events. These were in a dialectical relationship: the first event cannot be understood or assimilated by the victim until the second event triggers the memory of the first, that only then comes to be understood as traumatic. Thus, for Freud (12, 62–63), anxiety is linked to trauma through memory. His interpretation involves latency and retrospection, through which the first act takes on meaning—the return of the "outlaw" repressed (86). Hence, trauma is unstable because of the unconscious motives that confer meaning, which changes over time while retaining traces of its origins. These sedimented memories return to haunt the victim in the form of flashbacks, hypervigilance, and overreaction (Leys 2000, 2).

China, like many emerging economies, is always aware of how its heritage conditions its current policy activism, as shown in its constant references to its nineteenth-century history as the "Century of Humiliation." This interpretation conditions its response to the United States, which it perceives as continuing to subjugate it. But the Chinese state's hypervigilance is a response not only to the United States but also to those whom it perceives as threatening its control and coherence from within. Its response to the powerful United States has been largely tempered; its response to less powerful actors has been one of overreaction. The Chinese state, in this sense, is a split libidinal subject with ambiguous if not contradictory actions that it attempts to conceal ideologically. Despite its subordinate position to the United States, it is after all a state that reproduces capitalism, to the benefit of the party elites and capitalist classes, at the expense of workers. So if China openly declares its traumatic response when dealing with more powerful entities such as the United States, it simultaneously disavows its projection of trauma onto exploited workers and farmers, as well as subject populations in Hong Kong, Tibet, or Xinjiang. Herman's interesting insight (2015, 39–41) is that it is the sense that someone "gets away" with something that reinforces the sense of helplessness and humiliation: the perpetrator is too powerful to challenge, so the victim seeks scapegoats upon whom to project its narcissistic rage.

For those used to being in power, a challenge to their putative entitlement and privilege comes to be experienced as trauma. This is as true of the United States' trade response to China as of China's political response to internal resistance by its own citizens. Herman notes (2015, 1–2) that for trauma victims, knowledge is illusory, partial, and unspeakable, because shame is attached to the victims, not the perpetrators. As such, denial, repression, and disassociation operate at the level of politics, creating an "underground" history that underpins the state's "official" justification of policy actions. Thus, for example, when it comes to global economic matters, China appears readily willing to point to its past subjugation to Western powers but reluctant to acknowledge the shame that drives its technological mimicking of the West. Its decisions surrounding technology take on the weight of psychic survival.

In this regard, the defensive mechanism against anxiety is an unconscious process by which libidinal energy is displaced onto a fetish (Freud 1966, 448–515). In our case, this means that the abjected selfobject invests in technology as a defense against the anxiety of potential humiliation: in attempting to cover up its trauma, the subject cloaks its "inferiority" through the fetish of technology (introjection). But at the same time, as underlined by Bollas (2011, 83–87), the shame of narcissistic injury is projected elsewhere in the "circuit of depersonalization." Thus, as we shall see, the Chinese state asserts its mission toward technological dominance by turning its surveillance technologies upon its own citizens (projection).

In what follows, we study trade negotiations over technology as a series of gestures with diminishing degrees of psychological bowing by China as the recalcitrant selfobject. To this end, we begin by analyzing the assertiveness of China's "wolf warrior" diplomats and politicians, before moving on to the conciliatory public statements of some of the country's leaders, as well as the less publicized concessions of its negotiators. Finally, we examine how China's psychological bowing to the United States results in narcissistic rage that it projects onto its selfobjects.

Opening the Front

During a trip to Southeast Asia made by one us (Maureen) in 2012, there was a general air of anxiety at the news that the US 7th Fleet was patrolling the Straits of Malacca subsequent to the Obama administration's "Pivot to Asia" strategy (Clinton 2011). The "enemy" in the United States in 2012 tended to be the Middle East. Coincidentally, not long after Maureen returned to the United States, she met an intelligence officer who had just been stationed with the 7th Fleet. Even with security considerations restricting conversation about the officer's trip, they stated that US attention and anxiety was pivoting from the Middle East to China.

The following statistics are derived from Lau's (2020b) description of China's economic growth since 1978, when its GDP was under 5 percent of the United States'. In 2000, Chinese GDP was only 18.7 percent of the US GDP, but by 2019, this figure rose dramatically to 66.2 percent. The absolute size of China's GDP is projected to equal that of the United States by 2030, although Chinese per capita GDP would still only be one quarter of that of the United States. Not surprisingly, then, president Joe Biden has cast US competition with China as a Manichean ideological struggle between democracy and autocracy, disavowing its crucial economic/trade dimensions.

The current trade dispute between both countries, which began in March 2018, soon mutated into a battle for leadership in core technologies like 5G, AI, and semiconductors. Tech anxieties became a container for the libidinal anxieties of the waxing and waning of geopolitical power. The situation came to prominence in the 2016 US presidential campaign when the US trade deficit with China emerged as a flashpoint. Donald Trump accused China of unfair trading practices—intellectual property theft, forced technology transfer, restricting market access for American companies, and providing government subsidies for Chinese companies (SCMP Reporters 2020). In March 2018, the Trump administration announced tariffs on $50 billion, eventually increasing to tariffs on $550 billion worth of goods. China retaliated by imposing tariffs of $185 billion on US goods (Mullen 2021). Then, in December 2018, the Trump administration issued a warrant for the arrest of Huawei's CFO, Meng Wanzhou, who was visiting Canada at the time (Wintour 2021a). Meng's arrest opened a new front in the trade war. The arrest laid bare that the real stake of the trade war was technology.

In 2015 China announced its strategic plan "Made in China 2025" (MIC2025) to transform the country from a low-end manufacturer of consumer goods to a high-end producer of information. The MIC2025 initiative identified ten priority sectors for investment: advanced information technology; automated machine tools and robotics; aerospace and aeronautical equipment; ocean engineering equipment and high-tech shipping; modern rail transport equipment; energy-saving and new-energy vehicles; power equipment; new materials; medicine and medical devices; and agricultural equipment (Ramadori 2021). China's economic czar, vice-premier Liu He, identified technological innovation not only as an issue of development but also as a matter of survival as exemplified by the examples of South Korea, Singapore, and Israel, states that see themselves as under siege and whose economic and defensive capabilities are very much tied to their sophisticated technology (Tang 2021). Recall that Herman (2015, 33) identifies the common denominators of trauma as "intense fear, helplessness . . . and the threat of annihilation," which would apply to the official narratives of all the three countries referenced by vice-premier Liu He. For all three, technology is the fetish against the anxieties of potential annihilation—it "decides geopolitical reality," in the words of Andrew Sheng (2021). With tensions over technology increasing even after the departure of Trump, in November 2021, the Biden administration placed Chinese companies specializing in quantum computing, semiconductors, and drone manufacturing, as well as the country's Academy of Military Medical Sciences, on its trade and investment blacklist, ostensibly because of military ties or surveillance of Muslims in Xinjiang (O. Wang 2022). China nevertheless went on to release its fourteenth five-year plan on December 12, 2021, highlighting Beijing's strategic vision for a more powerful digital economy sector, while further exacerbating American trade anxieties (Yahoo Finance 2022).

Much of the tension in the trade war has centered on the development of 5G technology, soon to be succeeded by 6G technology, whose significance can be divided into three areas: (1) enhanced mobile broadband that enables faster data speeds; (2) ultrareliable low-latency connectivity, which is the basis for self-driving, industrial automation, and remote medical assistance applications; and (3) massive machine-type control to connect millions of devices per square kilometer. The last of these is what underpins the development of smart cities.

Between 2020 and 2025, the Asia-Pacific region will be the site of more than $400 billion of investment on infrastructure development, 80 percent of which will be on 5G technologies (Perez 2020; Pan 2022). China's pro-6G digital economy blueprint, issued in January 2022, signals the country's intention to take a leading role in shaping advanced mobile technology development and, more importantly, to set international standards for sixth-generation mobile communications technology (Pan 2022). While MIC2025 intends to secure China's position in the global supply chains of critical technologies, China Standards 2035 is intended to control the governing framework for the use of future strategic technologies (Gargeyas 2021). In this sense, following Freud (1966, 448–515), China's fetishization of advanced technology is its key defensive mechanism against the anxiety of its subordination by the United States. Such a strategy also prepares the ground for the country to create its own technological bloc by exporting standards through cross-border agreements such as those signed through the Belt and Road Initiative (see chapter 8). Since Chinese technology is usually more affordable than most Western technology, it is more attractive to developing countries. And China could leverage it into becoming the next international technology standard. In this sense, as innovator and leader of its own technological bloc, China is trying to contradict the script of international relations by posing a potential threat to the United States. But in so doing, it has become a "flaw" in the United States' self-perception by depriving it of an "approving mirroring response" (Kohut 1973, 628, 644).

Trade Wars: Contesting Hegemonic Identity in Globalization

In what follows, we show how the dynamic of the US-China trade war is performed through the relationship between the grandiose self and recalcitrant selfobject, as manifested in the degrees of psychological bowing performed by China toward the United States. Performing the grandiose self in globalization turns on a sense of entitlement to material, cultural, and psychological rewards. Lau (2020b) reminds us of an often-overlooked aspect of China's growth, which has become the source of resentment surrounding its success: its rapid rise has left competitors with little time to adapt to the new reality. Moreover, unlike Japan's economic success in the 1980s, which also generated its share of resentment, China is a non-Western country that is *not* willing to settle as simply a rule follower.

So adapting Hochschild's framework of emotional labor to the US-China trade-war-turned-tech-war, we analyze the contestations and concessions as emotional labor mobilized within the institutional setting of trade negotiations over technology. We argue that preeminence in technology becomes a synecdoche for a hegemonic masculine agency, because it enables revenue streams and military defense. Emotional labor on the part of China as the recalcitrant selfobject comes in the form of accepting payment of tariffs, loss of revenue, and, more significantly, loss of dignity if it makes concessions to the grandiose self of the United States to avoid such penalties. These practices constitute psychological bowing, in the Hochschildian sense. The stake in technological primacy comes in the form of the capacity to refuse psychological bowing. As previously noted, "feeling rules" transmute into the public domain, as a result of which the subordinate subject, China, bows psychologically to the dominant power, the United States.

PSYCHOLOGICAL BOWING I: WOLF WARRIORS

Disavowal is one of the most powerful tools of disempowerment (Sioh 2014a, 2014b). To disavow one's own desires is an act of emotional accommodation, since one is confronted with the recognition of how little one is valued socially with every act of disavowal. Sioh (2018b) reminds us that since the advent of colonialism, poorer countries in the international order have had to bow psychologically because of their relative economic, technological, and military weaknesses, even as they are expected to disavow their humiliation. China, like many other non-Western countries in the last 250 years, has made multiple concessions to Western powers, that is, until it began its spectacular growth. Yet, China's diplomats and politicians, following Deng Xiaoping's dictum of *taoguang yanghui* (loosely translated as "not exposing your knowledge but patiently waiting for the right moment"), have maintained a moderate stance in their international interactions (Nawrotkiewicz 2021). In the last decade, the behavior of Chinese diplomats, politicians, and technocrats has shifted to greater assertiveness. The latter have been dubbed "wolf warriors," after the 2015 hit Chinese movie of the same name (Martin 2021). This shift in foreign policy accelerated after Xi Jinping took the helm in 2012. Where earlier diplomats, such as Cui Tiankai, ambassador to Washington, and Fu Ying, ambassador to the United Kingdom, demonstrated a "spirit of humility and tolerance" (Zhu 2020), others, such as Foreign Ministry spokespersons Hua Chunying and Zhao Lijian, have taken to heart president Xi Jinping's promotion of "a fighting spirit."

Responding to external criticisms of China's handling of the coronavirus outbreak and the poor quality of exported Chinese medical equipment, Zhao tweeted that "if someone claims that China's exports are toxic, then stop wearing China-made masks and protective gowns." And in response to US politicians referring to COVID as a "Chinese virus," Zhou tweeted, "It might be (the) US army who brought the epidemic to Wuhan" (Wells 2021). At the US-China Alaska Summit in March 2021, when US secretary of state Antony Blinken criticized China for "cyberattacks on the United States" and "economic coercion toward our allies," China's foreign affairs chief Yang Jiechi responded that the United States "can't blame this problem on somebody else," raising Black Lives Matter as an example of historical US social failure. Responding to White House national security adviser Jake Sullivan's scolding of the Chinese for their "lectures or long, winding statements." Yang told reporters that it was the United States that had broken diplomatic norms: "When I entered this room, I should have reminded the US side of paying attention to its *tone* in our respective opening remarks, but I didn't." He then went on to say, "The Chinese side felt compelled to make this speech because of the *tone* of the US side" (Taylor and Rauhala 2021; emphasis added).

Our point is not that China's representatives are justified in their aggressive response, or that the US representatives are justified in their condescension, but that previously China would have not called out American criticisms. Contradicting the "feeling rules" (Hochschild 2012, 76) of international relations, China's representatives appear to no longer tolerate public displays of disrespect by American diplomats and politicians. In doing so, China declines to provide an unconditional approving mirror to the United States (Kohut 1973, 644).

Nonetheless, president Xi Jinping has provided contradictory messages by coming across as both aggressive and conciliatory in his public comments. Zhanna Malekos Smith (2021), quoting the *Tao-te Ching*, notes that "The great generals are not warlike. The great warriors do not get angry. . . . It is called the virtue of non-contention." To be sure, Xi's speech (2021b) to the UN General Assembly is an example of such noncontention, noting that differences between countries are unavoidable but could be addressed "on the basis of equality and mutual respect." Xi pointedly reminded his audience, "One country's success does not have to mean another country's failure." Even so, in his speech marking the one-hundredth birthday of the Chinese Communist Party, he vowed to defend China from those who try to bully or oppress it, by declaring that China would "crack their heads and spill blood on the Great Wall of steel built from the flesh and blood of 1.4 billion Chinese people" (quoted in Buckley and Bradsher 2021). Such hyperbolic language is revealing of the need to compensate for China's erstwhile subordinate position in the global hierarchy. The mixed messaging—tough on the outside, humiliated on the inside—speaks to the Chinese state's ideological attempt to cover up the contradictions by constructing an outwardly masculinist position.

If Xi is bowing psychologically while staying defiant, he can do so only because he is gambling that technological advantage will eventually put China beyond the risk of being militarily and economically insecure. It is noteworthy, in this regard, that "technology security" is one of the key areas covered by the country's security agenda from 2021 to 2025. Fetishizing technology forms the basis of China's "holistic approach to national security," which Xi introduced in 2014 as encompassing threats on ideological, economic, political, and military fronts. For him, the battlefield is technology, the heroes are scientific innovators, and the prize is China's dignity (Huaxia 2021). He notes, in fact, "Scientific and technological innovation has become the main battlefield of the international strategic game," and sees science and technology as "a sharp weapon for development" (Z. Wang 2021). Technological innovation is couched in terms beyond mere profit; it is the fetish that will deliver China from the trauma of another "Century of Humiliation."

If a scientific challenge provokes anxiety in Americans, Xi's emphasis on tying science to culture explains why scientific and technological supremacy are Chinese identity challenges. While mainstream Western scientific discourse argues for a universal model of science, Xi sees it differently: he appears to consider scientific standards as part of a particular cultural system, arguing that China should strive for science and technology with "Chinese characteristics, Chinese style, and Chinese manner," with the state as guide (quoted in Z. Wang 2021). For him, a key factor in China's ascendance to sovereignty will lie in its ability to create a technology that acknowledges its cultural roots as it "participate[s] in global science and technology governance. Science and technology are . . . the shared wealth of mankind" (Z. Wang 2021). The message is obvious: China will not allow the United States to subordinate it technologically.

In stressing cultural roots rather than the Western coding of "universalism" of science and technology—that is to say, a science that is paraded by the West as universal, all the while maintaining global control of it—Xi challenges the US narrative, at least outwardly and ideologically. In so doing, he deprives the United States of the approving mirroring response that the grandiose self has come to expect in the international order. The result, following Kohut, has been to trigger narcissistic rage in the United States. Yet, regardless of China's claim to a different approach to science and technology from the United States, in fetishizing technology as the answer to its anxieties, China has introjected the US model as its ego ideal.

PSYCHOLOGICAL BOWING II . . . IN SECRET

Central to the US-China trade tensions has been the issue of forced technology transfer (Qin 2019, 743), according to which, even if China is developing economically, it is able to do so only because it has acquired the knowledge through theft—by "forcing" Western corporations to provide it with the technology for free. The problem came to prominence in the 1990s with the advent of the dot.com boom, when the United States insisted on the enforcement of intellectual property rights (IPRs, covering patents, trademarks, and copyright), especially at the WTO (Sassen 2008, 241–42). Technology transfer can take place through education, technological aid, employment, commercial transactions, or outright theft, usually involving transnational transfers through licensing agreements. While Qin (2019, 745) argues that the term "forced transfer" is poorly defined, we use it here to refer to any situation in which a government requires a foreign firm to share proprietary information as a condition of conducting business in the country. This can be either for administrative purposes or because of mandatory joint venture requirements.

In this regard, US federal agencies, including the United States Trade Representative (USTR) and the United States International Trade Commission (USITC), have criticized the prevalence of Chinese state-sponsored unfair trade practices. In August 2017, the USTR initiated an investigation under Section 301 of the 1974 Trade Act against China. Based on the results of this investigation, President Trump ordered that China be put on USTR's Special 301 "Priority Watch List," which may have been the first time forced technology transfer emerged as a major world trade issue (Qin 2019, 743–44). Although a WTO panel ruled that the tariffs unilaterally imposed by the United States violated the General Agreement on Tariffs and Trade

(GATT), the US actions were supported by the European Union and Japan, who claimed that Chinese state industrial policy amounted to forced technology transfer, as it is a condition to market entry into China's lucrative telecommunications and financial sectors (Shang and Shen 2021, 4, 11).

Shang and Shen suggest that China made several moves to accommodate US demands, regardless of its tough public stance. Beginning in 2012, the United States had banned domestic companies from using Huawei Technologies equipment. The Department of Commerce issued a final rule in May 2019, adding Huawei and its sixty-eight non-US affiliates to the Bureau of Industry and Security "Entity List," thereby cutting Huawei off from acquiring US-originated hardware and software. The list was later expanded to include more Huawei affiliates and subsidiaries across the world. Moreover, the 2020 Economic and Trade Agreement between the United States and China Phase One (the "Phase One Agreement") addressed concerns regarding protection of IPRs, including increasing the transparency of foreign investment regulations. These sanctions are estimated to have doubled or tripled Chinese corporations' costs of doing business in the United States (Shang and Shen 2021). Critically, despite the public belligerence of its wolf warriors, China conceded to most of the US demands, agreeing to comply with a range of US IPR laws, including compliance monitoring by the United States (6–8).

The point we are making is that regardless of China's public wolf warrior diplomacy, it has continued to bow psychologically to a great degree. Lawrence Lau (2020a) estimates, in fact, that China's real trade surplus with the United States in 2020, after discounting for US repatriation of profits by its transnational subsidiaries, was $111 billion, as opposed to $285 billion as claimed by the US administration (US Trade Representative, n.d.). China appears not to have publicly challenged the US position, indicative once again of its unconscious psychoanalytic bowing. But the humiliation of the above concessions needs an outlet for the resulting narcissistic rage experienced. And since China cannot realistically challenge the United States, that rage must be projected elsewhere—onto the subjects of China's militant ideology of national renewal.

The Psycho-Political Costs of Bowing

Indeed, China's psychological bowing comes at a high cost: dignity forfeited to preserve access to markets triggers the latent trauma of China's "Century of Humiliation." These "sedimented memories" (Leys 2000, 2) appear to haunt the Chinese authorities, who are already hypervigilant of any humiliation. The legal jargon of the trade deals, for example, provides a fictitious sense of neutrality and fairness that, to recall Herman's (2015, 39–41) shrewd insight, exacerbates China's humiliation because it reinforces the sense that the United States "got away" with thwarting China of its rightful gains. This is likely why, psychoanalytically speaking, the Chinese state can be said to be projecting its humiliation-inflected narcissistic rage on its own recalcitrant selfobjects in the form of protestors in Xinjiang or Hong Kong (the latter of which signals the return of the earlier mentioned Freudian "outlaw" repressed). So the fetishization of technology as national salvation has now been trained on domestic targets.

Indeed, China, along with the United States and Russia, is regarded as a leader in cyber warfare research.[2] As early as 2014, the cyber security company Lacoon warned that the Chinese government was using smartphone apps to spy on prodemocracy protesters in Hong Kong (Associated Press 2014). The application (known as "mRat") targeted phones that ran Apple's iOS or Google's Android system; it represented a shift from attacking traditional PC systems to singling out mobile devices for providing access to users' address books and call logs. Similarly, facial and voice recognition software developed by Huawei has reportedly been deployed on the Uighurs in Xinjiang (Dou 2021). In this regard, Human Rights Watch (Shakir and Wong 2021) compares China's surveillance of the Uighurs to Israel's surveillance of Palestinians (recalling vice-premier Liu's linking of his country's pursuit of technological excellence as a matter of survival to that of Israel's; see Tang 2021). Shakir and Wong point out that China's big data system, Integrated Joint Operations Platform (IJOP), categorizes people into degrees of threats based on facial recognition— similar to Israel's Blue Wolf app, used by police to determine whether or not to detain Palestinians. In Xinjiang, those targeted by IJOP risk "political education" and imprisonment.

While the above are examples of the state using and abusing surveillance technology, more worryingly, the fetishization of technology-driven smart cities has seen willing collusion by Chinese citizens in their own surveillance, not unlike Westerners who trade privacy for convenience on social media. Projects such as the Golden Shield Project, Safe Cities, Skynet, Smart Cities, and Sharp Eyes have resulted in over two hundred million public and private security cameras installed across China (Gershgorn 2021). The German journalist Kai Strittmatter, who tracks the

Chinese government's surveillance programs, is skeptical about the success of such surveillance, but in a Foucauldian vein, he makes the valid point that like most surveillance programs, once the population subscribes to it, they begin to self-discipline (see Davis 2021). China may thus well insist that it uses science and technology in a culturally specific and more socially inclusive way than the United States, but its practices belie such an assertion, suggesting in fact an introjection of the US system as an ego ideal. A glaring example here is the Chinese state's recent purchase of CIA-backed Endeca software, developed by Oracle and used to spy on protestors in Chicago during the Occupy movement, and later on the George Floyd protesters (Hvistendahl 2021). If anything, it reveals the twisted psychic logic of reproducing the Master's oppression even as one aims at countering it.

What should not be lost in this melee, though, is that the psychic contradictions of the Chinese state—the fact that its global technological drive emanates from an anxious, not a coherent, subject—is itself revealing of the class antagonisms that beset it (see chapter 1). To be sure, it is the Communist Party apparatchiks and corporate industrial elites who are the main drivers and benefactors of the country's capitalist technological development, with the state acting as mechanism to discipline labor, enforce surplus extraction, and suppress dissent (Li 2008; Day 2013; E. Friedman 2014; Guo 2018). Technological supremacy thus helps both in advancing the country's outside standing and in reproducing the country's internal system of authoritarian capitalism. Such supremacy is needed and constructed as fetish to cover over state antagonisms—to prosecute the socioeconomic and political inequalities required to maintain the system, while at the same time serving as ideological cloak for the humiliated subject.

Conclusion

We have argued that the US-China trade-war-turned-tech-war negotiations are so intractable because they are driven by a libidinal calculus, rather than simply an economic calculus, as conventional IPE (or mainstream International Relations, for that matter) would have it. The focus on technology lies in the subject's anxious desires: the war over the control of technology is a container for the subject's anxieties about contesting hegemonic identities in globalization. Viewed through a GLE lens, therefore, the US-China trade negotiations can be taken as a contest between two performances: the current hegemonic identity and the one perceived as its challenger. We have argued that China's desire to lead in technological innovation and exert its independence from the United States is perceived by the latter as a "flaw in a narcissistically perceived reality," thereby responding with rage. For its part, China appears to see the negotiations as the historic moment in which to reject the emotional accommodation of the United States. It has done this through aggressive "wolf warrior" diplomacy. Yet its public rejection is contradicted in its less publicized capitulation to American demands for almost all trade concessions. This places the Chinese government in the delicate position of appearing defiant while simultaneously having to frame its concessions in a way that renders them acceptable domestically without losing face; it speaks to the split character of the Chinese state-as-subject, and the ideological-fantasmatic efforts required to smooth over its contradictions (masculinist power and performance yet diplomatic bowing to the United States; growing global economic clout yet continued humiliation by erstwhile Western trade rule makers). We have suggested that such thwarted desires result in narcissistic rage on the part of the Chinese state itself, which now finds a target in its own recalcitrant selfobjects. So fetishized has Chinese technological development become, in fact, that it has psychically transfigured into a technoideological maneuver in the service of population control.

6

Financialization

The Psychopathologies of Fictitious Capital

Our aim in this chapter is to investigate the libidinal economies integral to the rise of global financialization, which is perhaps one of the most crucial political economy events of the last three decades. Our main claim is that, under financialization, the search for *jouissance* (enjoyment) reaches fresh pathological heights[1] by enabling market subjects, not to invest in the production of useful commodities, but to "make money out of money" by betting on *future* accumulation (i.e., fictitious capital). The availability and spread of new financial instruments has effectively normalized risk, making many of us de facto risk takers and foregrounding both the thrill and peril—that is, the enjoyment—of so doing. The psychopathologies of such risk taking lie in leaving us as indebted subjects, increasingly invested in the market and hence unlikely to rebel against it, and providing strategic opportunities to produce a leaner, meaner capitalism that exploits, displaces, and indeed enslaves poor, gendered, and racialized people. Money that begets money is thus a capitalist's fantasy, ensuring the enjoyment of fictitious capital by short-circuiting the political (i.e., the antagonism of labor/class struggle).

Financialization: Fictitious Capital

Financialization or financial capitalism describes private accumulation that occurs through financial instruments rather than commodity production or trade. It involves pools of money leveraged to make returns by hedging (i.e., betting) against what are estimated as under- or overvalued prices, interest rates, currencies, or company stocks. Here capitalization commodifies claims based on anticipated future accumulation, so that the value of capital *precedes* rather than follows production in view of predicted future outcomes (Sotiropoulos, Milios, and Lapatsioras 2013, 157). Financialization is thus built on "fictitious capital," which allows risk to be traded without the actual assets being traded. In fact, the financial asset is not necessarily tied to a dedicated object; it can be applied to any object, with the result that anything can be capitalized and securitized: assets in the present can be linked to prices in the future (e.g., a ton of wheat today to its expected price in six months) just as much as assets linked to the prices of one asset can be linked to another asset form (e.g., interest rates to currencies or stock prices); in addition, assets can be sliced or bundled with a derivative and then traded as a "credit default swap," leading to a system that is highly flexible and complex, with the ability to penetrate and incorporate any sector anywhere, all in search of added value (Bryan and Rafferty 2005; Boltanski and Esquerre 2016).

The unprecedented expansion of financial capitalism has its origins in the 1980s, when growth of the productive sector in many (mostly Western) economies began to slow down, especially relative to the economic boom of the 1950s and 1960s. The fallout was the search by capital for new forms of accumulation, with financial speculation emerging as the main channel. Financialization thus arose as a result of the asymmetry between the sphere of production and the sphere of circulation, acting as the principal medium for absorbing investible surplus (Lapavitsas 2013, 793). This is also the period accompanied by the rise of neoliberal deregulation, which meant the removal of impediments to capital mobility and the dramatic expansion of access to credit by individuals and businesses. The overall consequence was that global capital flows rose by about 5 percent of world GDP in the mid-1990s to about 20 percent in 2007, three times faster than world trade flows during the same period (Blakeley 2018).

It is this mix of neoliberal deregulation and capital mobility that led to a massive speculative bubble that finally burst, leading to the 2008 global financial crisis. Financial institutions, particularly although not exclusively in the United States, had engaged in speculative mortgage lending to often poor working families, while fund managers had bought assets without paying full cost (i.e., they were allowed to borrow up to twenty times the value of hedge funds from banks in order to take leveraged positions). So when banks realized that many of the assets on their books were not really assets at all, general panic ensued and markets crashed, pointing up the fiction, excess, and unpredictability of speculative capital.

Despite the crisis, financialization continues to flourish today, bringing to the fore the rising global importance of financial institutions—from banks and brokerage firms to mortgage companies and insurance services. Not only do financial services account for an increasing share of national income relative to other sectors (24 percent of the world's economy in 2020), but profits of the financial sector have soared, reaching $20.5 trillion in 2020 in spite of the COVID-19 debacle (Research and Markets 2021). Crucial here has been the successful mobilization by financial institutions of the savings of individuals and households as a key source of profit, linking stock market trading with household savings and lending. As a result, speculative investing, which used to be the preserve of large corporations and the very wealthy, now counts huge sections of the population (and nonfinancial businesses[2]) worldwide, including not only the working class but also private/public sector unions investing their pension money (itself the product of declining state support for social security). Lapavitsas thus points out that financialization "represents a transformation of mature capitalism resting on the altered conduct of non-financial enterprises, banks and households" (2013, 802).

The neoliberal state has played a key facilitative role in this overall financial boom, with central banks emerging as the main supporter of financial sector interests. Accordingly, interest rates have been kept low, consumer debt has been encouraged (credit cards, home mortgages, consumer lines of credit, student loans, etc.), and taxes on corporations and the rich have often been lowered. Except for mostly face-saving state financial measures in the aftermath of the 2008 crisis, speculative capitalists have continued to be subject to few legal constraints or fiduciary responsibilities, with many economico-political elites choosing to operate from offshore centers, using tax havens to avoid taxes and capitalize on investment gains (as the recent Credit Suisse leaks and Pandora, Paradise, and Panama papers have revealed) (Pegg et al. 2022; The Guardian 2021; Pegg 2017; Harding 2016). Neoliberal deregulation has thus enabled not only the speed of global capital mobility—trillions of dollars are traded on markets almost every day—but also the complexity and obscurity of financial markets, now increasingly beyond the reach of the neoliberal state.

Enjoying Money

Because individuals, households, and nonfinancial businesses have increasingly been incorporated into the global financial system, financialization effectively means that more and more of us are now (speculative) capitalists: the mainstreaming of financial capitalism implies the integration of not just the petite bourgeoisie but also the middle-income and working classes as money savers and investors. Yet, psychoanalytically speaking, along with this "love for money" comes a host of neuroses and psychopathologies: (neo)classical economics may well insist that the love of money is self-interested (see chapter 1), but psychoanalysis points out that it is also accompanied by profound excess and irrationality.

Indeed, Freud (1977) was one of the first to dematerialize money (and economic relationships generally), seeing it as a symbolic expression of erotic desire. He focused on the infant's "anal phase," suggesting that the child's resistance to potty training revolves around a predisposition to hold on to what it first produces—feces—that is, an unwillingness to relinquish the latter, to give up an important part of itself. It is this infantile "interest in faeces" that for Freud continues "partly as interest in money" in later life (296, 299), manifesting as both covetousness and miserliness. Here, one measures one's worth in terms of money and possessions—as capitalists often do—but one is also stingy with money, even going so far as to hoard it as tangible proof of one's capacity to produce and hold on to something meaningful. Freud points to such slang German expressions as *Ducatsheisser* ("shitters of ducats," referring to German federal bank officials) and *ein großes Geschäft machen* ("doing big business," referring to defecating) as indicative of his equation of feces with money, and in English one could add such expressions as "shitload of money," "hot/holy shit," or "goldfinders" (a Victorian era expression for toilet cleaners). He even reflects on the relationship of his own discipline, psychoanalysis, to capital (1973, 170), remarking on the irony of making money off the recovery of his patients' libidinal expenditures!

While Freud's biologistic discussion might at times appear reductionist, if not tongue-in-cheek, his symbolic linking of sex and desire is certainly compelling, and it is in this direction that Lacan takes the analysis. To be sure, Lacan (2015, 177) equates money not with feces but with the *objet petit a*, the object cause of desire—that which lures us by its promise of redemption and full enjoyment (*jouissance*). Money, in other words, is a source of huge joy; it seduces us by covering up loss and alienation, portending instead (the illusion of) security, safety, omnipotence.

In this sense, it is not the material object per se—paper, metal, plastic, or electronic currency—that is the lure but the fantasy surrounding it, which serves to neutralize originary castration, while promising power and wealth. The love and enjoyment of money is thus an "expression of our deepest connection to a sense of internal plenty" (Carrington 2015, xvi, 110).

The advent of financial capitalism thereby opens up new and ever-growing opportunities for enjoyment. Since capitalist valorization no longer depends on material production but on fictitious capital, the promise of power and wealth becomes boundless. By inventing imaginary capital and borrowing on the future, financialization has developed both inexhaustible possibilities for accumulation and bottomless wells of enjoyment.[3] The principal manifestation of this has of course been consumerism, as chapter 3 underlined. The rise and spread of the minicapitalist classes under financialization—the power of their newfound wealth—has translated into an explosion of consumer lending and spending, enabling them to buy not just mass consumer items but luxury commodities (e.g., iPhones, computers, luxury automobiles, etc.) and real estate as well. This is evidenced by the fact that private consumption expenditures worldwide topped $20 trillion in 2000 (at the height of the "financial revolution"), a fourfold increase over 1960 (in 1995 dollars) (Worldwatch 2013).

Psychoanalytically speaking, such widespread spending and materialism appear as desperate attempts at "holding on to one's shit," that is, measuring and displaying one's worth through possessions as a way of soothing one's alienation. We are seduced by the fantasy of commodities (i.e., the branding and advertising surrounding them) and so inundate our lives with material goods as a way of covering over—filling up—the ontological hole in our lives. This is why Žižek (2006, 303, 307) contends that late capitalism represents the universalization of commodity fetishism, a system of generalized perversion governed by the post-Oedipal command to "Enjoy!" Here, as we have previously outlined (see chapters 1 and 3), early capitalism's call to temper our pleasure by working hard and saving is replaced by late capitalism's imperative to consume incessantly. The system needs (and commands) us to shop endlessly to overcome its contradictions (e.g., declining profits from mass production) and satisfy its goal of constant accumulation, all the more so under a regime of fictitious capital.

The irrationality of such late capitalist enjoyment comes through best when one considers the orgiastic concentration and display of wealth and waste in our times. Of note since the 1990s has been spectacular accumulation in the hands of the few, with the emergence of billion-aires, multimillionaires, and a highly remunerated corporate bourgeoisie (earning fat-cat salaries, bonuses, and stock options). The world's richest 1 percent today possess more than twice as much wealth as 6.9 billion people, with 2,153 billionaires holding more wealth than 60 percent of the planet (4.6 billion people). Meanwhile, in Brazil, the six richest men own the same wealth as the poorest 50 percent (100 million people) (Oxfam 2020a, 2020b, 2018). And such huge affluence is plainly exhibited—and meant to be plainly exhibited—everywhere: in the legendary shopping sprees by Saudi royal families and Grace Mugabe; billionaire Ambani's twenty-seven-story, 400,000-square-foot skyscraper home in Mumbai; Richard Branson and Jeff Bezos's billionaire "space race"; the luxury estates and cars of Hollywood moguls; the exclusive shopping malls for the rich and famous; and the Burj Khalifa and Shanghai and Petronas Towers (the latter of which often stand in sharp contrast to nearby shantytowns and poor neighborhoods, especially in the global South). Even philanthropic giving is taken to new heights with the likes of Bill Gates, Warren Buffett, and George Soros donating $50 billion, $42.8 billion, and $16.8 billion, respectively, to charity (Brown 2020; Forbes 2021).

All of such mediated public displays of wealth, consumption, and charity appear as a desperate search for thrill, a crying out for status, envy, glory, power. It is as if the superrich cannot simply spend or give (thousands of dollars)—they must spend and give spectacularly (millions and billions of dollars) (see Kapoor 2013, 47–82; 2015c; 2020, 94–122). Such excess, to be sure, is the very marker of enjoyment, which comforts by providing the *illusion* of omnipotence—illusion because no matter how much power, wealth, envy, or fame one racks up, it is never enough (to fill the ontological gap in human existence).

What should not be missed here is how the excess of enjoyment under late (financialized) capitalism implies massive waste: not only in the form of garbage, pollution, or e-waste from unprecedented global consumption but also as a result of the sheer prodigality of global wealth concentration (too many mobiles, cars, and houses; too much food, water consumption, and energy use, etc.), which alongside the relative indigence of so many on the planet appears nothing if not shockingly wasteful. Bataille (1986) is right to point to the tendency of societies to engage in the meaningless, orgiastic expenditure of surplus/waste; we might add that under late capitalist conditions, this is a generalized condition, most especially among the global elites. The economy of command enjoyment means that, despite being urged (or *because* we are urged) to spend rather than save, we have become hoarders (read: shit collectors), surrounding ourselves with ultimately empty—trivial, disposable—objects.

Enjoying Risk

But that is only part of the story: *jouissance*, recall, is about excessive pleasure to be sure, but one that is always mixed with pain—the pain of pleasure, the pleasure of pain—so that while we may derive joy and safety from something, we also, at the same time, experience discomfort and anxiety from it. Such is certainly the case with financialization. Since the value of financial securities precedes rather than follows the production process, financial capitalism presupposes risk; it is based on betting on the realization of future (fictitious) capital, all the more so in the case of such instruments as derivatives, which magnify risk in order to make as much money as quickly as possible. *Jouissance* here is multi-dimensional, involving not only the enjoyment of present value added and the prospect of future value added by betting on fictitious capital but also the peril of the unknown, of making the wrong bet, of failing, of losing. What keeps the whole system moving incessantly, in fact, is precisely this perverse cycle of real or prospective reward and disappointment, which as we have underlined before and will develop further below, is what psychoanalysis calls "drive."

This dimension of risk has become more and more generalized today, given, as we have noted, the incorporation of individuals and households into financial capitalism (Sotiropoulos, Milios, and Lapatsioras 2013, 167–69). People have increasingly come to rely on financial institutions for access to important goods and services—not just consumer commodities but also education, health, housing, transportation, and retirement. Mostly, this is the consequence of neoliberal austerity measures, with the state offloading its public responsibilities by cutting or privatizing higher education, public transit, pensions, and health services. Accessing any of these thereafter requires engaging in speculative capitalism, with all the joys and anxieties (i.e., the enjoyment) of betting that goes along with that. Market risk has thereby been mainstreamed.

A recent instance of such normalization is the 2021 controversy over "WallStreetBets": this is a Reddit online forum made up of millions of mostly young amateur speculators who engaged in aggressive trading to drive up the price of GameStop stocks that had until then been losing market value. The group was subsequently accused by Wall Street "insiders" (some of whom had suffered losses) of recklessness, ignoring basic risk management practices, and causing market instability (Harwell 2021; Daniel 2021). Yet, as Žižek points out, what WallStreetBets members had done was simply to bring the "surplus-enjoyment of stock-exchange gambling out into the open. The popular appeal of wallstreetbets means that millions of ordinary people participate in it . . . wallstreetbets is doing openly what Wall Street has been doing in secret for decades. The excesses of wallstreetbets brought into the open the latent irrationality of the stock exchange itself" (2021).

As this stock market insider-outsider distinction crumbles and the question of risk is increasingly generalized, the psychology of speculative trading is likewise also mainstreamed. To be sure, perhaps nowhere is manic depression so embodied institutionally than in stock exchanges, with traders often engaged in extreme and irrational displays of emotion, from excitement, rapture, and jubilation to anxiety, fear, and depression, passions that are frequently symptomatic of such underlying conditions as bipolar disorders, nervous breakdowns, and burnout. True, the normalization of risk across the world may not manifest quite so starkly as this,[4] but one can certainly detect a degree of it, perhaps especially in times of crisis, such as during the 2008 financial debacle, during which time scenes of generalized shock, disbelief, and hysteria were not uncommon, including panic buying, homeowner psychological distress, substance abuse, and sharp rises in "economic suicides" (Lambe and Wisniewski 2018).

But as harrowing and pathological as such behavior might seem, it is written into the very system of speculative capitalism. In fact, the system both spawns it and thrives on it. This is because, as noted in chapter 1, capitalism is *driven* by an unending quest to recover ontological loss. It is drive's insistent reenactment of this loss that brings forth the capitalist system's self-propelling circuit—the continuous cycle of C-M-C/M-C-M (commodity-money-commodity/money-commodity-money), or what Marx also calls "the law which gives capital no rest and continually whispers in its ear: 'Go on!,' 'Go on!'" (2000, 290). Under the speculative capitalist regime, such drive manifests not only as a search for greater personal gain/profit (i.e., M-M[5]—money that begets money) but, more importantly, as an enjoyable compulsion to perform and repeat the rituals of market speculation. In the same way that people end up enjoying the activity of shopping more than what they actually buy, so the activity of speculative capitalism itself becomes the object (of drive/enjoyment). To wit, the cycle of identifying the right stocks or portfolios, assessing them, purchasing them, anxiously anticipating their rise or fall, checking their (daily/weekly/monthly/yearly) performance, celebrating wins or mourning losses, reinvesting windfalls, and so forth—is what both drives and thrills the market speculator. The nugget of enjoyment lies not so much in the payoff but in the hustle of betting, the persistent repetitive effort of playing the market.

Here, the question of risk performs a central role. It is the not simply the risk of winning but especially the risk of losing the bet that makes a financial security valuable. As McGowan puts it, we "can value only what costs us some sacrifice because sacrifice—of money, of time, of possessions—produces desirability" (2013, 32).[6] This is surely why compulsive gamblers keep coming back for more: the guessing game, the thrill of not knowing, is partly why; but indeed the trauma of failing, of losing everything, is also what keeps one so transfixed on the play. Losing is painful, but it is painful such that we enjoy it. And that is why psychoanalysis insists that drive is never about getting the object but about encircling it; it is the process of constantly missing the object that is satisfying.

But the big glitch is that, as a consequence, financial markets seldom learn (belying neoclassical economics' insistence that, left to their own, markets self-correct). Speculators get so caught up in the rituals of speculation, so mesmerized by the thrill, stress, and risk of it all, that they end up engaging in excessive and irrational behavior. This is nowhere better illustrated than in the 2008 financial crisis, when the frenetic search for quick profits led to predatory mortgages being offered to households (a disproportionate number of whom were working-class, Black, and Latino, in the United States at least) (Dymski 2010). But as mortgage rates increased and housing prices declined sharply, mortgage delinquencies soared and the value of mortgage-based securities held by financial firms across the world plunged. Here, it is not just the callous yet enjoyable rituals of drive's circuit that this crisis exposes but also the ripple effects that drive's repetitive character has on global financial markets: the close interconnectivity of markets means that gains and losses (re)circulate and reverberate throughout the system. As Jodi Dean emphasizes, "At some point, doing the same thing over and over shifts from order into chaos. Persistent repetition can amplify patterns to the point of overload and collapse, as in the bursting of market bubbles" (2012, 61). This was all the more the case during *this* crisis because risky mortgage-based loans had been repackaged and sold multiple times throughout the global financial system.

It is because (financialized) capitalism is drive-ridden—that is, because it unthinkingly repeats and seldom learns—that it is so prone to failure and crisis. Drive propels and overwhelms the market, capturing its subjects, whose enjoyment-producing repetitive activities intensify to the point of peril and destruction. The self-interested calculus of *homo economicus* is easily transformed through drive into an incautious protection of not just general wealth but one's own personal wealth as well. Drive's *jouissance* animates the subject to the extent of self-sabotage. And yet even so, capitalism's dynamic flexibility enables it to rise up from the ashes: by capitalizing on crises, by exploiting fresh market inequities, by betting on recovery. So indeed was the case in the aftermath of the 2008 crisis, when new clusters of speculators scooped up undervalued properties, leveraging them for yet another drive-propelled cycle of accumulation.

Sociopolitical Implications

When the self-generating cycle of drive-ridden capital value becomes an end in itself, it has serious sociopolitical implications. Not only is there a pathological callousness and stupidity to drive/enjoyment because it answers to, and serves, only itself but, in addition, the abstractness and anonymity of financial markets blind (or inure?) speculators to the often exploitative social relations embedded in their activities.

For a start, financialization has brought about new configurations in terms of power and class, with financial elites at the top of the social pyramid capitalizing on middle- and working-class households (i.e., mobilizing their savings and loans for speculative purposes), while also exploiting (gendered and racialized) labor at the bottom of the pyramid to extract surplus value, as we shall see below. Fictitious capital has thus generated new capitalist power relations that reflect the contradictions of late capitalist political economy (i.e., declining production-based accumulation) (see Sotiropoulos, Milios, and Lapatsioras 2013, 155–79). The rising power of central banks and global financial/economic institutions (e.g., WTO, IMF, World Bank) is particularly noteworthy: since financial debt is the de facto means through which a good part of capital is now accumulated globally, it is these institutions that tend to dictate the rules of the game, holding sway not only over individuals and households but also states. Thus, Nancy Fraser writes,

Financialized capitalism has sharply altered the previous relation of economy to polity. Whereas the prior regime empow-
ered states to subordinate the short-term interests of private
firms to the long-term objective of sustained accumulation,
this one authorizes finance capital to discipline states and publics in the immediate interests of private investors. The effect
is a double whammy. On the one hand, the state institutions
that were previously (somewhat) responsive to citizens are
decreasingly capable of solving the latter's problems or meeting
their needs. On the other hand, the central banks and global
financial institutions that now constrain state capacities are
politically independent—unaccountable to publics and free to
act on behalf of investors and creditors. (2015, 176)

To be sure, the fact that multinational credit rating agencies such as Standard & Poor's, Fitch, and Moody's can downgrade the sovereign credit rat-
ings of countries (e.g., that of Portugal, Greece, and Spain during the 2008
financial crisis), that states must increasingly coordinate their financial
policies with the likes of the IMF, or that, as previously noted, at the behest
of their central banks, governments increasingly encourage consumer debt
to ensure high levels of spending—all speak to the power of finance in
today's world. This also speaks to the increasingly "postpolitical" environment in which much of the world operates: the de facto "consensus"
that global capitalism is the only game in town, the neoliberalization of
state policies and programs (from health care and education to water and
indeed finance), and the rising incapacity—if not unwillingness—of states
to meaningfully regulate the corporate sector.

Note here how, under financialization, this postpolitical consensus is
constructed at the level of the subject. Given the generalized extension of
credit, mortgages, and student and consumer loans, Tomšič underscores
that subjects are heretofore positioned as "debtors," who feel they owe
something to the (neoliberal) state, which is positioned, in turn, as the
"creditor":

The invention of national debt and the corresponding production of subjectivity expose the kernel of the capitalist form of
alienation that Marx indicates in the term "externalisation of
the state." . . . The externalisation of the state in the national
debt is accompanied by its internalisation, in the sense that
it shapes the nature of modern subjectivity. Being essentially

> grounded on indebting and standing for national debt as such, the modern state places every citizen in the position of the debtor, while the position of the creditor is assumed by the social institutions of capital: the central banks. . . . The equivalent of the placement of the citizen in the position of the debtor is the transformation of the subject into a quantifiable and exploitable subjectivity, which is indebted in advance and is also produced as such. (2015, 153; see also Lazzarato 2012; Samman and Sgambati 2022)

Indebtedness to the state/market makes us feel responsible—by tying us down to a career, training, property, assets. And so mortgagers, frequently counting double- or triple-income households, must keep their jobs to be able to pay back their debts. Student loans or state-sponsored refugee training programs, likewise, must be repaid through self-commodification after finding employment. The political consequence, then, is a tendency toward compliance and pliability. Our indebtedness to the system makes us not only consent to it but also give "credit" to it, literally and figuratively; we are (made) liable to "give back" to our employer, community, state, country. As indebted subjects, in short, we are interpellated to acquiesce to the postpolitical consensus, and hence much less likely to revolt against it.

Worse, though, is that this postpolitical consensus effectively sanctions the construction of a leaner, meaner global capitalism in which states not only become a proxy for economic elite interests but also ignore—or indeed facilitate—the systematic extraction of surplus on the backs of workers and marginalized groups. In fact, the normalization of risk, the drive-ridden accumulation of money for its own sake, has brought about new forms of class exploitation and social dispossession.

One such instance is that, because money is increasingly channeled into fictitious capital investments rather than production, production has stagnated if not decreased, resulting in declining employment and rising layoffs worldwide. Statistics indicate, for example, that even before the 2008 financial crisis, employment-to-population ratios were declining on average in most OECD (Organization for Economic Co-operation and Development) countries, and have continued to do so after the crisis, most adversely affecting young workers, and in the United States, especially Black and Latino workers (Fischer 2021; Freeman 2010, 171–72). Some countries (e.g., Germany, Sweden, South Korea) have tried to hide this joblessness by subsidizing firms to temporarily keep their workers on board. All of this reveals financialization's dependence on rentierism—the accrual of wealth from unproductive economic rents—which causes declining overall employment and increasing wealth and income inequalities.[7] It also underscores that profit, not production, is the primary goal of capitalists: to wit, as mentioned earlier, nonfinancial enterprises have themselves turned to fictitious capital investments as a way of maximizing their profits.

At the level of the firm, this means that management are using profits to engage in financial activities (hedge fund investments, shareholder payouts, interest payments, etc.) instead of hiring or expanding physical investments. Companies are sometimes unable to reinvest because of their financial debts: they must use their operating revenues to first pay off bondholders and banks. So not only does such failure to reinvest in production forestall economic growth and employment, it also negatively affects wages: recent data confirm a stagnation if not decline in the share of income accruing to OECD workers during the last decade, due at least in part to rising company dividend and interest payments (Fischer 2021; Dünhaupt 2013).

But in addition to threatening employment and wages, financialization also helps raise the rate of labor exploitation—on a global scale. Since hedge funds are interested only in quick, short-term returns, they frequently harm the long-term interests of workers. Bryan and Rafferty (2005) explain, for example, how derivatives, because they provide the real-time value of a company's assets, can put tremendous pressure on a company to intensify its competitive edge by lowering costs and increasing productivity. As a matter of fact, derivatives are frequently used to raid "underperforming" businesses and turn them around ("leveraged buyouts"). Assets or plants not meeting profit goals are then depreciated, restructured, or sold. Most often, such pressure ends up on the backs of labor: the demand to cut costs, increase profits, and deliver on share values means extracting greater labor flexibility and wage "competitiveness," while sometimes also providing an alibi for management to replace workers with robots. In this regard, on top of reducing long-term costs, automation is also a way for the capitalist/speculator to undercut unions and do away with labor politics—because, as they say, "robots don't talk back."

The situation is more dire in the global South: faced with rising labor costs and a comparatively more unionized work force in the global

North, financialized/multinational capital has resorted to offshoring and outsourcing production to the Third World, especially since the 1980s (see chapter 2). The result is a system that increasingly depends not just on labor flexibility but on hyperexploitation and indeed a renaissance of new forms of slavery (Kara 2017): the use of bonded, forced, and child labor (e.g., in South Asia and central Africa) for agro-industry and mineral extraction; the resort to sweatshop labor, often comprised of the most "vulnerable" workers—women, children, migrants—who are proffered low wages and quasi–concentration camp work and living conditions; and the employment of migrant construction and farm workers in the rich Gulf States, deprived of basic civil and political rights.

(Neoliberal) Third World states have often acted as facilitators to such hyperexploitation, opening up their economies to multinational capital or creating export processing zones that provide foreign corporations with favorable investment conditions (e.g., tax breaks, energy subsidies, low or no environmental regulations, unionization bans). Frequently, it is through the mechanism of debt that such states have been coerced into this position: in the wake of the 1980s "debt crisis," their continued borrowing from banks and international financial institutions has been contingent on neoliberal conditionalities ("structural adjustment") requiring them to throw open their economies (i.e., financial, investment, and trade liberalization). Not only has such indebtedness enabled said labor hyperexploitation, it has also yielded to "accumulation by dispossession" (Harvey 2003). Indeed, in order to pay back their loans and encourage multinational investment, states have privatized public services (health, education, sanitation, drinking water), frequently rendering these inaccessible to the poor and marginalized, while also expropriating public resources (land, water, forests, mines) for the benefit of private accumulation, often leading to the expulsion of millions of poor rural and indigenous communities from the commons. For example, hedge funds have been directly linked to the recent spate of "land grabs" in sub-Saharan Africa: facilitated by local governments (e.g., in Ethiopia, Tanzania, South Sudan, Sierra Leone, Mali, and Mozambique), Western and Chinese financial speculators have acquired large tracts of land, mainly for the cultivation of cash crops (e.g., cut flowers) or sugarcane for use as biofuel. In the process, however, millions of small farmers and landless peasants have been displaced, threatening sub-Saharan Africa's long-term ability to grow food (as opposed to cash crops) (BBC 2011; Shepard and Anuradha 2011; Edelman, Oya, and Borras Jr. 2016; Oliveira, Liu, and McKay 2021). Thus, as Fraser puts it, "Debt plays a major role, as global financial institutions pressure states to collude with investors in extracting value from defenseless populations. It is largely by means of debt that peasants are dispossessed and rural land grabs are accorded a veneer of legality in the capitalist periphery" (2016, 176).

There is an unmistakable gender and "race" dimension here that must be teased out: not only have (mostly white and Western) financial elites made the debts of poor and racialized workers in the global North fodder for their speculative pursuits (as underlined earlier), but their activities have also ended up preying on mostly racialized and gendered bodies in the global South in the process of hyperexploitation and expropriation. The racialized and gendered poor thus serve as both investment opportunity and object of exploitation and domination. As several analysts have stressed (Robinson 2000, 2019; Williams 2021; Gottfried 2013; Wright 2013), the system requires and feeds off socioeconomic differentiation and inequality to sustain its operations and excesses. And while it is certainly the material benefits of financial speculation that help propel the system, the drive/*jouissance* of it all should not be discounted (see chapter 1; and Kapoor 2020, 236–64): the sadomasochistic enjoyment derived from being on "top," from extracting surplus from one's subordinate, and from lording it over gendered and racialized bodies. Capitalist libidinal economy, like capitalist political economy, "gets off" on social hierarchy and domination. There is therefore a close relationship between the material and libidinal excesses of financialized capitalism and questions of gender and "race" (see also chapters 2 and 8).

Consequently, the search for surplus value is imbricated with the search for surplus enjoyment, with crushing sociopolitical consequences: a postpolitical acquiescence to a system that extracts surplus value and enjoyment through shopping and inventive but risky financial products, while also depending on racialized forms of exploitation, enslavement, and expropriation. Jodi Dean (2020) sees this as "neofeudalism," under which corporate lords extract value "through monopoly, coercion, and rent." Such consequences are not a deplorable accident but a structural necessity. Ensuring profitability and risk-oriented enjoyment in late capitalism requires the organization of new social power relations that commandeer labor and gendered/racialized bodies; absent such exploitation and domination, the system's material and libidinal profitability would be all but impossible to achieve.

Notable here is how this "neofeudal" system penetrates and sucks material and symbolic value from every sector globally, integrating workers, racialized subalterns, environment, consumers, states, borrowers/

lenders, banks, producers/corporations, and speculators. And not only is everything and everyone absorbed into global capital's orbit, but the abstractness and anonymity of both market and libidinal drive make them indifferent to distance (nearness or remoteness) or object (commodity, environment, animal, human relations) as long as surplus value and enjoyment can be extracted. What the psychoanalytic lens adds to the question of commodity fetishism, then, is the significant insight that it is both material *and* affective relations between things that are substituted for social relations between people (and environments) so that there is a close "interdependency between exploitation and fetishisation" (Tomšič 2015, 53). The distance between use value and exchange value—the fundamental inequality that sustains the global capitalist system—is intersected by the fetishist's disavowal, allowing capitalist speculators (but not exclusively them) to enjoy their world by ridding it of lack and difference (see chapter 3). This is why billionaires can relish their wealth because of—and despite—hyperexploitation and expropriation; why market subjects can (pleasurably) consent to the postpolitical system even if they are aware of its ills; and even why exploited sweatshop workers can buy and enjoy sweatshop products (like anyone can). It may well be the socioeconomic and political elites that derive by far the most material and libidinal value from the system, but everyone in the system derives something (or the promise of something). The inequalities that found the system do not prevent all subjects—whether at the top or the bottom of the socioeconomic hierarchy—from being complicit in the process of alienation, distancing, and anonymity. All are tainted with the negativity of *jouissance*, and hence captive to its irrationality and excess, irrespective of identity or social positioning.

The latter point is an important corrective to Marxist IPE, which tends toward essentialization of the proletariat—the working class as Subject of History. Not only does the Marxist view privilege workers as a universal class, ignoring the likes of the lumpenproletariat, precariat, or marginalized gendered and racialized groups (i.e., whom we refer to as "the part of no-part"), but it also tends toward a romanticized and moralistic position, as a result of which workers are glorified and the "evils" of superexploitation are deplored. GLE averts such tendencies by seeing all subjects—whether proletarian or not, and whether under a current capitalist or a future postcapitalist regime—as alienated, forever tainted by excess and antagonism. Thus, capitalist exploitation happens not because a presumed "basic" or "natural" need—that is, use value—is being violated (which is what leads to moral outrage), but rather because of the *inequality* between use value and exchange value.[8] Thus, under financialization, exploitation happens even when workers are well remunerated (as they sometimes are, especially but not exclusively in the global North) or when racialized working families engage in financial speculation (as they sometimes do, as per our earlier discussion). It is not the violation or corruption of some essential goodness or "need" of the worker/subaltern that is the problem but instead the commodification of labor and the socioeconomic inequality (i.e., the increasing *distance* between use and exchange value under financialized capitalism) required to generate massive surpluses. All of us may well buy into the excesses of the system, but the benefits of such excess accrue overwhelmingly to our new feudal lords—the global financial elites. Indeed, the proof of such excessive inequality is that sweatshop labor and shantytowns have expanded across the globe at the very same time as the hyperconcentration of wealth—or as Dean (2020) renders it, "a few billionaires, a billion precarious workers."

Conclusion

This chapter has underlined not simply the passionate underpinnings of financialized capitalism but also its pathological irrationalities and excesses. The mainstreaming of financial instruments and institutions has opened up limitless possibilities for both accumulation and surplus enjoyment, further feeding global capitalism's self-propelling circuit of drive. This drive—the system's impassioned frenzy to repeat and seldom learn—is evident in such contemporary phenomena as excessive consumption, massive waste, and environmental destruction, all to the point of failure and crisis. It is also evident in rising rates of exploitation and domination—layoffs, sweatshop labor practices, new forms of slavery, appropriation of the commons—hitting hardest those who are poor, gendered, and racialized.

Thus, it is not "greed" that is at the source of the excesses of contemporary capitalism—a commonly held view, whether by the Church, mainstream media, or indeed neoclassical economists (see Özselçuk and Madra 2010)—but drive/enjoyment. Greed assumes an egoistic yet stable and rational subject whose debauchery can be curbed and corrected with the right policies; drive/enjoyment (as stressed by a GLE perspective) are the inherent excess to an unstable and split subject, impossible to predict or contain (see chapter 1). As Özselçuk and Madra maintain, "While economic institutions and discourses try to administer and domesticate enjoyment, they always fail since it is impossible to balance out, apportion or stitch together enjoyment. This emphasis on the excessive and unstable nature of jouissance negates any form of reproductionism in which the practices of consumption, production and distribution are glued snugly together in a systemic cycle of social equilibrium and crisis" (2010, 335).

What is remarkable is drive/*jouissance*'s unrelenting tenaciousness under late capitalism, something standard IPE, whether (neo)classical or Marxist, is unable to account for. For GLE, it is enjoyment's "stuckness" that helps explain both the intensity and extensity of financial capitalism: how the thrill and risk of it all grips subjects on an unconscious level, mesmerizing them, while also thereby making capitalism seem inevitable, unavoidable, impossible to change; and how it magnetically attracts all that stands in its path, allowing capital to integrate into its orbit the material as much as the symbolic, the wealthy as much as the subaltern, civil society as much as the state, and the local as much as the global.

What is also remarkable, as Feldner et al. point out, is the fetishistic illusion of the financial speculator that capital can be valorized without class antagonism—the inconveniences of subaltern organizing or environmental crisis—so that full enjoyment can be finally reached: "Money-be-getting-money is the dream scenario of capitalist utopia" (2014, 26–27). True, to some extent, this scenario has panned out, given the generalized postpolitical consensus, the collaboration of the neoliberal state, and the successful hyperexploitation of poor, gendered, and racialized labor to extract value. Yet, as GLE emphasizes, the logic and necessity of capitalist accumulation and enjoyment inevitably bump up against contingency and unpredictability: their very own (i.e., immanent) irrationalism and excess is their downfall. Signs of such contingency and unpredictability abound today (see Žižek 2021): a system that may well absorb everything everywhere but is also thereby vulnerable to attacks from all sides (global warming, social protests, the continuing COVID-19 pandemic, recalcitrant states such as Bolivia, Nepal, or Cuba, etc.); fictitious capital's failure to generate adequate production and employment, leading to the rise of social unrest, especially among youth; the globalization of speculation, resulting in a nihilism immanent to the stock exchange itself (as witnessed by the likes of WallStreetBets) . . . *Jouissance*'s proclivities toward self-sabotage suggest that the threats to any system that depends on it arise from within the heart of the system itself, not from outside, thus potentially transforming the capitalist's dream of a world without antagonism into a nightmare.

Indeed, that financialized capitalism lures everything into its orbit may well be its strength, but it is equally its weakness, since such ensnarement involves so many points of contact, which is to say, as pointed out above, so many potential openings/antagonisms, whether along the axes of class, identity, or ecology. But at least two political challenges stand in the way here. One is devising a politics that *cuts across* antagonisms, rather than yielding to segmentation and ghettoization, which is what the system favors (particularistic identity politics poses no real threat to the globalization of capital, as we have mentioned before). Drawing on Žižek, Kapoor and Zalloua (2022) suggest precisely such a cross-cutting negative universal politics—solidarity forged on the basis of antagonism (i.e., shared experiences of exploitation and marginalization). The idea is that such varying groups as workers, Palestinians, or Black Lives Matter come together not on the basis of identity, which tends to divide people, but of shared forms of alienation, which our era of financialization makes all the more intensive and widespread. A second, related challenge is finding the resolve—the drive—to uncompromisingly work toward a postcapitalist future. This would entail inhabiting the very same drive that propels financial capital accumulation, but in this case, to obstinately refuse to accept global capitalism as our only horizon, while doggedly abstaining from compromising one's desire for radical systemic change (i.e., settling for reformist measures that end up helping to maintain the system; see chapter 4). It is indeed the same resoluteness and relentlessness of drive that enables global capitalism's revolutionary circuit that may also help us short-circuit and break out of its choke hold (see chapter 7). Yet, given the excess and unpredictability of drive, any such politics will always already be accompanied by a plethora of dangers and pitfalls (i.e., failure, creating a power vacuum for authoritarian rule, replacing old social hierarchies with new ones, etc.).

7

Ecology

Toward a Psychoanalytic Political Ecology

What is a psychoanalytic approach to political ecology? At a time when environmental degradation and climate change are widely seen as the most pressing concerns of our day, do we need another perspective? As political ecology tends to argue, the distinction between nature and society is a spurious one, the result of modernity's hubris of dominating the environment. Here, the human subject is seen as a small side story in the history of nature (the latter having its own dynamics), and any effort to understand the social outside of larger "natural" frameworks is seen as inherently reductive. Such a view appears to open the door to a resolution between people and nature ("we need to overcome our arrogance") and imply a postpolitical approach to ecology, one devoid of conflict or struggle, and one that assumes human beings will by necessity adopt conservation and mitigation policies (Swyngedouw 2016). Meanwhile, other more radical viewpoints have adopted a more expansive critique, arguing that we need not only overcome the human-nature dichotomy but that the human encounter with "otherness" can redeem us from Western modernity's degradation of nature, giving way to an alternative "futurality" (Escobar 2008). The latter perspective has been criticized for romanticizing the relationship between humans and ecology by advocating a return to nature as a way of overcoming the trauma of loss (Knudsen 2014; Kapoor 2020; Kapoor and Zalloua 2022). Psychoanalytic theory, in contrast, places emphasis on the constitutive nature of loss to the human experience, as we have previously underlined (see chapter 1). Nature is beyond good and bad, and the separation between being and nature is what makes human life exceptionally singular. As Žižek (2012) puts it, the prehistory of being entails a fall from nature. This is the "bad news" of a psychoanalytic political ecology: there is no redemption through reconciliation. Human loss has to be assumed as definitive, so that alienation is constitutive of being.

In this chapter, we offer a psychoanalytic political ecology that, while attending to the ontological struggles for territory and difference, refuses to fall back on romanticized notions of redemption through reconciliation. Nature is understood as sublime, beyond "full" comprehension for humans, grounded in fundamental instability and disharmony. Or to put it in Lacanese, nature is always already traversed by the Real, the latter standing for the antagonism immanent to reality. The Real of nature thus manifests as a constitutive failure to construct a stable relationship between ecology and society. Accordingly, a psychoanalytic political ecology centers on the political unconscious (Jameson 2015) of nature, where the Real compels us to make political decisions about how to reinvent socionatural relations as emancipatory by attending to antagonisms within nature, including human nature.

This chapter therefore explores the "bad news" of psychoanalysis, offering a critique of attempts to ground political ecology in an ontology of difference, and proposing instead the idea of the Real of nature as "extimate," that is, at the limit of nature/reality. The key question we pose is: What is it in nature that we think can redeem us from loss? We attempt an answer by focusing on the Colombian Pacific, a territory that has been historically subjected to the violence of colonization, slavery, and violent conflict, centering on the control of natural resources. We analyze such a territory as a laboratory for incorporating local populations into the global capitalist system as peasant smallholders, an effort initially resisted by Catholic missionaries bent on preserving people's ontological dignity (de Castro 2015) from the onslaught of Westernization. We claim that both sides of this conflict—the one aiming at modernization of the territory, the other at its protection—give way to the "invention of conservation" as a compromise formation in which the "natives" are reimagined as "natural" conservationists. What both sides have in common, in other words, is a disavowal of the instability of nature: each depends on the enjoyment of an assumed coherent nature as redemption from loss. What we suggest instead is a more politicized and psychoanalytically inflected political ecology—one that attempts to come to terms with rather than ignoring nature's lack, and one that foregrounds rather than assumes those most affected by crisis and instability—the part of no-part.

Political Ecology and the "Bad News" of Psychoanalysis

A conventional definition of political ecology is as follows: "[It] emerged in the 1980s as an interdisciplinary field that analyzed environmental problems using the concepts and methods of political economy. A central premise of the field is that ecological change cannot be understood without consideration of the political and economic structures and institutions within which it is embedded. The nature-society dialectic is the fundamental focus of analysis" (Neumann 2009: 228). Marxist anthropologists Erik Wolf and Michael Watts are often mentioned as precursors of the field (Roberts 2020). Both authors put at the center of their analysis changes in labor and property relations that ensue from the encounter between local communities in the global South and wider capitalist forces. Ecology here is seen as a constitutive part of the forces of production, through which local economies are incorporated into global capitalist economies. This position, it should be noted, was penned before climate change came to be considered the primary driver of global transformations.

From the 1980s onward, political ecology often distinguished itself from other mainstream approaches such as ecological modernization (Mol, Sonnenfeld, and Spaargaren 2010). The latter set out to provide relatively straightforward pathways for transitions toward sustainable futures; in contrast, political ecology became more interested in the distributional aspects of capitalist modernization—how the benefits and costs of ecological change are shared among different actors, classes, and groups (e.g., on the basis of gender, sexuality, ethnicity, caste, and so on). An "environmentalism of the poor" was thus seen as crucial in determining how nature-society relations are shaped (Martínez Alier 2002). Here the focus was on indigenous and environmental justice movements involved in extraction conflicts around the world.

But as virtuous as this framing may sound for taking on the position of the excluded/part of no-part, it is problematic from a psychoanalytic perspective. Indeed, as Watts himself suggests (2015), it is a view that emphasizes the role of maladaptation and instability as a political factor, which is to say that it assumes environmental harmony as a goal for creating sustainable futures for the poor. Yet, we ask, what if nature is inherently unstable and any stabilization of the nature-society dialectic is impossible *because* of human intervention? What if, since the onset of the Anthropocene, the environment has been so adapted and controlled that human intervention is *integral* to nature's fragility? The point not to be lost, accordingly, is that politics depends not on a moral position that ends up heroizing or romanticizing the poor but on the properly political condition of having to respond to society-nature relations that are beset by multiple antagonisms (socioeconomic, cultural, environmental, etc.).

Alain Badiou makes the cogent argument that the ecology has become the opium of the masses in our times: "Let's start by stating that after the 'rights of man,' the rise of the 'rights of Nature' is a contemporary form of the opium for the people. It is only a slightly camouflaged religion: the millenarian terror, concern for everything save the properly political destiny of peoples, new instruments for the control of everyday life, the fear of death and catastrophes . . . it is a gigantic operation in the depoliticization of subjects" (2008, 139). The pertinence of Badiou's statement here concerns the portrayal of the poor as victims, depriving them of historical agency. This is an important insight in view of our upcoming claim that "the rights of Nature" approach in the Colombian Pacific has led to two interpretations that depoliticize the political subjectivity of local subaltern populations: constructing them as "naturally" close to nature and/or targets of governmental interventions aimed at their incorporation into capital's expansionary drive. The part of no-part thus become a prop to serve and stabilize both capitalism and social-ecological relationships (more on this below).

In this regard, Erik Swyngedouw (2016) brings out the specifically depoliticizing dimensions of such maneuvers: he criticizes the postpolitical elevation of ecology by querying, for example, the contemporary role of carbon dioxide as a fetish, which ends up putting aside social contradictions in our struggle for the preservation of the planet. This is a powerful form of critique of the ideological investment in the dream of a stabilized and protected nature, as advocated by mainstream conservation policies and programs. In this light, what Badiou's critique of "the rights of Nature" brings out is political ecology's postpolitical sleight of hand: the depoliticization of the part of no-part, that is, our use and abuse of them to cover over—indeed to solve—our socioeconomic and ecological antagonisms.

What a psychoanalytic political ecology points to, in contrast, is the importance of viewing the part of no-part as the very incarnation of the political—that which reveals the processes of socioeconomic antagonisms and exclusion at the heart of the global capitalist system. To be sure, as we have previously stressed (see chapters 1, 4, and 6), the part of no-part are what the system crucially depends on (e.g., as reserve army of labor) yet abjects, giving them no "proper place." They are what the system needs to disavow in order to function and indeed constitute itself. This is why, as Žižek emphasizes (2009, 53), giving critical attention to ecological catastrophe without simultaneously addressing the socioeconomic antagonisms that produce the excluded can never yield a permanent or viable solution. Unless we confront the exploitative and exclusionary logic of global capitalism itself, "ecology turns into a problem of sustainable development" (Žižek 2016, 105), a problem that needs only to be managed rather than solved (Kapoor and Zalloua 2022, 7).

Importantly, what such a perspective implies is not just the instability of nature but also its "extimacy" (see chapter 4): that which is simultaneously intimate and outside, the "other" that is "strange to me, although it is at the heart of me" (Lacan 1997, 71). And it is precisely because nature is an "intimate disjunction" that remains unknowable despite being familiar (as opposed to coherent and controllable) that it must treated as an inherently political object: one devoid of any "natural" essence, which, because of its contingency, compels us to think politically about new ways of dealing with disjointedness and disharmony. So rather than trying to overcome the nature-society binary by using and abusing the part of no-part, the idea is to prioritize the construction of new socio-ecological forms in which the part of no-part (which embody the antagonisms of the system) are positioned center stage. It is such thoroughly political thinking that provides the opportunity to rethink a system that depends on systematic exclusion, while also reorganizing it in favor of the commons (of the environment, knowledge, biogenetics).

Thus, while an "environmentalism of the poor" tends toward a moral discourse that depoliticizes the part of no-part in an effort to stabilize the human-nature relationship and ignores the structural mechanisms that crucially depend on their subalternization, a psychoanalytic political ecology centers them precisely because they reveal systemic instability and antagonism. In this sense, political ecology often engages in a form of self-righteous blackmail, championing the excluded to stabilize ecological crisis. GLE, in contrast, attempts to confront the ecological crisis head-on by seeing it as an opening toward reconfiguring the capitalist system and its positioning of the part of no-part. Without this recognition, political ecology so often stabilizes that which it seeks to confront, offering a harmonious nature *outside* of capitalism, which is precisely what capitalism desires and demands as a site of "accumulation by dispossession" that can be readily integrated into the system (Harvey 2003).

A Critique of Political Ontology

After critiquing the drive of capital to overcome the nature-society binary, let us engage with the desire to protect populations who live close to nature from the onslaught of capitalist modernity. This stream of political ecology is particularly strong in Latin America, where political concerns stemming from socioenvironmental conflicts over dispossession from territory have become pervasive. Such a stream centers on the defense of indigenous people, their culture, and their territory. Here Arturo Escobar (1999b) is a major representative; he defends cultural and ontological difference by arguing that the encounter with radical otherness can redeem us from Western modernity's treatment of nature as a bundle of resources (see also Leff 2021).

The focus on difference has inspired important work in subaltern environmental history, analyzing diverse ways of relating to nature and underlining the possibilities of "other ways of knowing." The dialogue of knowledges—inherent to *buen vivir/sumak kawsay* ("living well")—has become mainstream in many Latin American countries, although some argue that its constitutionalization (in Bolivia, for example) may have deprived it of critical edge (Radcliffe 2012). Also relevant is work that focuses on alternative ways of constructing nonbinary/plural relationships between nature and society (Descola 2013), or alternate ways of perceiving the world, for example, through *sentipensar* (thinking by way of emotions/sentiments) (Fals Borda 2000).

Perhaps more radically, this stream of political ontology sets out to show the existence of other ways of being, what Blaser (2014) calls "world-making." The idea of the *pluriverse* (Escobar 2018) is key in this regard, deriding the violence of the universalization of Western modernity in favor of the need to acknowledge difference in order to construct "a world in which many worlds are possible." Escobar, drawing on the idea that different natures produce different ways of being, imagines plural futures ("futurality") as a way of avoiding the trap of Western modernity's separation of the market and politics, and the primacy of the individual over communal ways of being. The title of his book on the Colombian Pacific, *Territories of Difference* (2008), is a prime example of this "ontological turn," with territories standing for both the struggle against dispossession and the defense of place in a globalizing world. The idea of place is thus constructed as the common site for the communitarian and solidary against the onslaught of capitalist modernity.

But the problem with such a political ontology, psychoanalytically speaking, is its tendency to romanticize the relationship between humans and the environment by advocating a return to nature as a way of overcoming the trauma of loss. To be sure, Escobar has been roundly criticized for his proclivity to idealize and heroize local/indigenous communities (Kiely 1999; Pieterse 2000; Storey 2000; Kapoor 2008, 52–53). Kiely, for example, characterizes Escobar's gloss as the "last refuge of the noble savage," emphasizing how it celebrates the local while downplaying such problems as internal disagreements, gender violence, exploitation, and inequality. Kapoor concurs (2020, 41–45; Kapoor and Zalloua 2022, 94–104), suggesting that Escobar's is an attempt to construct the subaltern as somehow immune to ideological interpellation, which, despite their characterization as agentic subject, amounts ironically to depoliticizing them through their exoticization (their closeness to "territory"/nature). What is missing here, in other words, is the dimension of the Real—the fundamental blockage that prevents any subject, subaltern or not, from realizing its identity with itself.

So, like the "environmentalism of the poor," this strand of political ecology ends up using and abusing the part of no-part to buttress the promise of reconciliation and deny the antagonisms at the heart of both subject and nature. This proclivity is reproduced in the case study we discuss next, guiding the actions of the development establishment *and* the missionary-activists inspired by liberation theology.

The Colombian Case

The case of the Colombian Pacific brings together two (seemingly paradoxical) positions—dealing with the nature-society divide by both protecting "native" populations and integrating them into the logic of capitalism. The first position, as we will show, is taken by missionaries inspired by liberation theology, while the second is advocated by a Dutch development project (the DIAR). It is the encounter with the DIAR project that convinces the missionaries to take up the cause of the local population, ironically resulting in the "the invention of conservation." All this at a time when a prolonged conflict over territorial resources is being waged in the country.

REDEEMING THE FALL IN THE COLOMBIAN PACIFIC

In 2009 research was conducted by Pieter de Vries and Eduardo Restrepo on the genealogy and nonintended impacts of the DIAR, a Dutch Development Cooperation project in the Chocó department of Colombia (de Vries and Valencia 2010; Restrepo 2010). Both the DIAR and Catholic missionaries played a central role in the drafting of the Ley 70 land titling program in 1993, which recognized Afro-Colombians and indigenous people as subjects of land rights. The country's indigenous people had already been declared subjects of rights in the 1991 Colombian constitution. Significantly, in 2016, the Pacific region's Atrato River was also declared a subject of rights.

The Atrato flows from deep south in the Chocó department toward the Atlantic Ocean, operating as an "open vein" (Galeano 1997) through the rainforest. The river has been a geopolitical pawn since early colonial times, first in the contest between the Spanish and British empires, later in invasions by pirates, and later still in political interventions by the United States. The Chocó department borders with the Darien strait in Panama (formerly a Colombian territory that seceded under pressure from the United States). In the aftermath of the construction of the Panama Canal, this area was targeted as a possible site for the construction of a new canal connecting the Atlantic and the Pacific. Furthermore, since colonial times, the Pacific region had been the subject of extensive natural resource extraction, in particular gold mining and logging. The indigenous communities in the area resisted subjugation by the Spanish, many eventually escaping to inaccessible areas in the rainforest, far away from mining sites. As a consequence, miners resorted to the deployment of enslaved labor from Africa. The region also became a destination for maroon slave refugees (Restrepo 2008; Wabgou 2012) who settled on the shores of the rivers (henceforth denominated as the "river people"). Later, the area was subject to colonization by mestizo (mixed-race) colonists from the highlands. By the second half of the twentieth century, the pressure on land increased due to the southward advance of logging companies interested in tropical hardwood. Thus, through the ages, the Pacific became both the site for extraction/dispossession and a refuge for those trying to create livelihoods outside of the mercantile economy (fishing, hunting, forestry).

THE ENCOUNTER BETWEEN THE CLARETIANS AND THE DIAR

In the 1980s, under the administration of President Belisario Betancur, a negotiation process was initiated between the Colombian government and the Revolutionary Armed Forces of Colombia (Fuerzas Armadas Revolucionarias de Colombia, or FARC) and M19 guerrilla armies. Around the same time, the Dutch and Colombian governments negotiated the implementation of three integrated rural development projects, one in the Amazon, a second in the northeastern banana plantation area of Urabá, and a third in the Pacific department of Chocó. The Dutch ministry of development cooperation and the Colombian planning agency chose these areas because they were peripheral and hence vulnerable to armed conflict.

The DIAR in the Chocó started in 1979 and lasted until 1989. Like the other two projects, it aimed to improve the living conditions of the local peasant population by introducing new technologies, providing extension and health services, supporting local institutional development, and improving local infrastructure. In contradistinction to the classical "Green Revolution" development projects, it aimed to do this in a participatory and programmatic way. This involved the establishment of local organizations (mainly marketing organizations) to embark on a peasant road of development so as to integrate local populations in wider markets. This programmatic approach meant that no clear-cut objectives or indicators were seen as necessary: design and project implementation would take place in a step-by-step, experimental fashion, exploring (in a participatory way) different alternatives. The project had a large budget (twenty-nine million florins in 1980, with a current value of thirty million Euros) and substantial transportation equipment and personnel.

One problem encountered from the start was the absence of cash crops in an area where people lived largely off fishing and forest products. Integration into local markets therefore became the first goal. An early assessment established that there was a lack of salt in the region, so project staff started providing salt to the community in order to generate goodwill. The next step was finding a suitable cash crop. After much experimentation (pigs, plantains, maize, sugar cane, peach palm, *borojo*), the project finally settled on the introduction of rice. This was an immediate success, creating an economic boom, but it was short-lived, as the riverbank soil became exhausted and the introduction of fertilizers and pesticides led to diminishing returns.

The DIAR drew significant criticism, not only from local elites who distrusted the sudden growing power of the project leader and foreign experts but also from Claretian missionaries who had been active for decades in small development projects in the area. The missionaries had until then operated mills and established local exchange networks (through funerals, baptisms, catechisms) independently from the regional political and institutional system that was notorious for its corruption. Along with other missionaries in the region, the Claretians were among the foremost practitioners of liberation theology, creating ecclesial base communities for the defense of people's territory.

In order to understand the Claretians' mistrust of the DIAR, it is important to explain the evolvement of their thinking and missionary practice. The first Claretian missionaries were Spaniards who started their activities in the Chocó in the nineteenth century with a focus on conversion. In the twentieth century, most missionaries came from Colombian seminaries that had been exposed to the progressive thinking of Pope John XII, under whose papacy the second Episcopal Conference of Latin America was organized in Medellin, Colombia, which endorsed the "option of the poor" advocated by liberation theology. Gonzalo de la Torre, the head of the Claretian congregation, grew up in Chocó and was strongly involved with this theological current. As he put it, "For us it was very strange to see our mission as that of converting the people into Christians when we saw that their spirituality and religiosity was much stronger than in other areas where the Catholic Church had a strong presence. The idea of going to the rivers to marry young couples proved to be nonsensical when we saw that the community itself had provided the sacrament according to the thinking of Jesus" (de Vries, interview, September 2010). Furthermore, liberation theology thinking was critical of the past complicity between the Church and the country's elite, in particular of their racist mission to extirpate pagan and, later, indigenous and black elements, so as to convert them into Catholics. The role of the base communities was that of harnessing the spirituality of the river people to create a consciousness about their right to live at peace in their territory.

Hence the missionaries resented the DIAR's attempts to introduce new crops that would make local populations dependent on broader, global markets, and lure them into a consumerist culture. Furthermore, they suspected that the DIAR operated in tandem with logging companies in trying to expand commodity production in Chocó. Conversely, the DIAR project directors viewed the missionaries as feudal priests determined to keep the local population "ignorant."

During the 1983–89 period, the DIAR started employing more Colombian extension workers, social workers, and anthropologists to motivate the river people to engage in market activities, drawing on a pro-peasant discourse. Some of these young Colombian professionals established close connections with Dutch cooperants, many of whom had been strongly influenced by pro-peasant Third World solidarity movements in Dutch universities.

By the end of the project in 1989, the encounter between the Claretians and DIAR staff had led to a shift in perspective by both parties. The Claretians, on the one hand, had become convinced that the outside forces of the market could be countered only by establishing alliances with progressive development agencies and the Colombian state; in other words, they believed the only way of preserving the "ontological dignity" (de Castro 2015) of the river/indigenous people was by *opening up* to globalization processes in select ways. The DIAR team, on the other hand, had come to accept the missionary principle of protecting Afro-Colombians and indigenous people from the onslaught of extractivist enterprises, in particular logging companies. These companies, after having established themselves in the Low Atrato (the northern part of the Chocó), had begun invading communal lands in the Middle Atrato.

But the idea that it was possible to find a cash crop that could act as the mainstay of a peasant transition to modernity proved wrongheaded. A household economy research exercise conducted by two DIAR staff members (Leesberg and Valencia 1987) revealed that indigenous and black communities were not "peasants," and that their economy was based on a plurality of activities in which monetary exchanges played a minor role relative to the importance of community and kin exchange networks. The report further claimed that the river people's "close relationship with nature" was what made their livelihoods sustainable, and that this "closeness" reflected a kind of local knowledge that should be preserved. This was an enormous blow to the modernist idea of a "peasant" road to economic development. The problem, the research argued, was not poverty or resource scarcity (as was so often the case in peasant areas in the highlands were *minifundismo* was prevalent), since land and water were abundant. The failure of the programmatic approach revealed, in fact, the inability of "development" to recognize that the river people had always been involved in the management of natural resources (e.g., timber) and that they possessed precious knowledge about how to use and manage the forest without compromising its regenerative capacity. This led to a pivotal shift in the DIAR's strategy, toward a conservationist strategy aimed at giving local populations a new role as custodians of the rainforest. Thereafter, timber became the sought-out cash crop (still aimed at local and global market integration), premised on the belief that its rational use and management would be ensured by "traditional knowledge systems."

The growing rapprochement between DIAR and the missionaries was strengthened by the fear that local people's livelihoods were being threatened by powerful logging companies, which enjoyed the strong support of the national political elite. This paved the way for the creation of the Integral Peasant Association of the Atrato in 1987, a producer's association that drew on the experiences of the ecclesial base communities and the marketing organizations established by DIAR. In turn, these events were accompanied by the surge of a strong black consciousness movement in the region. Traditionally, blacks from Chocó were seen, and saw themselves, as former enslaved people with few ethnic commonalities. But with "the invention of black ethnicity" (Restrepo 2008), the groundwork was established for a movement that contested regional subordination to national patron-client networks. The movement thereby became instrumental in debates about black ethnicity and the possibility of making claims to communal territories, comparable to those of indigenous communities.

It is during this time that negotiations of the Ley 70 began. In 1991, a new constitution conceded indigenous peoples' legal rights to communal (as opposed to state) land. This established a legal precedent, taken up in Chocó to initiate a struggle for the recognition of local people as subjects of communal land rights. A process started in which the DIAR, the Claretians, and the National Planning Agency pressured the Colombian government to recognize the "original" rights of Afro-Colombians and indigenous people in the Pacific region. The result was the 1988 agreement of Buchadó, which led to the promulgation of Ley 70 in conferring collective titles to black and indigenous communities.

THE INVENTION OF CONSERVATION

The attribution of land titles to local Pacific communities was part of a wider discussion among actors about how to create a territorial governance system that would give these communities a central role in the rational production and management of timber as a prime commodity. The concern was to ward off the dispossession of the river and indigenous people by logging companies. A communal forestry approach was thus created to protect communal lands while at the same time integrating them into the nation as territories inhabited, owned, and managed by "native" populations.

Implied here was a reconceptualization of the role of Afro-Colombians and indigenous people as stewards of the rainforest, given their close ties to nature as "river people" rather than as peasant agricultural producers. Also implied was the idea of tropical rainforest as a source of valuable biodiversity. Both assumptions led to the creation of a communal forest approach (*bosques comunales*) to natural resource planning, seen as a sustainable forest resource management system in which the river people would be the "natural" custodians of the rainforest. Timber, according to this view, became a natural resource managed by native populations and assisted by conservation experts.

But such a new form of governmentality was short-lived: the region saw the arrival of corporate logging, mining, and cattle ranching, much of which sought, with the complicity of the state, to fund paramilitary groups to displace local populations and occupy their territory. In response, the guerrilla armies FARC and ELN (National Liberation Army) expanded their theater of operations to the Pacific in their war against the state and the paramilitaries, often funded through coca production. In 2000, the United States and Colombia signed Plan Colombia, an agreement outwardly aimed at eradicating coca production but in practice devoted to training the Colombian military to fight against guerrilla insurgent groups (see LaRosa and Mejía 2017). Plan Colombia also organized the air spraying of glysophate (a highly poisonous herbicide) to combat coca production in the Amazon, causing many colonists to start moving their agricultural operations to other regions, notably the Pacific. In this quickly changing context, the role of the missionaries became once again that of defending the rights of local populations now being displaced by the maneuverings of external forces.

While these recent political dynamics reflect a new and more intense phase of "developmentalization" in the region (Restrepo 2010), they still reveal an ongoing process of integration into the global capitalist economy going back to the nineteenth century and, more recently, to the 1980s under the guise of "conservation." We argue that the situation is thus best understood as the "invention of conservation" as a *means* to capitalist integration: it involves depoliticizing Afro-Colombians and indigenous people by constructing them as the best "protectors" of nature—but in the service of capitalism. Despite the beginnings of political organization by these river and indigenous people, they nonetheless became prey to powerful desires—principally those of the Claretians and the DIAR, who wished to "protect" and/or "develop" them (but later also those of corporate elites, state, and guerillas, who wished to use or displace them for economic or geopolitical purposes). Constructing them as "naturally" close to nature was an appropriate fantasy to guide such desires: stabilizing the nature-society divide through community conservation was at the same time a way to stabilize capitalist development, with the part of no-part as the medium. So, in this sense, a depoliticized and exoticized conservation *had* to be invented to harmonize and reproduce the system. In this melee, the voices of the part of no-part were obscured; that they may have seen themselves as, say, conservators, farmer-peasants, communitarians, and/or revolutionaries had no bearing. As Spivak would put it, between conservation and development, "subject-constitution and object-formation, the figure of the [subaltern] disappear[ed]. . . . There [was] no space from which the . . . [river and indigenous people could] speak" (1988, 306–7).

Conclusion

We have outlined a few theoretical and empirical positions on political ecology, which while distinct also have much in common: a moralizing "environmentalism of the poor"; a romanticizing and exoticizing political ecology; and an environmental-developmental conservationism aimed at protecting and/or modernizing the part of no-part. All appear to share two proclivities.

One is the tendency toward the stabilization of nature and/or capitalism. It is this same tendency that is the answer to the question posed at the start of the chapter: What is it in nature that we think can redeem us from loss? Answer: (the comfort and enjoyment of) its stability. Indeed, both the environmentalism of the poor and Escobar's environmental futurality, as we have seen, are hypothesized on the promise of reconciliation with nature, one that ends up denying the antagonisms at the heart of ecology (and the subject). The Claretians and the DIAR proceed to make the same assumption through their "invention of conservation," although the idea there is not just harmonization with nature but, despite initial reservations by the Claretians, also the sustainability of the system through subaltern integration into global capitalism. We want to suggest, in fact, that "protecting," "saving," "modernizing," and "developing" the subaltern (and nature) are all an implicit acceptance of the system, since all aim only at sheltering the subaltern and ecology from systemic colonization rather than reconfiguring the very system that necessitates people's (and nature's) "protection." Even the two academic streams of political ecology appear to fall victim to this tendency: despite their criticisms of capitalist modernity, does not their desire to stabilize nature prepare the very ground for capitalist colonization of territory? Are not their moralizing and romanticizing impulses—their depoliticizing propensities—an implicit acceptance of, and accommodation to, global capitalism? What we are suggesting, then, is that their desire for a harmonious and depoliticized world/nature is revealing of their fetishization of the system itself: capitalism enjoys and demands nothing more than smooth territory to facilitate its mobility and accumulation.

The second tendency is surely the depoliticization of the subaltern. This is evident in the moralism of the "environmentalism of the poor" aimed at creating sustainable futures; in Escobar's inclination to protect subaltern territories, which often ends up undercutting subaltern agency; and in the Claretian and DIAR's construction of the river and indigenous people as "protectors" of nature. All of them end up speaking for the subaltern to buttress their own ideological positions; they each use and abuse it to cloak constitutive socioeconomic and ecological antagonisms.

So what does GLE offer up instead? A highly politicized and psychoanalytically inflected political ecology that foregrounds the antagonism of the part of no-part. Here, the subaltern does not become a prop to justify a narrow position or reproduce the system; rather, it is seen as the very site of antagonism, revealing the systemic deadlocks—exploitation, domination, inequality—that subalternize *in the first place*. The very presence of the part of no-part thus becomes the political opportunity to rethink and rework, not rationalize or maintain, a system premised on exclusion, violence, and dispossession. Political ecology is thus right to prioritize the subaltern but misses the point in its tendency to essentialize the latter by idealizing, romanticizing, and exoticizing it. GLE averts that mistake by desubstantializing the part of no-part, seeing them as symptomatic of the *system*'s deadlocks.

If we are right that, whether through disavowal or calculation, it is the increasing enclosure of the commons that depoliticizes the subaltern—subjecting it to the private interests and desires of others—then it is precisely a rethinking and reconfiguration of the political economy in favor of the commons (of the environment, knowledge, biogenetics) that points to ways of empowering the subaltern—enabling it with the space, literally and figuratively, to be self-determining, although never without struggle. Here again, Escobar is right to point to the idea of shared communal territories, but his nostalgic and romanticized view of a stable subaltern-nature relationship disempowers the subaltern by fixing, so to speak, its species-being. He opens up the part of no-part's material and geographic space even as he closes down their agentic subjectivity. In contrast, by imagining a more open and common territory *that is always already unstable and contingent*, a psychoanalytic political ecology enables the part of no-part to be self-determining, but never with any guarantees (including, from an environmental perspective, the guarantee that the subaltern will "naturally" choose conservation and harmony with nature to the benefit of us all, especially those superconsumers in the global North disproportionately responsible for climate change). It is precisely the instability and contingency of the material world that brings forth the political, making life a continual struggle (for the subaltern as much as anyone)—agentic and liberating, but at the same time risky and unpredictable. In this sense, the instability and contingency of the world is the price to pay for the properly political; or, to put it the other way around, there is no meaningful politics without (ant)agonism.

Thus, rather than harmonizing the nature-society divide by using and abusing the part of no-part, a GLE implies new socioecological forms that face nature's instability while prioritizing the part of no-part. The coupling of the two—nature's instability and subaltern politics—is fundamental: confronting ecological volatility and crisis without simultaneously addressing the socioeconomic antagonisms that produce the excluded can never yield a viable solution because it only perpetuates elite-subaltern inequalities and reproduces discourses that disavow the need for systemic change. And we are suggesting that a movement toward a thoroughly politicized commons is a way of encapsulating that coupling, since it empowers the subaltern *first* in times of volatility and crisis. As Kapoor and Zalloua put it, this is a way of

> concretizing *égaliberté* [equality-freedom] so that when the next environmental shock hits, it is liable to impact people and places around the world more equally: regulating the commons will better ensure that the part of no-part does not pay

the highest price (in order that the wealthy pay the lowest). We cannot fully guard against crisis—it is part and parcel of human-nature relationships, as argued earlier—we can only try to make sure that when it strikes, it does so in more equal ways. (2022, 226)

The commons helps minimize the divide between the excluded/included, allowing the former—that is, entitling it with the material and symbolic space—to better cope with insecurity and disaster, while also disabling the latter to exploit, dominate, and/or expropriate. The part of no-part thus embody the "negative universal" (2022, 226): they point to the kinds of systemic politico-economic and environmental changes that need to happen in order for *everyone*, not just the privileged, to lead more self-determining—albeit still always struggling—lives.

8

The State

How China's Belt and Road Initiative
Breaks the Cycle of Race and Trauma

We will never allow anyone to bully, oppress or subjugate China.

—Xi Jinping 2021a)

China's Belt and Road Initiative (BRI), previously referred to as the One Belt One Road initiative, is the biggest development project in the world. Officially known (in Mandarin) as the "Silk Road Economic Belt" and the "Twenty-First-Century Maritime Silk Road," it was launched in 2013 and, as of 2021, involved projects in 139 countries (Sacks 2021). Although estimates vary depending on the source,[1] figures on funds allocated to BRI as of November 2020 range from $4 trillion to $762 billion over a seven-year period (Dezan Shira and Associates, n.d.; Business Wire 2021). The BRI has the potential to be globally transformative, not just for China but also for the countries along the BRI corridors, which, by some estimates, require 70 percent more FDI to fulfill their infrastructure needs, which could increase trade by 30 percent (Ruta et al. 2019). Despite its scale, the BRI remains largely unknown to the wider public in the West, or, when referenced, is often described pejoratively as "debt trap diplomacy" (Abi-Habib 2018; Arežina 2019; Shepard 2020; O'Connor 2021; Davidson 2021). Ferchen and Perera (2019) and Jones and Hameiri (2020), however, argue that there is no real evidence that China set out to entrap its partners. We should not forget, moreover, that the austerity programs for developing countries long championed by the IMF and the World Bank, as well as by US aid programs during the Cold War, have long been described as debt trap diplomacy.

China's explosive economic growth in the last forty years has put it in the anomalous position of being both a "developing" or "emerging" country and the second-biggest economy in the world (World Bank 2020). China's development trajectory has been marked by extraordinary milestones: the renminbi was designated by the IMF as a reserve currency in 2016; two Chinese COVID vaccines were accepted by the WHO in June 2021; and, perhaps most significantly, the *Zhurong* rover landed on Mars on May 15, 2021. But the BRI remains the crowning project, not as a massive infrastructure project but as a project of modernity that is meant to signal China's break from its impoverished past. The BRI is Wagnerian in its all-encompassing scale and scope and in the hysterical response it has often generated from Western politicians and pundits, especially from the United States, who depict the BRI as nothing less than an attempt to overturn the world order and hijack geopolitics as we have known it in the last two centuries (Wintour 2021b; O'Connor 2021; Brinza 2021). The fear that China's economic rise poses a geopolitical threat is underpinned by a more insidious, if barely concealed, racial anxiety in the West, mirrored by China's suspicion of Western motivations in its policy responses at the international level (Mishra 2020). Central to the Western narrative of China upending the international hierarchy as much as to Chinese confidence that they can break the Western cordon (which is *not* the same thing as replacing the United States) is the role the state plays in economic growth. Maçães (2018), Mishra (2020), and Weber (2021) have all argued that this is less a role of mere mimicry of the West and more a new model of political economy, thus challenging Western subjectivity.

This chapter takes the hysterical Western response as its starting point, so that from China's perspective, the BRI can be understood by examining the role of the state in the libidinal economy of race in globalization. We argue that the state is the active agent, and BRI the process through which China breaks the repeated trauma of racial humiliation. We define the term "agency" using Brennan (1993, 80–81) as a directed, motivated will with the means for actualizing itself. In making our argument, we are not attempting a Manichaean tactic of simply reversing the good and evil dichotomy of the West and China. The Chinese state has been rightly criticized for its authoritarianism and oppression of its own populations in its policies toward the Uighurs, Hong Kong, and Tibet; but if psychoanalysis teaches us anything, it is that the theoretical dreams of a perfectible world are fantasies when confronted with the ambiguities and heartbreaks of lived experience.

This chapter is not a comprehensive overview of the BRI, nor do we attempt to predict its success. Instead, our challenge is to show how an understanding of the libidinal economy, even if it is partial and not named as such, can guide policy activism. In theoretical terms, we use Brennan's "Foundational Fantasy" to explain how China perceives externally imposed obstacles to its development as repeated trauma and, conceptualizing the Chinese state as an agentic subject, we use Latour's network theory to argue that the BRI can be understood as a network strategy to dismantle the foundational fantasy. We begin with a brief overview of orthodox models of the role of the state in economic development, particularly the developmental state, before moving on to a discussion of psychoanalytic approaches to studying the nation-state. The latter studies have almost entirely focused on a critique of essentialized national identities. We provide an alternative perspective by focusing on the state as the entity that combines both the sovereign territory comprising a country and its government. The second half of the chapter applies the psychoanalytic framework to state subjectivity to make sense of the BRI as a strategy to break the cycle of racial trauma.

Theories of the State's Role in Development

One of the most pressing problems for non-Western countries, most of which were newly decolonized in the 1950s and 1960s, was how to grow their economics. In the wake of Bretton Woods, the prevailing climate of Keynesian-influenced welfare economics in the former colonizing countries and, crucially, in the context of the Cold War, governments of non-Western countries were allowed a share in implementing economic development, but under the guidance of Western countries. These provided experts, financing, and access to some technology, although on highly unequal terms, with the most advanced stages of science and technology reserved for and protected by the West. The dependency on external factors of production and the enduring trade inequalities, carried over from the colonial era, set up a power dynamic that inevitably handicapped attempts at economic growth (see McMichael and Weber 2021, 27–92, for an overview). Concurrently, Marxist-influenced political economists, several from South America, extended Lenin's analysis of imperialism to diagnose underdevelopment in non-Western countries as a function of unequal trade relations between the rich core countries (that exported high-value manufactured goods) and the poor peripheral countries (that depended on low-value primary resource exports). The solution for poor countries was then to decouple economically and replace exports with state-induced domestic production, a process that became known as "import substitution industrialization" (see Sheppard et al. 2009; Simon 2006).[2]

But it was not until the rise of the Japanese economy in the 1960s–1970s that a non-Western country appeared to have found the formula for rapid economic development (Johnson 1982). For a while, Japan appeared to be an anomaly, until the economic success of South Korea, Taiwan, and Singapore in the 1980s and 1990s (Amsden 1989; Castells 1992; Studwell 2013; Golub 2016; Chua 2017). The Commission on Growth and Development (2008, 19) noted that nine of the thirteen countries that achieved sustained high growth of 7 percent over twenty-five years were located in East Asia. But the basis of that growth was a source of contention. The World Bank (1993), referring to the phenomenon as "the East Asian miracle," attributed success to giving free reign to the market. In contrast, many scholars (Johnson 1982; Amsden 1989; Castells 1992; Studwell 2013; Golub 2016; Chua 2017) saw the state as central to the successful industrial policies of what became known as "the developmental state." This was controversial because there appeared little consensus on what defines the developmental state (Beeson 2004). Even those who give it credence argue that its policy prescriptions were too historically specific (Lin 2012; Beeson 2011; Wade 2017; Takagi, Kanchoochat, and Sonobe 2019).

China, of course, has produced its homegrown models of economic development, most notably Mao Zedong's Marxist model and Deng Xiaoping's pragmatic mixed economy—the starting point of China's successful growth trajectory (Schell and Delury 2013, 197–323). But China's spectacular growth and geographic scale prompts a discussion of whether it fits the developmental state model. For the purposes of this study, the real significance is whether the state has a role to play, and if so, what the basis of its policy activism is. Yet the discourse of the developmental state has always been fraught with undertones of cultural essentialism, at the very least, if not outright racism, because of its association with the concept of "Asian values"—the subject of much debate in Western circles in determining the roots of Asian economic success (Sioh 2010, 2018a, 2018b). Moisi (2011) has highlighted the absence of analysis of emotion in highly charged contemporary geopolitical issues, while Zvogbo and Loken (2020) take international relations scholars to task for ignoring questions of race. Taking a psychoanalytic perspective, Kapoor (2014) notes that a prominent "blind spot" in development discourse is ignoring the significance of colonialism, thus denying the complicity of the West in development failures. Kapoor (2020) then turns the perspective around by also asking what psychoanalytic elements "drive" development. Yet, although the development has spawned an industry of consultants in the public, private, and nonprofit sectors, from the perspective of developing countries, it is still largely within the purview of the nation-state.

Psychoanalytic scholarship on nation-states tends to focus on the *nation* half of the equation because of the interest in essentialized identities and their impact on political dysfunction (Chowdhry and Rai 2009; Garner 2017; Mercer 2017; Gniazdowski 2018; Salaam Abdel-Malek 2019). In studies of immigration, ethnic conflict, citizenship, and genocidal wars, the focus is on the essentializing mission of the political subject. In returning the focus to the *state* as the site of policy activism, the developmental state model recovers the state as a site of political agency, even if its proponents acknowledge the nation as the site of affects that energize state actions. Gallagher's (2018) is a rare attempt to theorize the state, rather than only the nation, psychoanalytically. The focus on the state is valuable because it is not essentialized even if it *could* function as a vehicle to realize the agency of the nation. While Gallagher argues that newly independent Ghana's attempts at statecraft were simply in the service of the evolution of a national identity, she sees "state-subjectivity as analogous to self-consciousness" (883). In Freudian terms, the state stands in for the ego to the nation's id. But if the state can embody both the identity and aspirations of its (most powerful) citizens, then its policies are a manifestation of the state-subject's agency. Fridell (2014, 1180) points out that conventional development discourse, in privileging the fantasies of market agency, ignores the power of statecraft in delivering higher standards of living. Thus, focusing on the state rather than the nation is politically hopeful because policy activism, by definition, is agentic, with "sovereignty" as the code for psychoanalytic agentic subjectivity. So, building on Gallagher's psychoanalytic understanding of the state, we argue that the concept of a developmental state is valid for China. We would also argue that the East Asian developmental states all recognize that the state acts as an agent whose policy activism is driven by a libidinal economy. Unlike Western governments that enact protectionist policies under the fantasy of protecting the free market, East Asian developmental states *openly* admit the identity anxieties that drive their policy activism and draw attention to the power dynamic inherent in the racialized discourse invoked to justify global governance policies and discourse.

Building on this, it is necessary to explore how the state, as the embodiment of its class antagonism (see chapter 1), "experiences" trauma in the gendered terms of the foundational fantasy. If a political subject experiences trauma because of its perceived cultural identity, the practices to impose the trauma are realized through the interstate system. Sioh (2018b), using a framework derived from Christopher Bollas (2011, 81–87), argues that hypercompetition in globalization creates shame that must be projected elsewhere so that the psychopathic subject dehumanizes their victims in the name of a militant ideology, in this case, the free market. Simultaneously, the proponents of the free market assert their higher purpose to create a prosperous world because of their intellectual superiority. For Bollas (168–71), a militant ideology involves seduction, the promise of a false safe space, and the development of dependency. Yet under the intense emotional pressures of envy or anxiety, the psychopathic subject will project their negative traits externally to coalesce into stereotypes that belittle and caricature their victims (88–89). Herman (2015, 80) argues that a key symptom of trauma is isolation, because of the inability to trust and form relationships with others, thus compounding the trauma further. In what follows, we graft the above trauma framework onto Teresa Brennan's foundational fantasy to show how geopolitical trauma plays out in constraints to development. We then move on to show how the BRI functions as an active response to trauma through the construction of a libidinal ecosystem of allies linked by their anxieties to circumvent the economic and political constraints imposed upon China by the United States and its allies. But we also see that while China pushes back against Western constraints, the effects of trauma may translate into a lack of trust that cascades into the relationships with BRI member countries.

Brennan (1993, 11–22) argues that we live in an age of social psychosis, characterized by an insatiable anxiety, of which key symptoms are aggression and the inability to tolerate difference. This is the era of the dominant ego, which she associates with the active masculine subject. This subject relies on scientific rationality, in turn manifested through use of technology to control the subject's environment. Brennan argues that the

"Ego's era" is composed of active, self-contained, and invulnerable subjects who arrive at their identity through the psychical fantasy of controlling the passive object as a fixed reference point. For Brennan, the object is symbolized by the psychical fantasy of "Woman," which she terms the "Foundational Fantasy." Points in the psyche are paralleled and reinforced by constructions in the social world (xii). Brennan's (52–53) central thesis is that an objectifying projection is a condition of subjectivity because it is only through creating the fantasy of a fixed inferior that the subject can overcome the anxiety of its own unstable identity. For our purposes, the Other could be the racial other, nature, or any fixed category of identity not necessarily "feminine." While Brennan (79–81) keeps her thesis abstract, she also notes that the dynamics for the foundational fantasy is located in political economy. When history intersects with the psyche, the foundational fantasy manifests itself in a territorialization imperative on the part of the active subject, while spatial constraint is the fate of the pacified object (5–11). In Freudian terms, castration manifests itself as spatial constraint, the fate of colonized and imperial subjects. Masculinity and femininity are terms in which the war of the foundational fantasy is played out (Brennan 1993, 113). Brennan (12) suggest that objectification requires knowledge, which is why science and technology are so important in ego's era.

Extending Brennan's thesis to analyzing the BRI, we argue that in the current global conjuncture, the West, especially the United States, conceives itself as the superior active geopolitical and economic subject of modernity, contingent quite literally through spatially constraining China. The process of putting China in its place is reinforced by the narrative that invokes racial stereotypes to criticize the BRI. However, Brennan (1993, 18–19) places the state in a contradictory position of facilitating the spatial constraints on its pacified objects while also reigning in the foundational fantasy depending on the state's relationship to capital. The state invariably serves as both subject and object. In the case of China, the state takes on the powerful role of dismantling the externally imposed foundational fantasy, using capital to further the aims of the state as the active subject on behalf of its people. Since Brennan (44–46, 111) reminds us that imperialism generates scarcity as byproduct, while concomitantly guaranteeing the dependence of its victims on those oppressing them, both activities generate further anxiety and aggression so that even active subjects fear retaliation from their pacified objects. Putting Brennan in conversation with Bollas, we can see how capitalism creates a dependent relationship between states in globalization, while the fixing of subject-object relationships takes place through the division of labor in the global value chain (see chapter 2).

We use Latour's (1987) network theory to argue that the BRI began as a defensive strategy to break the cordon of the foundational fantasy imposed on China by the West. While the foundational fantasy is an attempt to impose a fixed identity on a group, network theory allows for the group to break the material and, in turn, psychological cordon off the pacified identity of nation through the agency of the state. Latour (93) defines "reality" as the temporary hegemony of a material claim. And to wit, the current tense standoff between China and the United States and its allies can be interpreted as a divergence between China's perspective that hegemony is temporary, and the United States' perspective that hegemony is its prerogative. The BRI is thus China's attempt to overturn the current US hegemony. China may not expect to replace the American hegemon, let alone believe that any replacement would be permanent, but it seems indisputable to us that it seeks to subvert the hegemony of the United States.

Using science as the example of how power is attained, Latour's (1987, 124) network theory explains how scientific information becomes an indisputable fact in two stages: the acquisition of allies and the control of the narrative. This is not to say that Latour (25) is a relativist who dismisses material reality. Rather, he argues that certain statements and practices become accepted as standards only if they become embedded within a *network* of statements and practices. The difference is that while Brennan (1993, 12) sees science and technology only as tools for fixing in place the object position, Latour (1987, 221) sees technology as significant in creating a counternetwork by counting the inanimate tools of science and technology as well as scientific facts (e.g., the speed of a Wi-Fi connection) as allies themselves, not just as the tools of allies. The one who controls the network will thus crucially be the one who accumulates the most allies. The recruitment process of allies that will link strongholds or nodal points to create a network involves multiple small translations to create commensurabilities among allies so that they see themselves as having common goals and, following the methodology of the network controller, will deliver greater success in achieving individual goals (108–11, 180).

This has indeed been the case with the BRI, where China has persuaded its allies that buy-in will deliver their national goals. The end goal of controlling the practices and narrative is to become a passage point. Latour (1987, 41) cautions us that "fact" construction is a collective process, so that isolated persons or groups only "build dreams or make claims, not facts." But he also argues that starting and controlling a counternetwork is very different from simply being enrolled in one, however successful that participant may be (167). Thus, he reminds us, like Sassen (2008, 227) and Brennan (1993, 61), that economic wealth alone is an insufficient condition of transforming from the object to subject position. The truly revolutionary change that BRI seeks to bring about is that, unlike Japan and South Korea, China seeks not to be a wealthy junior ally of the United States but to create a *state with real agentic possibilities* in the international system. But we extend Latour's thesis to argue that it is the very powerful drive of anxiety that links China to the majority of its allies in the BRI to create a libidinal ecosystem. In this sense, China is attempting to create an alliance that is connected organically through emotion (anxiety)—in this case, the past and continuing experience of humiliation.

The Western Foundational Fantasy of China

China signed the Treaty of Nanjing with Britain in 1842, in which it ceded Hong Kong to the British, while opening five ports to Western traders, where trade would be taxed at very low tariffs. It was also forced to pay an "indemnity" to Britain as compensation for the loss of British lives during the Opium War (Schell and Delury 2013, 11–32). This was the beginning of the "Century of Humiliation" for China, which would officially end only with the return of Hong Kong in 1997. But China's path to ending the Century of Humiliation began long before its current economic trajectory, when, on September 21, 1949, Mao stood before the Chinese People's Consultative Congress and declared, "Ours will no longer be a nation subject to insult and humiliation" (quoted in Schell and Delury 2013, 229). On October 1, 1949, Mao (1949) would declare the founding of the People's Republic of China in Tiananmen and claim that the "government is willing to establish diplomatic relations with any foreign government that is willing to observe the principles of equality, mutual benefit, and mutual respect of territorial integrity and sovereignty." But if China could protect its sovereignty internally, it would still be relatively constrained within its borders, despite its allies fighting the Korean

War to a stalemate and being victorious against the United States in the Vietnam War.

The emphasis on linking humiliation in military and geopolitical matters to a lack of economic growth seems the consensus regardless of whether we are talking about an orthodox Marxist, such as Mao, who chose autarky, or the less orthodox Deng, who set China on the path to capitalist success in 1978 by enrolling in Western-controlled GVCs to become the "world['s] factory" (Zhang 2006). But to enroll in an economic network is still to be constrained by the terms set by others (Latour 1987, 167), in other words, abiding by a benign form of gunboat diplomacy.[3] The BRI can be seen as the latest, but perhaps most ambitious, attempt to finally end the gunboat diplomacy of Western imperialism, including its contemporary incarnation in the form of economic pressure (Sioh 2010). Until the COVID crisis in 2020, China had averaged a growth rate of almost 10 percent a year, lifting over eight hundred million people out of poverty (World Bank 2021). To do so, it adopted a variant of the developmental state model (Studwell 2013). But the pressing issue now is how to escape the middle-income trap, a condition in which countries escape poverty but fail to transition to fully "developed," high-wage economies (Kharas and Kohli 2011; Lewin, Kenney and Murmann 2016). And even if they do, another hurdle awaits them, whereby high income does not necessarily translate into political power or symbolic status (Brennan 1993, 61; Sassen 2008, 227).

The reason for this is that countries entering the global economy belatedly, and relying on secondhand technology to industrialize, have had to contend with three handicaps. First, economic growth and, ultimately, survival is dependent on continued access to technology controlled by others. Second, such dependency implies, in turn, the humiliation of knowing that others have power over one's fate. And, third, as a result of the other two, one is stereotyped as intellectually inferior for not being able to develop the technology oneself. All three handicaps are materially manifested in the politics of intellectual property rights (see chapter 5). Now recall that for Bollas (2011, 168–71) trauma is experienced as a function of powerlessness, dependence, and belittlement. These practices are played out geographically through the new international division of labor. Subsidiaries, after all, are dependent on the controlling brand, and decisions are made at the headquarters located in Western countries and Japan (Suwandi 2019). And while Japan, and later South Korea, Taiwan, and Singapore, would achieve incomes that qualified for "developed" country status, their dependence on the United States militarily has meant that their roles and places in the geopolitical hierarchy have always been set by others. Japan, for example, has far less global institutional power than Britain and France, which have smaller GDPs. Brennan's foundational fantasy (1993, 113), in which trauma is born of constraint, powerlessness, and humiliation, maps onto race geopolitically here.

Notwithstanding China's phenomenal growth, it has also been subject to the various forms of trauma and consequent anxieties of late-catchup countries. China may function as the world's factory, but its manufacturing is also often pejoratively labeled "poorly made in China."[4] Its state-owned enterprises have become synonymous with "crony capitalism" in the West, so much so that a recent Google search of the term brought up 2,280,000 references.[5] The BRI is part of the larger project to escape the constraints of the middle-income trap, but as Brennan (1993, 75) noted, success in imposing spatial constriction rebounds on the active subject who fears retaliation. The United States, as active subject, fears retaliation from those it has pacified historically. Thus, China's BRI is perceived as retaliation, an endeavor to displace the United States as the preeminent superpower. The consequent attempt at castrating China comes in two forms: ring-fencing China physically in the form of military exercises, and seeking to deny China access to technology and markets. The United States and its allies have reinforced their existing alliance with new agreements such as the Blue Dot Network, the Trilateral Infrastructure Partnership, and, more recently, Build Back Better World, a US-led G-7 infrastructure initiative as an alternative to the BRI (Brinza 2021; O'Connor 2021).[6] Most significantly, denial of access to technology highlights how China's growth has depended on borrowed technology, especially from the United States, which is slated to dry up in the wake of the Strategic Competition Act of 2021.[7] European countries now view China as a "systemic rival" and have clamped down on Chinese acquisitions of strategic European companies (Karnitschnig 2020). As pointed out in chapter 5, the Chinese high-tech company Huawei no longer has access to US technology or markets, nor can Chinese companies buy US-made high-performance chips (Morozov 2020). Unsurprisingly, China has had to create alternative routes for growth. As Brennan (1993, 12) understands, technology is the core to objectification through control. Indeed, as we have previously suggested, the current trade war between the United States and China is more accurately a tech war.

When applied to the BRI, the second prong of the foundational fantasy, which calls for the projection of the superior subject's negativity onto the pacified object (Brennan 1993, 57), is evident in the demonizing of China. The United States' Strategic Competition Act of 2021 uses pejorative vocabulary in which to "expose the PRC's use of corruption, repression, coercion, and other malign behavior to attain unfair economic advantage and deference of other nations to its political and strategic objectives" (Hsu 2021). The document goes on to accuse China of (a) "promoting its governance model," thereby "undermining democratic institutions"; (b) "subverting financial institutions"; and (c) "coercing businesses to accommodate the policies of the PRC." The act also accuses China of deliberate disinformation to disguise the nature of its actions (see Hsu 2021 for summary). Elsewhere, as noted above, the BRI has been described as "debt trap diplomacy," that is, as an expensive public relations exercise with no substance to its projects (Brinza 2021).

Network Theory and the Libidinal Ecosystem of the BRI

China's economic success from its opening to the global economy in 1978 rested on enrolling and specializing in stages of the GVC. To do so, it hosted Western and Japanese subsidiaries that relocated their lower-value manufacturing to take advantage of China's vast pool of cheap labor (Zhang 2006). By the early 2000s, Chinese policymakers had already recognized that a growth model relying on producing low-value goods with secondhand technology would consign the country to the dreaded middle-income trap. Moreover, the flow of technology from the West started to peter out, and markets began to close off to Chinese high-tech exports as Western countries increasingly recognized the former's aspirations to be an equal, rather than a junior, ally. China's finance minister publicly estimated that China had a 50 percent chance of succumbing to the middle-income trap (Maçães 2018, 76). To escape, it would have to update the developmental state for the digital age. In 2015, it announced "Made in China 2025 (MIC2025)" as the strategic response to the dilemma of the middle-income trap (State Council of the People's Republic of China, 2021). The BRI, while predating MIC2025, is thus an industrial policy for an updated version of the developmental state. China recognizes that survival in globalization requires policies that embed the global economy, not just the domestic economy, in the state. MIC2025 is meant to guide future industrial policy aimed at upgrading China's manufacturing sector and putting it on the path to high-income status. To do so, the Chinese government plans to direct investment into smart cities, greener production, social security, and, crucially, high-tech innovation, which will drive economic growth to pay for the other policy prescriptions (McBride and Chatzky 2019; Yang 2020). In cutting across different sector needs—projects cover education, agriculture, health, transportation, telecommunications, energy, and finance—the BRI, as the practical realization of a transnational industrial policy (TNP) to fulfill MIC2025's goals—can achieve a comprehensive approach to development for its allied countries—in contrast to the piecemeal approach generally taken by Western agencies. It has the potential to enable domestic industrial policy in partner countries by tapping into the TNP of the BRI: in Latour's (1987, 25) terms, the BRI embeds local networks of development within the global network of the BRI's TNP. And given the austerity programs attached as conditionalities to obtaining funding from Western institutions, the BRI speaks to an audience that implicitly understands the humiliations, as well as the economic and social failings, inherent in the current Western-led development agenda. This reinforces a network of allies that is key to withstanding the anxieties of powerlessness, which itself is symptomatic of a traumatized psyche (Herman 2015, 80).

As noted earlier, the BRI extends over four continents through memorandums of understanding signed between China and partner countries, although the actual number of countries and projects has been contested.[8] Even so, a very partial list of projects conveys the scale and scope of the BRI. These include the Agadem Oil integrated project and the Niamey referral hospital in Niger; the Mirador copper mine and the Minas San Francisco hydro power station in Ecuador; the Hulhamae housing project in the Maldives; a port, an airport, a fiber-optic cable production, and Pakistan-China Friendship Hospital in Gwadar, Pakistan; and the Milanovic-Stip Expressway and the Kicevo-Ohrid Expressway in Macedonia. As well, state-owned companies have taken on steel plants in Thailand, Indonesia, the Philippines, and Serbia; transportation corridors connecting the Balkans to Hungary; and the COSCO installation at the Port of Piraeus in Greece (China State Information Center, n.d.; Yang and Zhang 2016; Maçães 2018, 83; Ivanić and Savović 2020).[9] One of the more ambitious projects is the Bangkok-Nakhon Ratchasima high-speed railway, which will link Thailand to Laos, and eventually extending from China to Singapore (Oxford Business Group 2018).

It should be noted that China does not simply engage in hard infrastructure projects that directly contribute to Chinese development; it also sweetens the agreements with its partners by investing in projects that benefit local communities such as hospitals and schools. This accords with Latour's point (1987, 132, 110, 180) that recruiting allies is a consequence of not only finding commensurabilities between the allies' aims but also allowing for a margin of negotiation that permits shifting goals. In the case of Pakistan, China has encouraged oversight by a relatively autonomous regulatory body, thus allowing customization of the BRI projects by local companies (Maçães 2018, 101–2). This reinforces the alliance with efforts that are not restricted to a specific project. Perhaps another instance of Western development's "blind spot" here is to ignore the fact that by tapping into the anxieties of economic survival in their allies, the BRI is creating a libidinal ecosystem from a network of alliances linked by anxiety-driven goals underpinned by the common trauma of Western imperialism. This is a not insignificant emotional current that links BRI allies.

If the accumulation of allies determines the winning network (Latour 1987, 220), then counting the inanimate tools of technology in the 1.38 billion smartphones that were sold worldwide in 2020, the majority made by Huawei (O'Dea 2021; Sin 2020), indicates a significant step in the creation of a winning network. This is before accounting for other digital devices such as tablets, and in a world that is projected to run on the "Internet of Things," the owners of the standard essential pattern technologies stand to reap exorbitant gains. Fifth-generation technology (5G), in which China-based Huawei is a leader,[10] sets the technical standard for standard essential patterns and currently accounts for $13.1 trillion dollars in revenue (Qualcomm, n.d.). The RPX Corporation, which provides risk management for patents, estimates that there are 250,000 patents involved in producing and using a cellphone (Patent Progress, n.d.). Although contested because of the different forms of value assessment, China's Huawei is thus currently the biggest owner of 5G-patented technologies (GreyB 2022); others argue that those patents are in less essential technologies (Townsend 2019). We aim here not to settle the controversy but to point out that for a global South country to even feature in such a controversy signals the country's claim to be a major economic and, ultimately, intellectual equal to the West.

While this fits in with the broader economic aims of MIC2025, denigrating Chinese products as synecdoches of Chinese inferiority has been refuted by the seriousness with which the West now takes technological competition with China. The latter is already a leading researcher and home of patents in a number of technologies, such as wind and solar power, online payment systems, digital currencies, facial recognition, quantum computing, satellites and space exploration, 5G telecoms, drones, ultra-high-voltage power transmission (Kynge and Sandbu 2021; Council on Foreign Relations 2022). The BRI could not exist without technology; moreover, it also allows for the practical experimentation of large-scale sophisticated technological projects in the real world. This is a significant dimension of how the BRI will dismantle the stereotype of a pacified inferior China in the Western foundational fantasy.

If each project represents a node or diffusion point in the network (Latour 1987, 136), then the railways, shipping lines, and circulation of credit and technology form the actual links in the BRI. Technology is probably the most crucial link, so much so that the BRI is sometimes referred to as the Digital Silk Road (*Economist* 2020). Each technological device or standard adopted translates into another ally in the race to accumulate allies. As Brennan (1993, 12) argues, technology is important in successful objectification because knowledge underpins the ability to control and pacify the inferior object. By the same token, technology is also key to overturning the foundational fantasy by creating alternative networks, and the emphasis here is on the network in the sense of communication. An example of how technology is used to control the pacified object came to light in Edward Snowden's leaks, where it was revealed that the NSA listened in on China and other NSA targets in Operation Shotgiant by breaking into Huawei's servers (Morozov 2020). Unsurprisingly, China now prioritizes developing more secure communications. The Pakistan East Africa Cable Express, a marine link, will connect Gwadar and Karachi in Pakistan to Djibouti, with eventual projected extensions to Egypt and South Africa and the final goal of being routed to France through the Mediterranean (Peace Cable 2018). For China and its non-Western allies, this is an opportunity to finally create a communications network beyond the control of the West. Contemporary sovereignty is technological sovereignty (Morozov 2018).

Credit is the other key link in all the projects across space. Financing is one of the most controversial aspects of the BRI. As we noted in our chapter introduction, Western and regional critics of the BRI have decried the lines of credit as debt-trap diplomacy. Economic and development aid, particularly between highly unequal partners, as Kapoor (2008, 60–75) has noted in his critique of Western aid, can never be a true "gift." Instead, it invariably involves a degree of "grift," with interest-bearing loans providing leverage for the giver to demand or expect official and unofficial conditions that meet their foreign policy objectives. Thus, China has provided much-coveted economic assistance and investment to Caribbean states in difficult economic straits (see chapter 2), but with its goals always in mind, including convincing recipients to support the "One China" policy and break ties with Taiwan (Fridell 2015). Similar patterns are emerging with BRI, in particular with highly uneven relations with smaller states. For instance, political conflict has emerged in the Maldives over growing debt to China, representing 22 to 63 percent of the nation's entire GDP, and in 2017 Sri Lanka had to sell its controlling share of the newly constructed port of Hambantota to a Chinese firm when it was unable to service its debt to China (Abi-Habib 2018; Ethirajan 2020; Davidson 2021). Whether the leverage that China accrues in these instances will be used for specific political goals in the future remains to be seen, but either way China has been clear that BRI funding brings with it a trade and investment regime in which China sets the rules and standards. At the same time, subordinate governments are well aware that with loans and debt comes influence, deference, and a degree of compulsory compliance, regardless of the source. Chinese assistance tends not to be accompanied with the direct conditionalities associated with Western aid, and often supports projects that Western-dominated donors will not. For this reason, Chinese economic assistance is often welcomed by partners, who see its conditions as better than those involved in traditional Western "debt-traps" (Brautigam and Rithmire 2021).

A related criticism of the BRI is that financing from state-owned banks constitutes an unfair advantage for Chinese companies when in competition with Western companies.[11] BRI project funding mainly comes from the China Development Bank and the China Export-Import Bank, as well as new capital from the Silk Road Fund, the Asian Infrastructure and Investment Bank, and the New Development Bank (Lubin et al. 2018). When more countries adopt BRI standards for financing, these will gain greater purchase as non-Chinese businesses that seek to partner with BRI partners conform to the same standards. BRI project funding is notably denominated in US dollars (Lubin et al. 2018), which has two disadvantages: it benefits the US economy by creating a demand for dollars; and it constrains project operations through dependence on the availability of dollars, whose supply is controlled by the United States. Although the renminbi is a reserve currency,[12] currently the yuan, the actual Chinese currency used in finance and international trade, accounts for only 2.4 percent, versus 38 percent of dollar-denominated receipts (Barton 2021).

Despite this, the BRI, with its access to 139 countries and counting, sets the stage for the renminbi to become a truly global currency that may break the stranglehold of the US dollar. Moreover, China's gamble on digital financing means that the two networks, technology and finance, are projected to reinforce each other symbiotically.

So the stakes for controlling technology extend beyond the calculus of profits from direct sales in the current market. Instead, whoever controls the patents gets to set the standard for future technologies. This process sets up stable revenue streams, as there is no way of entering the market without compatibility with existing technologies. Instead, the BRI aims to create new standards and get them adopted by the majority through BRI projects (Maçães 2018, 89; Morozov 2020). In this manner, it delivers on dismantling the foundational fantasy because in hosting BRI projects, the host countries adopt Chinese standards for railways, construction, data management, communications, and financial transactions.[13] Each standard is embedded within a network of standards that will eventually set the stage for an alternative political economy. One way of thinking about how statements and practices become accepted as standards is to track how they become embedded within a network of existing statements and practices. The end goal of controlling the practices and narrative is to become a passage point; as Latour (1987, 41) cautions us, as long as the subject stays isolated, it builds only dreams, not facts. And in the case of China, this means never being in control of its own destiny, invoking Brennan's (1993, 61) and Sassen's (2008, 227) point that simply becoming wealthy does not turn a country into a rule maker. Instead, the BRI has begun to transform China into a rule maker through Chinese leadership on standards in the International Electrical Commission, the International Electrotechnical Commission, the International Telecommunications Union, and the International Organization for Standardization, and the launching of China Standards 2035 (Morozov 2020). It is this scenario, and the end of unilateral Western (especially US) control of the world *system*, not just economy, that has triggered the generally widespread current hysterical response of the West.

Conclusion

If the BRI succeeds as the launching pad for a whole new set of technical and financial standards, China will become a meaningfully active subject in a way that other economically successful East Asian countries have not. It will become a rule maker, not a rule taker. To be sure, we have argued in this chapter that the BRI, on the part of China as well as its opponents, is a project that can best be understood through the lens of GLE as driven by the libidinal economy rather than simply an economic project. The BRI is the spearhead for China to seek out its more ambitious goal of dismantling the foundational fantasy of a subservient, pacified, inferior object to the active Western subject that sets the terms of reference for China's existence. In the BRI, China aims to create a libidinal ecosystem as a defense against being isolated and constrained in fulfilling its ambitions for successful capitalist growth. In this particular sense, the BRI sets out to construct a somewhat different modernity than Western modernity, which has held up relatively unchanged for the last 250 years. In psychoanalyzing the BRI to understand China's anxieties, we are not claiming that the BRI will create a development utopia for its participants or allow them to rethink the global capitalist model; the BRI is clearly founded on accepting and reproducing capitalism, with all the problems of inequality and exploitation associated with it (see chapter 5). Nor do we dispute that the BRI may simply set up a different foundational fantasy between China and its BRI partners (see chapter 5). But what is remarkable from the point of view of a GLE approach is how China's end goal and terms of reference for success are anxiety-driven. Here, the Chinese state is outwardly performing the role of a "collective ego" and challenging the fantasies of its Western critics, who take entitlement so much for granted that any challenger to Western predominance needs to be punished. Even claims of security concerns seem to ignore that digital sovereignty is not the prerogative of the United States only, or, to a lesser extent, other Western countries. Moreover, if we can accept the premise that non-Western countries are entitled to seek realistic agency in Brennan's sense of the term—as directed, motivated will with a means for actualizing them—then the Chinese state is attempting to actualize that agency through policy activism manifested in the BRI.

Conclusion

We have centered this book on the libidinal by relying on key IPE categories—production, consumption, informal economy, trade, financialization,
ecology, the state—for two main reasons. First, to bring out their constitutive libidinal ingredients, overlooked by mainstream IPE with significant
consequence. Our claim is that global capitalism cannot escape the stain
of the unconscious, with the result that there are no pure economic activities. The administration of the libidinal—from anxiety, desire, and drive/
jouissance to racial and gender domination and sadomasochism—is thus
integral to production, consumption, informality, trade, and so forth, with
several important implications.

One implication is that, in contrast to the subject of rational calculation upheld by mainstream IPE, which sees reason triumph over blind
irrational instincts, GLE stresses the subject of unconscious desire, which
sees desire obeying its own grammar. Here, the subject is divided, unable
to master its own house, overwhelmed as it is by the libidinal, which subscribes to a logic of anxiety, excess, and instability rather than calculation
and predictability. Indeed, so caught up in the movement of the Freudian
"death drive" can the subject get that it is often willing to do anything,
sacrifice everything, so long as it can enjoy—as evidenced, for example,
by the massive waste generated by the delights of (over)consumption, or
the libidinal kick derived from following the routines of GVC production
or speculative investment (see chapters 2, 4, 6, and 7).

A related implication is that it is the power of the libidinal that
helps explain not just the exuberant irrationality but also the seductions of
capitalism—once again something that mainstream IPE critically underestimates. By exploiting desire, by inciting enjoyment, capitalism is able
to "grip" the subject, ensuring, for example, commodity fetishism or a

ritualistic devotion to Capital. It is such libidinal "stuckness" that helps explain both the intensity and extensity of contemporary global capital-ism—why it is able to reach everywhere, mesmerize everyone, and con-tinuously reproduce itself, even (and perhaps especially) in the face of obstacle or crisis. The subjective grammar of libidinal economy supports, and is supported by, the structural grammar of capitalist political econ-omy, each cofacilitating the ongoing circuit of capital.

Indeed, the seductive powers of capitalism are the very reason why knowledge and rational calculation cannot be counted on today. If the subject never learns because it prefers enjoying, if it is aware of, say, the environmental dangers of overconsumption or carbon-based production but still pleasurably engages in them, then the libidinal has beguiled and hoodwinked the rational. This is what we have previously referred to as "fetishistic disavowal," as a consequence of which the subject is con-scious of the risks and dangers of its actions in the economic sphere but remains so enchanted by them that it chooses the path of recklessness and self-sabotage.

The dirty underside of such recklessness is the systematic violence of global capitalism. The drive-ridden circuit of capital ends up pursuing its goal of both libidinal and material profits, callously impervious to how this affects the social and the ecological. The information age may well enable market subjects to be aware of the ills of inequality or sweatshop labor, but still they engage in destructive, yet libidinally charged, activi-ties—the *jouissance* of consumption, production, and speculative invest-ment that depend on gendered and racialized forms of labor exploitation and enslavement, as well as environmental degradation (see chapters 2, 3, 5, 6, and 7); the dispossession and displacement of the part of no-part in favor of "development" and gentrification (see chapters 4, 5, 6, and 7); or the sadomasochistic, racially inflected humiliation of the global South (see chapters 1, 5, 6, and 8). The systemic violence of late capitalism, in this sense, emerges not from corrupt or evil market subjects but from the unrelenting circuit of drive whose libidinal enjoyment knows no bound-aries and serves only itself.

What enable and support such systemic violence are social power relations, which in the present global conjuncture appear to be increas-ingly neofeudal, with the financial-techno-corporate sectors at the top of the social hierarchy, and poor, gendered, and racialized groups at the bottom (see chapter 6). It is upon such unequal social power relations, after all, that capitalism is founded: the extraction of material and libidinal surplus would be impossible without the domination and exploitation of labor (and nature). Implied here is the notion of social antagonism—the political struggle that undergirds capitalist economy/society. It is what Žižek, as previously noted (see chapter 1), calls "class struggle," and is to be understood as the Real, the traumatic limit that structures and helps reproduce (capitalist) society. Such class antagonism, in fact, is what makes GLE (and IPE for that matter) *political*, underlining the political struggle that inevitably cuts across the economic. Class antagonism signals the division, difference, and hierarchy at the heart of the capitalist economy (i.e., *homo economicus*), which is what prevents any attempt at instituting a stable or harmonious organization of production, consumption, informality, trade, financialization, or ecology.

The second (closely related) reason we have focused on key IPE categories is to emphasize the dialectical materialist basis of GLE. Our point is that while material reality comes first, it is always already fissured. In fact, it is because of the rupture in our material world that signification emerges (the realm of the symbolic order, culture, consciousness), so that the very notion of materiality is able to come to light. Without such a cut in reality, reality itself would be meaningless. The subject, accordingly, is to be viewed as the bona fide embodiment of materiality's antagonism: it is the site for thinking (i.e., investigating, detecting, representing) antagonism. Yet like materiality itself, said subject is also divided and unstable—it is an anchorage point for the excess of the libidinal that permanently disrupts the rational, logical, or stable. Signification, in this sense, is forever accompanied by a surplus, an extra that disjoints and derails even the best-made plans.

And so that is why we have arranged our chapters according to key IPE categories—to underline the significant economic dimensions of our contemporary global reality, while at the same time foregrounding the libidinal ruptures immanent to all of them. In contrast to mainstream IPE—whether (neo)classical or Marxist—which tends to view the economy as a "positive" or historically "real" order, with culture serving as a secondary or illusory realm, GLE seeks not to reverse the dialectic by positivizing culture (as postmodern identity politics tends to do) but instead to reconceive of the dialectic of materiality itself by desubstantializing the economy: the economy is thereby non-all—contingent, incoherent, unstable—forever traumatized by the Real/unconscious. Or to put it another way, the economy as a whole "does not exist"; it is forever traversed by lack, division, and unpredictability. This is why chapter 4 insisted on the impossibility that lies at heart of the capitalist economy, with informality as the evidence—however contingent—of the former's incompleteness and inconsistency. This is also why chapters 2, 3, 5, 6, and 8 emphasized the *extra*-economic technologies that capitalist economies critically depend upon to ensure their operations—the mythologies/fantasies required to drive consumption and production (e.g., commodity fetishism, fictitious capital, technological sovereignty), or the gendered and racialized domination needed to ensure labor exploitation, surplus extraction, and the economic supremacy of the global North. Thus, the global capitalist economy is impossible (i.e., non-all), and its vital need to deploy the extra-economic is the living proof.

Transformative Politics

Politics is to be seen here as a reply to the antagonism of the social: faced with the rupture at the heart of the economy (e.g., social difference, hierarchy, alienation, exploitation, domination), the political subject is moved to intervene, either by facing it, or, as is often the case, by trying to disavow and cover it up. Often downplayed in IPE, as chapters 2, 3, 5, 6, and 7 underlined, is the intense devotion to, and tireless energy spent on, reproducing capitalism rather than changing it. Yet what should not thereby be lost is that, despite the market's significant libidinal grip on the subject, despite the general tendency around the world toward political acquiescence to capitalism, antagonism always trips up the system, preventing it from totalization while at the same time opening up possible avenues for change. This is the return of the Real/unconscious that chapter 4 accentuated: the resurrection of stilt houses that, in spite of the power of Recife's elite-driven project of urban gentrification, interrupted it.

What, then, does GLE offer as a transformational politics, one that tarries with the Real? We have outlined several possibilities across the pages of this book, although we make no claim to have been exhaustive. For a start, there is the important task of ideology critique. To the extent that the system attempts to patch up fundamental social antagonisms (e.g., the denial of the rapaciousness of the market, the North's avoidance of complicity in global South "underdevelopment") through the construction of ideological fantasies (e.g., "free trade," the rationalism of the market, "the West is best," "technology/nature can save us"), then the role of ideology critique is to demystify such fantasies. This is indeed what all the chapters in this book have tried to do. Accordingly, our task has been not simply to identify the gaps, blind spots, exclusions, and contradictions of market ideologies; rather, the key psychoanalytic point, as Žižek (1989, 125) insists upon, has also been to unearth the libidinal investment of such fantasies, that is, their kernels of unconscious desire and enjoyment. If anything, psychoanalysis reminds us that speaking truth to power, deconstructing discourses, is never enough: this is because of the just-mentioned problem of fetishistic disavowal, as a result of which subjects are critically aware of a problem yet are so libidinally embroiled in it that they act as if they don't know. Ideology critique, like the one we have been engaging in, requires this additional step of psychoanalytic demystification to take into account the libidinal economy.

Given that the fantasies of capitalism—from commodity fetishism to "freedom of opportunity"—activate and orientate our desires, then another possible transformatory politics is to reorient our desires by constructing alternative politico-economic fantasies—postcapitalism, social and environmental justice, global regulation of transnational corporations, and so forth. The challenge, though, is for such alternate (Left) fantasies to be seductive—to somehow replace the late capitalist superegoic injunction to enjoy commodities with one that beguiles us into desiring, say, egalitarian justice, most especially as it concerns the part of no-part. This was the implication of chapter 3, which suggested ways of directing desire away from the commodity fetishism of both free trade and fair trade toward "trade justice," which prioritizes instead the elimination of broader global economico-political inequalities. Ultimately, such a move requires a politics of "traversing the fantasy," that is, changing the ideological parameters of what is permitted under the global capitalist order, which is what drive, as opposed to desire, is more likely (although once again never guaranteed) to achieve.

The more radical route indeed is the one that inhabits drive, whose impetus and relentlessness can capacitate the subject to break through, rather than reform or tinker with, the status quo. Unlike desire and fantasy, which often work within the coordinates of the system and may thus end up perpetuating the very hegemony they oppose (the symbolic order on which they rely is one they inherit rather than invent anew), drive is aligned with the disruptive presence of the Real. It is impelled not by the futile quest for a lost object (like desire) but by "a push to directly enact the 'loss'—the gap, cut, distance—itself" (Žižek 2012, 63), rendering it all the more excessive, antagonistic, and destructive. Drive is therefore more conducive to radical acts aimed at subverting the operations of capital (see chapters 6 and 7). The idea here is to be inspired by the same obdurateness and engagement as the drive of capital in order to undo capital, to firmly and creatively turn the system's own antagonisms (social inequality, political alienation, environmental crisis) against it.

Key here will be the role played by the part of no-part, as we have previously pointed out (chapters 1, 4, 6, and 7): unlike established social groups under the capitalist system (elites, bourgeoisie, middle classes, working classes) who have a stake in the system, subalterns—poor, gendered, indigenous, and racialized communities; the lumpenproletariat; slum dwellers; immigrant workers, and so on—do not. They may be used and abused by the system (as a disposable reserve army of labor, for instance), but they have no "proper" place in it, with the result that they add a nonconformist, subversive edge to politics; their demands putatively seek not to join a system that abjects them but, consistent with a politics of the drive, reconfigure the system to prevent the very problem of subalternization (chapter 7).

But of course, it cannot fall upon the part of no-part only to bear the burden of transformation. The sheer power and hegemony of global capitalism will require that multiple actors engage in transformation on multiplex issues at multiple levels—local, regional, and global; class, gender, "race," sexual orientation, indigeneity, disability; economic, environmental, informational, biogenetic; and so on—all aimed at trying to exploit the many antagonisms that beset the system. The challenge, as we have previously stressed (chapters 1, 6, and 7), will be devising a politics that is able to cut across these multiple levels, issues, actors, and movements, one that forges solidarity based not on identity (which most often divides groups on the basis of belonging and privilege) but antagonism. This is what Kapoor and Zalloua (2022), following Žižek, denote as a negative universal politics, on the basis of which varying actors work together contingent on shared experiences of systemic exploitation and marginalization (see also McGowan 2020). What will make such a solidary politics transformative, as opposed to reformist or palliative, will be its close relation to the part of no-part, so that action in relation to, say, the environment becomes not another exercise in technomanagerial "sustainable development" but attends to the environmental apartheid that deprives the subaltern of access rights to the commons (see chapter 7).

But beyond the politics of movements and classes, there is also the pivotal politics of the state. While capitalist globalization has meant increasing intensity and extensity of economic flows below and above the state, the latter nonetheless continues to be a key political actor, as chapters 5 and 8 have made clear. The overwhelming hegemony of capitalism today has meant that the state has become the de facto facilitator for the reproduction of the system. This is plain in the vast majority of capitalist liberal democracies across the world, but to prove the point, it is also evident in such "communist" countries as China and Vietnam, which have followed a path of authoritarian capitalism. To be sure, China may well have pursued trade and investment strategies aimed at breaking the cycle of racial trauma (see chapters 5 and 8), but it has done so by sticking firmly to a global capitalist framework, ensuring the country's long-term access to resources and trade partnerships, while benefiting its ruling elites (party technocrats, capitalist classes).

Yet, to the extent that the state is the site of class/social antagonism, as we have claimed (see chapter 1), then the challenge for a transformatory politics becomes not bypassing or doing away with it—it is too important a political site—but struggling to reconfigure it so that it serves the part of no-part instead of ruling elites. It is by identifying first with those who are excluded, those who have no stake in the system, that, when the state accedes to subaltern demands for equality, it is acting in the interests of all. As some save argued (Žižek 2009, 155; Žižek 2019; Wolff 2019; Kapoor and Zalloua 2022, 164–69), perhaps the Bolivian state under Morales gives us a glimpse of what such a reconfigured, if flawed, state might look like: it attempted to prioritize the demands of, and maintain close links with, poor and indigenous groups, while at the same time resisting (ultimately unsuccessfully) the power of foreign and domestic elites and extractive corporations.

But perhaps one of the most important sites for transforming the global capitalist order is transnational governance. The Westphalian nation-state system has proven sorely inadequate for combatting the globalization of capital or addressing pressing world problems such as climate change, COVID-19, or the refugee crisis (the latter two of which are critically imbricated with questions of socioeconomic inequality). Only the advent of supranational collaboration and coordination that prioritizes the interests of the part of no-part, and the construction of progressive/Left global agencies (e.g., a World Environment Organization), may better be able to both regulate capital mobility and counter the power of such neoliberal global agencies as the IMF, World Bank, or the WTO.[1] This would, of course, be a massive and treacherous undertaking, not least of which is working out, for example, that such alternative transnational systems would indeed be accountable to the part of no-part, the extent to which they would involve soft versus hard law (i.e., self-regulation versus command and control legislation), what role would be played by nation-states, and so forth (see Djelic and Sahlin-Andersson 2006; Morgan, Gomes, and Perez-Aleman 2016). Such suggestions may seem pie in the sky, yet it appears to us that, without daring, without imagining meaningful alternatives outside the parameters of our current global capitalist horizon, no egalitarian and socially just postcapitalist futures would be possible.

To be sure, GLE as we see it would be the first to insist that all the foregoing political proposals are flawed and incomplete: precisely because all of them are necessarily politically and libidinally inflected, they run the distinct risk of unpredictability and failure. The political as much as the libidinal are the very names for the antagonisms that always already beset us, exposing any serious transformation of the system to the power of the status quo (e.g., repression, co-optation, defeat), as well as the vagaries of the unconscious (e.g., compromising one's desire by settling for reform rather than revolution; replacing old social hierarchies with enjoyment-inducing new ones; and encountering antagonisms even after a miraculous postcapitalist transition).

Notes

Preface

1. Another significant and influential critical approach to the study of modernity is the Foucauldian one, centered on a cultural-discursive analysis that explicitly shuns questions of political economy. For a Lacanian psychoanalytic critique of this approach, see Kapoor (2020, chap. 2) and Kapoor and Zalloua (2022, 64–69).

2. We employ the term "Third World" well aware of its current pejorative associations, yet also cognizant of its significant political origins: it became popular in the 1950s–1960s, in the wake of the rise of the nonaligned movement aimed at charting a course different from either the capitalist West or the communist Soviet Bloc (see Prashad 2012; Kapoor 2015a). We identify with such political "nonalignment" and thus use the term approvingly but advisedly throughout this book, while also adopting "global South" and "emerging countries" where appropriate. Given the history of global economic and cultural colonialism, all terms associated with this part of the world are problematic, so it often becomes a question of choosing the lesser evil.

3. We seek to radicalize Marxist IPE by going forward from Marx to Freud-Lacan-Žižek (and back again), that is, steadfastly subjecting Marxist IPE to a psychoanalytic politico-hermeneutics (Hamza 2016, 172); in particular, by insisting on investigation of the unconscious-as-antagonism when treating the question of materiality as much as the subject. See our discussion of this later in this chapter.

Chapter 1

1. We are aware that focusing on (neo)classical and Marxist IPE is a limited, binary presentation of the field. But we consider them to be the "main" represen-

tatives, while venturing that such approaches as the constructivist, institutionalist, poststructuralist, or performative ones still fail to consider unconscious desires and non-rational motivations. Our book is of course just a modest beginning; much more thought and work is required at the intersection of psychoanalysis and IPE.

2. The Lacano-Freudian tradition differs markedly here from the likes of Marcuse (1955) and Reich (1974), who, while drawing on Freud and Marx, tend to view capitalism as repressing eros, while envisioning a post-capitalist society that encourages its free play rather than restraining it. The project of Lacano-Freudian psychoanalysis, in contrast, is not sexual liberation: it believes, instead, in the unavoidability of a structural impasse, so that society can never rid itself of antagonism; and moreover, that sexual repression is not imposed from outside (e.g., through social regulation) but is inherent to sex itself: it is part-and-parcel of our symbolic order, embodying the latter's very structural impasse (see Zupančič 2017).

3. Gammon and Palan (2006) draw our attention to Josephson's study (*The Robber Barons*) of late nineteenth-century US capitalism, during which the likes of the Morgans, Vanderbilts, Harrimans, Stillmans, and Rockefellers, despite spending their massive wealth profligately (on estates, luxury houses, art, fast cars, etc.), remain deeply bored, disappointed, and unhappy. "As one society commentator of the time noted 'Limited in their capacity of enjoyment and bored, yet prompted to outdo each other in prodigality, the New Rich experimented with ever new patterns and devices of consumption. . . . One season, it is a ball on horseback which is the chief sensation . . . finally, a costume ball given by Bradley.' In their attempt to foreclose on the future, to close the next deal, the pathology is revealed, as their attempts to accumulate ever more, their drive to combine and amass, leaves their drive to obliterate unabated. It is an unchecked narcissism that ultimately works against the subject. Think of a Michael Jackson or a Howard Hughes" (Gammon and Palan 2006, 110–11).

4. Of course, consumption patterns vary around the globe, at least in part shaped by class and local cultural norms (i.e., elites or middle-classes in the United States and China may not consume either as much or the same commodities as one another) but the point is that capitalist culture induces everyone—whether elite or subaltern—to consume (or at least, to buy into the fantasy of consumption), exploiting our proclivity to fill our ontological void with commodities. See chapters 3 and 6.

5. A politics of the drive is more "radical," because, in the Lacanian scheme of things at least, desire is mainly associated with the Symbolic, which tends to be the realm of the conventional, safe, and banal (since it comes to us from the Other, and in fact is often referred to in Lacanese as the Big Other). In contrast, the drive is associated with the Real, and hence is comparatively more subversive, unpredictable, and relentless. This is why it is drive more than desire that Žižek,

for one, takes up as a pathway to a radical politics (see chapter 6). As Jodi Dean suggests, "while some theorists focus on the subject of desire . . . Žižek has opened up the category of drive, confronting what it is that impels us, that invests us in activities or patterns or objects exceeding interest, life, even our own good" (2012, 2). A politics of the drive requires going beyond—traversing—the limits of desire-fantasy, so as to reconfigure the system, making what seemed "impossible" within the coordinates of that system, possible (see also the Conclusion).

6. Note that although the main philosophical approach of Marxism is called "dialectical materialism," Marx himself never used the term; it was coined instead by Joseph Dietzgen, a German socialist philosopher-journalist who became an ally and friend of Marx and Engels. See Burns (2002).

Chapter 3

1. The term "Fairtrade" is used here to refer specifically to the Fairtrade International system and its standards, which is commonly used to differentiate it from "fair trade," a wider social movement, of which Fairtrade and its member organizations are only a part. See Raynolds and Bennett (2015); Fridell, Gross, and McHugh (2021).

2. For more on the struggles of fair trade producer groups to have greater voice and control of the Fairtrade system, see E. Bennett (2020); Melo Maya and Pittoello (2021); Pruijn (2021); and Reed (2021).

3. See Raynolds and Bennett (2015); Fridell, Gross, and McHugh (2021); and the websites of the Fair Trade Advocacy Office at https://fairtrade-advocacy. org/ and the Canadian Fair Trade Network at https://cftn.ca/.

Chapter 4

1. In the wake of Keith Hart's work, the concept of the informal sector was introduced into international usage in 1972 by the International Labor Organization (ILO) in its Kenya Mission Report, which defined informality as a "way of doing things characterized by (a) ease of entry; (b) reliance on indigenous resources; (c) family ownership; (d) small scale operations; (e) labor intensive and adaptive technology; (e) skills acquired outside of the formal sector; and (g) unregulated and competitive markets" (quoted in Belev 2003, 11). The 1999 ILO International Symposium on the informal sector proposed that the informal sector workforce be categorized into three broad groups: (1) owner-employers of microenterprises, which employ a few paid workers, with or without apprentices; (2) own-account workers, who own and operate one-person businesses, who work alone or with

the help of unpaid workers, generally family members and apprentices; and (3) dependent workers, paid or unpaid, including wage workers in microenterprises, unpaid family workers, apprentices, contract labor, homeworkers, and paid domestic workers. See Belev 2003.

2. "Extimacy" is a Lacanian term that combines "exteriority" and "intimacy" and points to that which is at the limit of a discourse: "Something strange to me, although it is at the heart of me," as Lacan puts it (1997, 71). For Lacan, the Real/ unconscious is thus "extimate" to any discursive formation.

Chapter 5

1. Note that, in this chapter, the terms "China" and "United States" refer not just to political entities but to the state in its performance of the role of a collective Ego (Gallagher 2018). See also chapter 8.

2. China now exports mass surveillance technology, notably to the Middle East. In fact, an employee at a facial recognition laboratory in China mentioned their hiring of Middle Easterners, some of whom were asked to wear facial coverings and hijabs, to help perfect the software in recognizing specific "ethnic" features (Sioh, personal communication, 2019). Of course, Chinese companies are not alone in such exports. The Pegasus spyware, developed by the Israel-based company NSO Group, was revealed to have been used to hack into the devices of a range of people and politicians in 45 countries (Kirchgaessner 2021).

Chapter 6

1. Unlike Freud, who tends to oppose neurosis/(psycho)pathology (chronic mental distress) and psychosis (loss of touch with reality, leading to delusions and hallucinations) with "normality," Lacan refers to them not as symptoms but as clinical structures. That is, neither neurosis nor psychosis are "normal," since the subject is always divided/split—something that cannot then be cured (as Freud claimed) but only reckoned with by coming to terms with it. See D. Evans (2006, 125–26) and Lacan (1977, 168; 2015, 374–75). We use "psychopathology" here in the Lacanian sense.

2. Nonfinancial businesses have also increasingly engaged in speculative investing as a way of broadening their asset portfolios and growing their profits.

3. Özselçuk and Madra point out how corporate boards of directors get "something for nothing," typically by being paid twice, "first when Board members appropriate the entire surplus value, and then second, when they (handsomely) remunerate themselves [i.e., with bonuses and stock options] from the surplus value that they just appropriated for doing the job of appropriating surplus value! . . . 'all

individuals really active in the production from the manager down to the lowest day-labourer' have to perform 'something' to receive 'something'—except for the Board of Directors" (2010, 336). It could be argued, in fact, that the board is paid *four* times, since they also get the libidinal rewards (enjoyment) associated with profit making and bonuses. Which means that they are then getting not just "something" but *a lot* for nothing!

4. There is undoubtedly a close link between the recent rise of mental disorders globally and the onslaught of capitalist globalization, accompanied as the latter is by inequality, unemployment, dispossession, social insecurity, and financial instability (see Walker 2007).

5. Marx (1887, 104) presciently notes that a money circulation-based economy (i.e., financialized capitalism) will appear as M-M alone with no need for commodities per se (i.e., money will be the only capital that counts).

6. McGowan continues, "This is why it is impossible to enjoy objects that are given away for free. . . . The problem with free objects is not that one gets what one pays for—though this is often the case—but that they inevitably appear as simply empirical objects rather than as objects imbued with the elevating quality of the privileged object, which is a product of the association with loss. Loss is the creative act, the source of value" (2013, 32). See also Samman (2022).

7. Blakeley (2018) points out, in fact, that the global " 'rentier share' increased from 4 percent to 14 percent of total income between 1970 and 2000." Jodi Dean (2020) calls this development "platform capitalism," under which technology companies, in particular, "employ a relatively small percentage of the workforce, but their effects have been tremendous, remaking entire industries around the acquisition, mining, and deployment of data. The smaller workforces are indicative of digital technology's neofeudalizing tendency. Capital accumulation occurs less through commodity production and wage labor than through services, rents, licenses, fees, work done for free (often under the masquerade of participation), and data treated as a natural resource."

8. Tomšič (2015, 50) writes, in this regard, "[From Marx's claim about] the double character of commodities it seemingly follows that language is situated in exchange-value, while use-value stands outside language [i.e., "needs" are natural or given]. The critical axis of the idea of commodity language [deployed by GLE], by contrast, consists in the fact that it places the couple of use-value and exchange-value in language, thereby determining the relation between two linguistic levels, human language and commodity language, communication and autonomous difference."

Chapter 8

1. All amounts are in US dollars.

2. While the United States saw the countries espousing import substitution as socialist, the United States itself adopted similar thinking in the eighteenth and nineteenth centuries—Lin-Manuel Miranda created a hit musical from that history!

3. In turn, former Malaysian prime minister Mahathir Mohamad has criticized the BRI as "new colonialism" (Lubin et al. 2018).

4. The title of the book by Paul Miller (2011).

5. A Google search of "US and crony capitalism" yielded 5,780,000 references (March 16, 2022).

6. Build Back Better World is not just a counter to the BRI but also the latest in a series of attempts to ring-fence China going back to the Trans-Pacific Partnership, signed between the United States and eleven other Pacific Rim countries in 2016, which president Barack Obama described as ensuring that "the US—and not countries like China—is the one writing this century's rules for the world's economy" (McBride, Chatzky and Siripurapu 2021).

7. 117th Cong., 1st Sess., "To Address Issues Involving the People's Republic of China," accessed October 16, 2022, https://www.foreign.senate.gov/imo/media/doc/DAV21598%20-%20Strategic%20Competition%20Act%20of%202021.pdf.

8. Signing a memorandum of understanding does not imply that there are any ongoing projects, as evidenced by China's own website. And, as with every other economic activity, the BRI has been affected by the pandemic—up to one-fifth of its projects have stalled or been renegotiated due to pandemic-related delays (Coy 2021).

9. For all of these projects either ground has been broken or at a memorandum of understanding has at least been signed. The list does not imply successful completion. For a review of problems encountered by several BRI projects, see Hiebert (2020).

10. The brand is best known to the Western public for both the arrest of its Chief Financial Officer Meng Wenzhou in Canada over bank fraud for allegedly misleading HSBC about Huawei's business dealings in Iran (Warburton and Berman 2021) and Donald Trump's charge that the technology is "spyware" (O'Brian, 2020). Huawei is an employee-owned firm that is one of two Chinese communications technology giants, the other being the state-owned ZTE.

11. This is despite the fact that Western aid agencies have almost always specified that aid money to recipient countries should be used to hire consultants or purchase goods from the donor country ("tied-aid").

12. China's official currency.

13. In turn, this will likely impose the foundational fantasy on the countries participating in the BRI.

Conclusion

1. Our proposal is, of course, in strict opposition to such proposals for global governance as those promoted by the likes of the 1990s' Washington

Consensus or the current World Economic Forum–inspired "Great Reset," which, despite outward rhetoric of sustainability and "social entrepreneurship," amount to a top-down, elite-centered reproduction of the global capitalist status quo. See Peet (2013) and Klein (2020).

Bibliography

Abi-Habib, Maria. 2018. "How China Got Sri Lanka to Cough Up a Port." *New York Times*, June 25. https://www.nytimes.com/2018/06/25/world/asia/china-sri-lanka-port.html.

Akram-Lodhi, A. Haroon. 2018. "Alternatives: Fair Trade in Theory and Practice." *Studies in Political Economy*. https://doi.org/10.1080/07078552.2018.1492081.

Allison, Graham. 2017a. *Destined for War: Can America and China Escape Thucydides's Trap?* New York: Houghton Mifflin Harcourt.

———. 2017b. "China vs. America: Managing the Next Clash of Civilizations." *Foreign Affairs* 96 (5): 80–89.

Althusser, Louis. 1991. "On Marx and Freud." Translated by Warren Montag. *Rethinking Marxism* 4 (1): 17–30.

Amsden, Alice. 1989. *Asia's Next Giant: South Korea and Late Industrialization*. Oxford: Oxford University Press.

Anderson, Matthew. 2015. *A History of Fair Trade in Contemporary Britain: From Civil Society Campaigns to Corporate Compliance*. Basingstoke, UK: Palgrave Macmillan.

Arežina, Sanja. 2019. "U.S.-China Relations under the Trump Administration: Changes and Challenges." *China Quarterly of International Strategic Studies* 5 (3): 289–315. doi:10.1142/S2377740019500210.

Ariely, Dan. 2009. "The End of Rational Economics." *Harvard Business Review* 87 (7/8): 78–84. https://hbr.org/2009/07/the-end-of-rational-economics.

Arrighi, Giovanni. 2009. *Adam Smith in Beijing: Lineages of the 21st Century*. London: Verso.

Associated Press. 2014. "Hong Kong Protests: China May Be Spying with Smartphone Apps." *CBC*, October 2. https://www.cbc.ca/news/world/hong-kong-protests-china-may-be-spying-with-smartphone-apps-1.2785019.

Auld, Graeme. 2014. *Constructing Private Governance: The Rise and Evolution of Forest, Coffee, and Fisheries Certification* New Haven, CT: Yale University Press.

Badiou, Alain. 2007. *Being and Event*. London: Bloomsbury.

———. 2008. *Live Theory*. London: Continuum.

———. 2012. *The Rebirth of History: Times of Riots and Uprisings*. London: Verso.

Bair, Jennifer, ed. 2009. *Frontiers in Commodity Chain Research*. Stanford, CA: Stanford University Press.

Bair, Jennifer, and Marion Werner. 2011. "Commodity Chains and the Uneven Geographies of Global Capitalism: A Disarticulations Perspective." *Environment and Planning A* 43:988–97.

Baldwin, Richard, and Javier Lopez-Gonzalez. 2015. "Supply-Chain Trade: A Portrait of Global Patterns and Several Testable Hypotheses." *World Economy* 38. doi:10.1111/twec.12189.

Bamber, Penny, and Cornelia Staritz. 2016. *The Gender Dimensions of Global Value Chains*. International Center for Trade and Sustainable Development (ICTSD) (Geneva, Switzerland). http://www.ictsd.org/sites/default/files/research/the_gender_dimensions_of_global_value_chains_0.pdf.

Barrientos, Stephanie, Catherine Dolan, and Anne Tallontire. 2003. "A Gendered Value Chain Approach to Codes of Conduct in African Horticulture." *World Development* 31 (9): 1511–26. https://doi.org/10.1016/S0305-750X(03)00110-4.

Barton, Susanne. 2021. "Yuan's Popularity for Global Payments Hits Five-Year High." *Bloomberg*, February 17. https://www.bloomberg.com/news/articles/2021-02-18/yuan-s-popularity-for-cross-border-payments-hits-five-year-high.

Bataille, Georges. 1986. *Erotism: Death & Sensuality*. Translated by Mary Dalwood. San Francisco, CA: City Lights.

Bayliss, Kate, Ben Fine, and Mary Robertson. 2013. "From Financialisation to Consumption: The Systems of Provision Approach Applied to Housing and Water." *Financialisation, Economy, Society and Sustainable Development (FESSUD), Working Paper Series* (2): 1–46. http://fessud.eu/wp-content/uploads/2013/04/FESSUD-Working-Paper-021.pdf.

BBC. 2011. "Hedge Funds 'Grabbing Land' in Africa." *BBC News*, June 8, sec. Africa. https://www.bbc.com/news/world-africa-13688683.

Beeson, Mark. 2004. "The Rise and Fall (?) of the Developmental State: The Vicissitudes and Implications of East Asian Interventionism." In *Developmental States: Relevancy, Redundancy, or Reconfiguration?*, edited by Linda Low, 29–40. New York: Nova Science.

———. 2009. "Developmental States in East Asia: A Comparison of the Japanese and Chinese Experiences." *Asian Perspective* 33 (2): 5–39.

Belev, Boyan. 2003. "Informal Sector in Transition Economies." Washington, DC: World Bank, Europe and Central Asia Group (ECA).

Belt and Road Initiative. N.d. *Belt and Road Factsheets*. Accessed February 10, 2022. https://www.beltroad-initiative.com/factsheets/.

Bennett, David. 1999. "Burghers, Burglars, and Masturbators: The Sovereign Spender in the Age of Consumerism." *New Literary History* 30 (2): 269–94.

———. 2010. "Libidinal Economy, Prostitution and Consumer Culture." *Textual Practice* 24 (1): 93–121.

———. 2011. "'Money Is Laughing Gas to Me' (Freud): A Critique of Pure Reason in Economics and Psychoanalysis." *New Formations* 72 (72): 5–19.

Bennett, Elizabeth A. 2018. "Voluntary Sustainability Standards: A Squandered Opportunity to Improve Workers' Wages." *Sustainable Development* 26 (1): 65–82. https://doi.org/https://doi.org/10.1002/sd.1691.

———. 2020. "The Global Fair Trade Movement: For Whom, by Whom, How, and What Next." In *The Cambridge Handbook of Environmental Sociology*, edited by Michael Bell, Michael Carolan, Julie Keller, and Katharine Legun, 459–77. Cambridge: Cambridge University Press.

Bentham, Jeremy. 1996. *An Introduction to the Principles of Morals and Legislation*. Oxford: Clarendon Press.

Bernstein, Henry, and Liam Campling. 2006. "Commodity Studies and Commodity Fetishism I: *Trading Down*." *Journal of Agrarian Change* 6 (2): 239–64.

Bhagwati, Jagdish. 2002. *Free Trade Today*. Princeton, NJ: Princeton University Press.

Bhattacharyya, Gargi. 2018. *Rethinking Racial Capitalism: Questions of Reproduction and Survival*. London: Rowman & Littlefield.

Bissio, Roberto. 2017. "Is 'Gender' a Trojan Horse to Introduce New Issues at WTO?" Accessed April 20, 2018. *Third World Network*. https://dawnnet. org/2017/12/is-gender-a-trojan-horse-to-introduce-new-issues-at-wto.

Black, John, Nigar Hashimzade, and Gareth Myles, eds. 2013. *A Dictionary of Economics*. Oxford: Oxford University Press. https://www.oxfordreference. com/view/10.1093/acref/9780199696321.001.0001/acref-9780199696321-e-3 168?rskey=ATgxhY&result=3256.

Blakeley, Grace. 2018. "The Latest Incarnation of Capitalism." *Jacobin*, September 5. https://jacobinmag.com/2018/09/financialization-capitalism-debt-globalization-crisis.

Blaser, Mario. 2014. "Ontology and Indigeneity: On the Political Ontology of Heterogeneous Assemblages." *Cultural Geographies* 21 (1): 49–58.

Böhm, Steffen, and Aanka Batta. 2010. "Just Doing It: Enjoying Commodity Fetishism with Lacan." *Organization* 17 (3): 345–61. https://doi.org/10.1177/ 1350508410363123.

Bollas, Christopher. 2011. *The Christopher Bollas Reader*. London: Routledge.

Boltanski, Luc, and Arnaud Esquerre. 2016. "The Economic Life of Things." *New Left Review*, no. 98 (April): 31–54.

Borrell, Brent. 1994. *EU Bananarama III: Policy Research Working Paper*. International Economics Department, The World Bank.

Boström, Magnus, Michele Micheletti, and Peter Oosterveer, eds. 2019. *The Oxford Handbook of Political Consumerism*. New York: Oxford University Press.

Bousfield, Dan. 2018. "Faith, Fantasy, and Crisis: Racialized Financial Discipline in Europe." In *Psychoanalysis and the GlObal*, edited by Ilan Kapoor, 3–24. Lincoln: University of Nebraska Press.

Brautigam, Deborah, and Meg Rithmire. 2021. "The Chinese 'Debt Trap' Is a Myth." *Atlantic*, February 6. https://www.theatlantic.com/international/archive/2021/02/china-debt-trap-diplomacy/617953/.

Breman, Jan. 2013. "A Bogus Concept? The Precariat: The New Dangerous Class." *New Left Review* 84:130–38.

Brennan, Teresa. 1993. *History after Lacan: Opening Out*. London: Routledge.

Brewster, Havelock, Norman Girvan, and Vaughan Lewis. 2008. *Renegotiate the EPA*. Memorandum submitted for the consideration of the Reflections Group of the Caricom Council for Trade and Economic Development on February 27. http://normangirvan.info.

Brinza, Andreea. 2021. "Biden's 'Build Back Better World' Is an Empty Competitor to China." *Foreign Policy*, June 29. https://foreignpolicy.com/2021/06/29/biden-build-back-better-world-belt-road-initiative/.

Bromley, Ray, and Tamar Wilson. 2018. "Introduction: The Urban Informal Economy Revisited." *Latin American Perspectives* 45 (1):4–23.

Brooks, Andrew. 2015. *Clothing Poverty: The Hidden World of Fast Fashion and Second-Hand Clothes*. London: Zed.

Broude, Tomer. 2018. "A Crafty Madness Kept Aloof: Anti-Dumping as Faulted Global Governance." In *Grey Zones in International Economic Law and Global Governance*, edited by Daniel Drache and Lesley A. Jacobs, 23–44. Vancouver: University of British Columbia Press.

Brown, Matthew. 2020. "Fact Check: Bill Gates Has Given over $50 Billion to Charitable Causes over Career." *USA Today*, June 11. https://www.usatoday.com/story/news/factcheck/2020/06/11/fact-check-bill-gates-has-given-over-50-billion-charitable-causes/3169864001/.

Bryan, D., and M. Rafferty. 2005. *Capitalism with Derivatives: A Political Economy of Financial Derivatives, Capital, and Class*. Basingstoke, UK: Palgrave Macmillan.

Buckley, Chris, and Keith Bradsher. 2021. "Marking Party's Centennial, Xi Warns That China Will Not Be Bullied." *New York Times*, July 1. https://www.nytimes.com/2021/07/01/world/asia/xi-china-communist-party-anniversary.html.

Burns, Tony. 2002. "Joseph Dietzgen and the History of Marxism." *Science & Society* 66 (2): 202–27.

Bush, Simon R., Peter Oosterveer, Megan Bailey, and Arthur P. J. Mol. 2014. "Sustainability Governance of Chains and Networks: A Review and Future Outlook." *Journal of Cleaner Production* 1–12. https://doi.org/10.1016/j.jclepro.2014.10.019.

Business Wire. 2021. "The Modern Silk Road: China Belt and Road Initiative Growth Opportunities Report 2021." *ResearchAndMarkets.com*. Berskhire Hathaway, June 29. https://www.businesswire.com/news/home/20210629005526/en/

The-Modern-Silk-Road---China-Belt-and-Road-Initiative-Growth-Opportunities-Report-2021---ResearchAndMarkets.com.

Cardoso, Fernando H., and Enzo Faletto. 1977. *Dependência e desenvolvimento na América Latina: Ensaio de interpretação sociológica. Quarta Edição.* Rio de Janeiro: Zahar Editores.

Carrington, Anca. 2015. *Money as Emotional Currency.* London: Routledge.

Castells, Manuel. 1992. "Four Asian Tigers with a Dragon Head: A Comparative Analysis of the State, Economy and Society." In *States and Development in the Asia Pacific Rim*, edited by Richard Appelbaum and Jeffrey Henderson, 33–70. Newbury Park, CA: Sage Publications.

Carveth, Donald L. 2018. *Psychoanalytic Thinking: A Dialectical Critique of Contemporary Theory and Practice.* New York: Routledge.

China State Information Center. N.d. Belt and Road Portal. https://eng.yidaiyilu.gov.cn/gbjj.htm. https://english.www.gov.cn/2016special/madeinchina2025.

Chowdhry, Geeta, and Shirin Rai. 2009. "The Geographies of Exclusion and the Politics of Inclusion: Race-Based Exclusions in the Teaching of International Relations." *International Studies Perspectives* 2009 (10): 84–91.

Chua, Beng Chuat. 2017. *Liberalism Disavowed: Communitarianism and State Capitalism in Singapore.* Ithaca, NY: Cornell University Press.

Clinton, Hillary. 2011. "America's Pacific Century." *Foreign Policy*, October 11. https://foreignpolicy.com/2011/10/11/americas-pacific-century/.

Coleman, James Samuel. 1990. *Foundations of Social Theory.* Cambridge, MA: Belknap Press.

Commission on Growth and Development. 2008. *The Growth Report: Strategies for Sustained Growth and Inclusive Development.* Washington, DC: The World Bank.

Connell, R. W., and Julian Wood. 2005. "Globalization and Business Masculinities." *Men and Masculinities* 7 (4): 347–64.

Copjec, Joan. 2015. *Read My Desire: Lacan against the Historicists.* London: Verso.

Council on Foreign Relations. N.d. *Assessing China's Digital Silk Road Initiative: A Transformative Approach to Technology Financing or a Danger to Freedoms?* Accessed February 12, 2022. https://www.cfr.org/china-digital-silk-road.

Coy, Peter. 2021. "China's New Belt and Road Has Less Concrete, More Blockchain." Bloomberg Businessweek, March 24. https://www.bloomberg.com/news/articles/2021-03-24/china-s-new-belt-and-road-has-less-concrete-more-blockchain.

Cramer, Chistopher, Deborah Johnston, Carlos Oya, and John Sender. 2014. *Fairtrade, Employment, and Poverty Reduction in Ethiopia and Uganda: Final Report to DFID.* SOAS, University of London (London). http://ftepr.org/wp-content/uploads/FTEPR-Final-Report-19-May-2014-FINAL.pdf.

Daly, Glyn. 2006. "The Political Economy of (Im)Possibility." In *International Political Economy and Poststructural Politics*, edited by Marieke de Goede, 177–94. Basingstoke, UK: Palgrave Macmillan.

Daniel, Will. 2021. "WallStreetBets Traders Are Pushing Risky Stocks to All-Time Highs." *Business Insider*, January 31. https://markets.businessinsider.com/news/stocks/wallstreetbets-traders-equities-all-time-highs-quotes-forum-explain-phenomenon-2021-1.

Da Silva, Sven, and Pieter de Vries. 2021. "The Ambivalence of Slum Politics in Reactionary Times in Recife, Brazil." *Dialectical Anthropology* 45 (5): 383–401.

Da Silva, Sven, and Pieter de Vries. 2022. "The Trajectory of the Right to the City in Recife, Brazil: From Belonging towards Inclusion." *Planning Theory* 21 (3): 291–311.

Davidson, Helen. 2021. "China Owed $385bn—Including 'Hidden Debt' from Poorer Nations, Says Report." *Guardian*. September 30. https://www.theguardian.com/world/2021/sep/30/42-nations-owe-china-hidden-debts-exceeding-10-of-gdp-says-report.

Daviron, Benoit, and Stefano Ponte. 2005. *The Coffee Paradox: Global Markets, Commodity Trade, and the Elusive Promise of Development*. London: Zed.

Davis, Dave. 2021. "Facial Recognition and Beyond: Journalist Ventures Inside China's 'Surveillance State.'" *NPR*, January 5. https://www.npr.org/2021/01/05/953515627/facial-recognition-and-beyond-journalist-ventures-inside-chinas-surveillance-sta.

Dawson, Michael. 2003. *The Consumer Trap: Big Business Marketing in American Life*. Urbana: University of Illinois Press.

Day, Alexander F. 2013. *The Peasant in Postsocialist China: History, Politics, and Capitalism*. Cambridge: Cambridge University Press.

Dean, Jodi. 2012. "Still Dancing: Drive as a Category of Political Economy." *International Journal of Zizek Studies* 6 (1): n.p.

———. 2020. "Neofeudalism: The End of Capitalism?" *Los Angeles Review of Books*, May 12. https://lareviewofbooks.org/article/neofeudalism-the-end-of-capitalism/.

De Castro, Eduardo Viveiros. 2015. *Cannibal Metaphysics*. Minneapolis: University of Minnesota Press.

De Janvry, Alain. 1981. *The Agrarian Question and Reformism in Latin America*. Baltimore, MD: Johns Hopkins University Press.

De Neve, Geert. 2009. "Power, Inequality, and Corporate Social Responsibility: The Politics of Ethical Compliance in the South Indian Garment Industry." *Economic & Political Weekly* 44 (22): 63–71. http://re.indiaenvironmentportal.org.in/files/Corporate%20Social%20Responsibility.pdf.

Descola, Phillipe. 2013. *Beyond Nature and Culture*. Chicago, IL: University of Chicago Press.

De Soto, Hernando. 1989. *The Other Path: The Invisible Revolution in the Third World*. New York: Harper and Row, 1989.

———. 2000. *The Mystery of Capital: Why Capitalism Triumphs in the West and Fails Everywhere Else*. London: Basic.

de Sousa Santos, Boaventura, ed. 2005. *Democratizing Democracy: Beyond the Liberal Democratic Canon*. London: Verso.

de Vries, Pieter. 2007. "Don't Compromise Your Desire for Development! A Lacanian/Deleuzian Rethinking of the Anti-Politics Machine." *Third World Quarterly* 28 (1): 25–43.

———. 2016a. "The Inconsistent City, Participatory Planning, and the Part of No Part in Recife, Brazil." *Antipode* 48 (3): 790–808.

———. 2016b. "Participatory Slum Upgrading as a Disjunctive Process in Recife, Brazil: Urban Coproduction and the Absent Ground of the City." *Singapore Journal of Tropical Geography* 37 (3): 295–309.

de Vries, Pieter, and Valencia, Emperatri, eds. 2010. *El DIAR: ¿Un fracaso o una promesa Cumplida?* Chocó, Colombia: Universidad Technológica del Chocó.

Dezan Shira and Associates. N.d. "Silk Road Briefing." Accessed February 9, 2022. https://www.silkroadbriefing.com/about-us/overview.html.

Djelic, Marie-Laure, and Kerstin Sahlin-Andersson, eds. 2006. *Transnational Governance: Institutional Dynamics of Regulation*. Cambridge: Cambridge University Press.

Dou, Eva. 2021. "Documents Link Huawei to China's Surveillance Programs." *Washington Post,* December 14. https://www.washingtonpost.com/world/2021/12/14/huawei-surveillance-china/.

Dünhaupt, Petra. 2013. "The Effect of Financialization on Labor's Share of Income." Working Paper #17. Berlin: Institute for International Political Economy Berlin.

Dymski, Gary A. 2010. "Understanding the Subprime Crisis: Institutional Evolution and Theoretical Views." Kirwan Institute for the Study of Race and Ethnicity, Ohio State University. http://kirwaninstitute.osu.edu/FairHousing_FairCredit/gary_dymski_subprime_crisis_merge.pdf.

Economist. 2020. "The Digital Side of the Belt and Road Initiative Is Growing." Special report in *Economist,* February 6. https://www.economist.com/special-report/2020/02/06/the-digital-side-of-the-belt-and-road-initiative-is-growing.

Edelman, Marc, Carlos Oya, and Saturnino M. Borras Jr., eds. 2016. *Global Land Grabs: History, Theory, and Method*. London: Routledge.

Edgeworth, Francis Ysidro. 1967. *Mathematical Psychics: An Essay on the Application of Mathematics to the Moral Sciences*. New York: A. M. Kelley.

Edmonds, Kevin. 2020. *Legalize It? A Comparative Study of Cannabis Economies in St. Vincent and St. Lucia*. PhD thesis, University of Toronto Press.

Elson, Diane. 1988. "Market Socialism or Socialization of the Market?" *New Left Review* 172:1–44.

———. 2002. "Socializing Markets, Not Market Socialism." In *Socialist Register 2002: Necessary and Unnecessary Utopias*, edited by Leo Panitch and Colin Leys, 67–85. Black Point, Nova Scotia: Fernwood.

180 | Bibliography

————. 2009. "Gender Equality and Economic Growth in the World Bank World Development Report 2006." *Feminist Economics* 15 (3): 35–59.

EPA. 2008. *Economic Partnership Agreement between the CARIFORUM States, of the One Part, and the European Community and Its Member States, of the Other Part.* Official Journal of the European Union. http://trade.ec.europa.eu/doclib/docs/2008/february/tradoc_137971.pdf.

Escobar, Arturo. 1995. *Encountering Development: The Making and Unmaking of the Third World.* Princeton, NJ: Princeton University Press.

————. 1999a. "The Invention of Development." *Current History* 98 (631): 382–86.

————. 1999b. "After Nature: Steps to an Anti-Essentialist Political Ecology." *Current Anthropology* 40 (1): 1–30.

————. 2008. *Territories of Difference.* Durham, NC: Duke University Press.

————. 2018. *Designs for the Pluriverse: Radical Interdependence, Autonomy, and the Making of Worlds.* Durham, NC: Duke University Press.

Ethirajan, Anbarasan. "China Debt Dogs Maldives' 'Bridge to Prosperity.'" BBC News, September 17. https://www.bbc.com/news/world-asia-52743072.

European Commission. 2018. *The CARIFORUM-EU Economic Partnership Agreement (EPA): A New Partnership for Trade and Development: Factsheet: How the EU Is Putting the EPA into Practice.* (Belgium). http://trade.ec.europa.eu/doclib/docs/2012/april/tradoc_149286.pdf.

Evans, Dylan. 2006. *An Introductory Dictionary of Lacanian Psychoanalysis.* London: Routledge.

Evans, Peter B. 1979. *Dependent Development: The Alliance of Multinational, State, and Local Capital in Brazil.* Princeton, NJ: Princeton University Press.

Evans, Peter B., Dietrich Rueschemeyer, and Theda Skocpol. 1985. *Bringing the State Back In.* Cambridge: Cambridge University Press.

Fals Borda, Orlando. 2000. Socialismo raizal y ordenamiento territorial. Bogotá: Ediciones Desde Abajo.

Fanon, Frantz. 1963. *The Wretched of the Earth.* New York: Grove.

Feldner, Heiko, Fabio Vighi, and Slavoj Žižek. 2014. *States of Crisis and Post-Capitalist Scenarios.* Farnham, UK: Ashgate.

Ferchen, Matt, and Anarkalee Perera. 2019. *Why Unsustainable Chinese Infrastructure Deals are a Two-Way Street.* Carnegie-Tsinghua Center for Global Policy. https://carnegieendowment.org/files/7-15-19_Ferchen_Debt_Trap.pdf.

Ferguson, James. 1990. *The Anti-Politics Machine: "Development," Depoliticization, and Bureaucratic Power in Lesotho.* Minneapolis: University of Minnesota Press.

Fine, Ben. 2013. "Consumption Matters." *ephemera* 13 (2): 217–48. http://eprints.soas.ac.uk/15968/7/13-2fine.pdf.

Fine, Ben, Michael Heasman, and Judith Wright. 1996. *Consumption in the Age of Affluence: The World of Food.* London: Routledge.

Fischer, Amanda. 2021. "The Rising Financialization of the U.S. Economy Harms Workers and Their Families, Threatening a Strong Recovery." Washington, DC: Washington Center for Equitable Growth. https://equitablegrowth.org/the-rising-financialization-of-the-u-s-economy-harms-workers-and-their-families-threatening-a-strong-recovery/.

Forbes. 2021. "America's Top Givers: The 25 Most Philanthropic Billionaires." *Forbes*, January 19. https://www.forbes.com/sites/forbeswealthteam/2021/01/19/americas-top-givers-the-25-most-philanthropic-billionaires/.

Frank, Andre Gunder. 1967. *Capitalism and Underdevelopment in Latin America.* New York: Monthly Review Press.

Fraser, Nancy. 2015. "Legitimation Crisis? On the Political Contradictions of Financialized Capitalism." *Critical Historical Studies* 2 (2): 157–89. https://doi.org/10.1086/683054.

———. 2016. "Expropriation and Exploitation in Racialized Capitalism: A Reply to Michael Dawson." *Critical Historical Studies* 3 (1): 163–78.

Freeman, Richard B. 2010. "It's Financialization!" *International Labour Review* 149 (2): 163–83.

Freud, Sigmund. 1959. *Inhibitions, Symptoms and Anxiety.* Translated by the Institute of Psycho-Analysis and Angela Richards. New York: W. W. Norton.

———. 1961. *Beyond the Pleasure Principle.* Translated by James Strachey. New York: Norton.

———. 1966. *Introductory Lectures on Psycho-Analysis.* Translated by James Strachey. The standard edition. New York: W. W. Norton.

———. 1973. *The Psychopathology of Everyday Life.* Edited by James Strachey. Harmondsworth, UK: Penguin.

———. 1977. "On Transformations of Instinct as Exemplified in Anal Erotism." In *On Sexuality: Three Essays on the Theory of Sexuality and Other Works,* edited by James Strachey, 295–302. Harmondsworth, UK: Penguin.

Fridell, Gavin. 2007a. "Fair Trade Coffee and Commodity Fetishism: The Limits of Market-Driven Social Justice." *Historica Materialism* 15 (4): 79–104. https://doi.org/doi.org/10.1163/156920607X245841.

———. 2007b. *Fair Trade Coffee: The Prospects and Pitfalls of Market-Driven Social Justice.* Toronto, Canada: University of Toronto Press.

———. 2014. "Fair Trade Slippages and Vietnam Gaps: The Ideological Fantasies of Fair Trade Coffee." *Third World Quarterly* 37 (5): 1179–94. https://doi.org/doi.org/10.1080/01436597.2014.926108.

———. 2015. "On the Margins of the Rising South: ALBA and Petrocaribe in the Caribbean." In *Beyond Free Trade: Alternative Approaches to Trade, Politics, and Power,* edited by Kate Ervine and Gavin Fridell, 211–28. Houndsmill, UK: Palgrave Macmillan.

———. 2019. "Conceptualizing Political Consumerism as Part of the Global Value Chain." In *The Oxford Handbook of Political Consumerism*, edited by Magnus Boström, Michele Micheletti, and Peter Oosterveer, 249–72. New York: Oxford University Press.

———. 2022. "The Political Economy of Inclusion and Exclusion: State, Labour and the Costs of Supply Chain Integration in the Eastern Caribbean." *Review of International Political Economy* 19 (3): 749–67.

Fridell, Gavin, Zack Gross, and Sean McHugh, eds. 2021. *The Fair Trade Handbook: Building a Better World, Together.* Halifax, Nova Scotia: Fernwood.

Fridell, Gavin, and Chris Walker. 2019. "Social Upgrading as Market Fantasy: The Limits of Global Value Chain Integration." *Human Geography* 12 (2): 1–17. https://doi.org/10.1177/194277861901200201.

Friedman, Eli. 2014. *Insurgency Trap: Labor Politics in Postsocialist China.* Ithaca, NY: Cornell University Press.

Friedman, Milton. 1957. *A Theory of the Consumption Function.* Princeton, NJ: University Press.

———. 1963. *Capitalism and Freedom.* Chicago, IL: University of Chicago Press.

Galeano, Eduardo. 1997. *Open Veins of Latin America: Five Centuries of the Pillage of a Continent.* New York: Monthly Review Press.

Gallagher, Julia. 2018. "Misrecognition in the Making of a State: Ghana's International Relations Under Kwame Nkrumah." *Review of International Studies* 44 (5): 882–901. doi:10.1017/S0260210518000335.

Gammon, Earl, and Ronen Palan. 2006. "Libidinal International Political Economy." In *International Political Economy and Poststructural Politics*, edited by Marieke de Goede, 97–114. Basingstoke, UK: Palgrave Macmillan.

Gargeyas, Arjun. 2021. "China's 'Standards 2035' Project Could Result in a Technological Cold War." *Diplomat*, September 18. https://thediplomat.com/2021/09/chinas-standards-2035-project-could-result-in-a-technological-cold-war/.

Garner, Steve. 2017. *Racisms: An Introduction.* London: Sage Publications.

Geertz, Clifford. 1978. "The Bazaar Economy: Information and Search in Peasant Marketing. *American Economic Review* 68 (2): 28–32.

Gereffi, Gary, John Humphrey, and Timothy Sturgeon. 2005. "The Governance of Global Value Chains." *Review of International Political Economy* 12 (1): 78–104. https://doi.org/10.1080/09692290500049805.

Gereffi, Gary, and Miguel Korzeniewicz, eds. 1994. *Commodity Chains and Global Capitalism.* Westport, CT: Praeger.

Gershgorn, Dave. 2021. "China's 'Sharp Eyes' Program Aims to Surveil 100% of Public Space." *OneZero*, March 2. https://onezero.medium.com/chinas-sharp-eyes-program-aims-to-surveil-100-of-public-space-ddc22d63e015.

Gibson-Graham, J. K. 1996. *The End of Capitalism (as We Knew It): A Feminist Critique of Political Economy.* Cambridge, MA: Blackwell.

Gniazdowski, Andrzej. 2018. "The Politics of Regression: The Idea of the Nation State in the Thought of Ernst Cassirer and Aurel Kolnai." *Eidos* 3 (5): 27–41. doi:10.26319/5813.

Goldman, Michael. 2006. *Imperial Nature: The World Bank and Struggles for Social Justice in the Age of Globalization*. New Haven, CT: Yale University Press.

Golub, Phillip. 2016. *East Asia's Reemergence*. Cambridge: Polity Press.

Goodman, Michael K. 2010. "The Mirror of Consumption: Celebritization, Developmental Consumption and the Shifting Cultural Politics of Fair Trade." *Geoforum* 41 (1): 104–16. https://doi.org/10.1016/j.geoforum.2009.08.003.

Gottfried, Heidi. 2013. *Gender, Work, and Economy: Unpacking the Global Economy*. Cambridge: Polity Press.

Green, Benjamin. 2020. "Excising a Malignant Tumour in US Political Discourse: The Thucydides Trap." *Educational Philosophy and Theory*, 2–3. https://doi.org/10.1080/00131857.2020.1799739.

Green, Cecilia A. 2007. "Between the Devil and the Deep Blue Sea: Mercantilism and Free Trade." *Race & Class* 49 (2): 41–56.

Green, Ginelle. 2015. "The CARIFORUM Economic Partnership Agreement: Lessons from Implementation." *Commonwealth Trade Hot Topics Series* (121): 1–7. https://www.oecd-ilibrary.org/content/paper/5jrqgv0rznq6-en.

Grey, B. 2022. *Who Owns 5G Patents?* February 12. https://www.qualcomm.com/5g/what-is-5g.

Guardian. 2021. "Pandora Papers: What Has Been Revealed so Far?" October 6, 2021. https://www.theguardian.com/news/2021/oct/04/pandora-papers-at-a-glance.

Gunawardana, Samanthi J. 2017. "Clothing." *International PoliticalEconomy of Everyday Life (I-PEEL)*.

Guo, Yingjie. 2018. "Bringing Politics into Class Analysis: State Power and Class Formation in Post-Mao China." *Australian Journal of Political Science* 53 (3): 370–84.

Guthman, Julie. 2002. "Commodified Meanings, Meaningful Commodities: Re-thinking Production-Consumption Links through the Organic System of Provision." *Sociologia Ruralis* 42 (4): 295–311. https://doi.org/https://doi.org/10.1111/1467-9523.00218.

Gutiérrez, Alejandra, and Eduardo Restrepo. 2017. *Misioneros y organizaciones campesinas en el río Atrato (Chocó)*. Medellín, Colombia: Uniclaretiana.

Hamza, Agon. 2016. "Going to One's Ground: Žižek's Dialectical Materialism." In *Slavoj Žižek and Dialectical Materialism*, edited by Agon Hamza and Frank Ruda, 163–75. Basingstoke, UK: Palgrave Macmillan.

Hannah, Erin, James Scott, and Silke Trommer, eds. 2016. *Expert Knowledge in Global Trade*. London: Routledge.

Harding, Luke. 2016. "What Are the Panama Papers? A Guide to History's Biggest Data Leak." *Guardian*, April 5, sec. News. https://www.theguardian.

com/news/2016/apr/03/what-you-need-to-know-about-the-panama-papers.

Hardt, Michael, and Antonio Negri. 2000. *Empire*. Cambridge, MA: Harvard University Press.

Hart, Keith. 1973. "International Labour Office Incomes, Employment and Equality in Kenya." *Journal of Modern African Studies* 11 (3): 61–89.

———. 2008. "Between Bureaucracy and the People: A Political History of Informality." Sussex, UK: DIIS Working Paper, No. 27.

Harvey, David. 2003. *The New Imperialism*. Oxford: Oxford University Press.

———. 2006. *Spaces of Global Capitalism*. London: Verso.

Harwell, Drew. 2021. "As GameStop Stock Crumbles, Newbie Traders Reckon with Heavy Losses." *Washington Post*, February 2. https://www.washingtonpost.com/technology/2021/02/02/gamestop-stock-plunge-losers/.

Hass, Ryan, and Abraham Denmark. 2020. More Pain Than Gain: How the US-China Trade War Hurt America. Washington, DC: Brookings Institute.

Havice, Elizabeth, and Liam Campling. 2013. "Articulating Upgrading: Island Developing States and Canned Tuna Production." *Environment and Planning A* 45:2610–27. https://doi.org/10.1068/a45697.

Herman, Judith Lewis. 2015. *Trauma and Recovery: The Aftermath of Violence from Domestic Abuse to Political Terror*. New York: Basic.

Hickel, Jason. 2014. "The 'Girl Effect': Liberalism, Empowerment and the Contradictions of Development." *Third World Quarterly* 35 (8): 1355–73.

Hiebert, Murray. 2020. "China's Belt and Road: from Malaysia to Philippines, ASEAN Projects Face Roadblocks, *South China Morning Post*, September 8. https://www.scmp.com/week-asia/opinion/article/3100628/chinas-belt-and-road-malaysia-philippines-asean-projects-face.

Hirsh, Michael. 2019. "Economists on the Run." *Foreign Policy*, October 22. https://foreignpolicy.com/2019/10/22/economists-globalization-trade-paul-krugman-china/.

Hochschild, Arlie Russell. 2012. *The Managed Heart: The Commercialization of Human Feeling*. Berkeley: University of California Press.

Homans, George Caspar. 1961. *Social Behaviour: Its Elementary Forms*. London: Routledge & Kegan Paul.

Hopkins, Terence K., and Immanuel Wallerstein. 1977. "Patterns of Development of the Modern World-System." *Review* 1 (2): 111–45.

Hsu, Serena. 2021. "Senate's Strategic Competition Act Will Make China-US Relations Worse, Not Better." *Diplomat*, April 27. https://thediplomat.com/2021/04/senates-strategic-competition-act-will-make-china-us-relations-worse-not-better/.

Huaxia. 2021. "Xi Focus: Xi Stresses Sci-Tech Self-Strengthening at Higher Levels." Xinhua, May 29. http://www.xinhuanet.com/english/2021-05/29/c_139976311.htm.

Hudson, Ian, and Mark Hudson. 2021. *Consumption*. London: Polity.

Hudson, Mark, Ian Hudson, and Mara Fridell. 2013. *Fair Trade, Sustainability, and Social Change*. New York: Palgrave MacMillan.

Humphrey, Errol. 2011. *Implementing the Economic Partnership Agreement: Challenges and Bottlenecks in the CARIFORUM Region: Discussion Paper No. 117*. European Centre for Development Policy Management (ECDPM) (Maastricht, The Netherlands). http://www.ecdpm.org.

Hung, Ho-fung. 2016. *The China Boom: Why China Will Not Rule the World*. Contemporary Asia in the World. New York: Columbia University Press.

Hvistendahl, Mara. 2021. "Oracle Boasted That Its Software Was Used against U.S. Protesters. Then It Took the Tech to China." *Intercept*, May 25. https://the intercept.com/2021/05/25/oracle-social-media-surveillance-protests-endeca/.

ILO (International Labour Organization). 2022. *World Employment and Social Outlook Trends 2022*. Geneva: ILO. https://www.ilo.org/global/research/global-reports/weso/trends2022/WCMS_834081/lang--en/index.htm.

Irigaray, Luce. 1985. *This Sex Which Is Not One*. Ithaca, NY: Cornell University Press.

———. 1986. "Women, the Sacred and Money." *Paragraph* 8:6–18.

Ivanić, Mladen, and Aleksandar Savović. 2020. *Belt and Road Initiative and Bosnia and Herzegovina*. Budapest: China-CEE institute.

İzdeş Terkoğlu, Özge, İpek İlkkaracan, Emel Memiş, and Yelda Yücel. 2017. *The UN Women, Gender, and Economics Training Manual*. UN Women (New York).

Jaffee, Daniel. 2007. *Brewing Justice: Fair Trade Coffee, Sustainability, and Survival*. Berkeley: University of California Press.

Jameson, Frederic. 1982. *The Political Unconscious: Narrative as a Socially Symbolic Act*. Ithaca, NY: Cornell University Press.

———. 1994. *The Seeds of Time*. New York: Columbia University Press.

Jenkins, Rhys Owen. 2014. *Transnational Corporations and Uneven Development: The Internationalization of Capital and the Third World*. London: Routledge.

Jevons, William Stanley. 1970. *The Theory of Political Economy*. London: Penguin.

Johnson, Chalmers. 1982. *MITI and the Japanese Miracle: The Growth of Industry Policy, 1925–1975*. Stanford, CA: Stanford University Press.

Jones, Lee, and Shahar Hameiri. 2020. *Debunking the Myth of Debt-Trap Diplomacy: How Recipient Countries Shape China's Belt and Road Initiative*. Research Paper Asia-Pacific Programme, Chatham House. https://www.chathamhouse.org/sites/default/files/2020-08-25-debunking-myth-debt-trap-diplomacy-jones-hameiri.pdf.

Kapoor, Ilan. 2008. *The Postcolonial Politics of Development*. London: Routledge.

———. 2013. *Celebrity Humanitarianism: The Ideology of Global Charity*. New York: Routledge.

———. 2014. "Psychoanalysis and Development: Contributions, Examples, Limits." *Third World Quarterly* 35 (7): 1120–43.

————. 2015a. "The Queer Third World." *Third World Quarterly* 36 (9): 1611–28.

————. 2015b. "What 'Drives' Capitalist Development?" *Human Geography* 8 (3): 66–78.

————. 2015c. "Billionaire Philanthropy: 'Decaf Capitalism.'" In *International Handbook of Wealth and the Super-Rich*, edited by Jonathan Beaverstock and Iain Hay, 113–31. Cheltenham, UK: Edward Elgar.

————. 2017. "Cold Critique, Faint Passion, Bleak Future: Post-Development's Surrender to Global Capitalism." *Third World Quarterly* 38 (12): 2664–83.

————. 2020. *Confronting Desire: Pyschoanalysis and International Development*. Ithaca, NY: Cornell University Press.

Kapoor, Ilan, and Zahi Zalloua. 2022. *Universal Politics*. Oxford: Oxford University Press.

Kara, Siddharth. 2017. *Modern Slavery: A Global Perspective*. New York: Columbia University Press.

Karnitschnig, Matthew. 2020. "How Germany Opened the Door to China—and Threw Away the Key." *Politico*, September, 10. https://www.politico.eu/article/germany-china-economy-business-technology-industry-trade-security/.

Kharas, Homi, and Harinder Kohli. 2011. "What Is the Middle Income Trap, Why Do Countries Fall into It, and How Can It Be Avoided?" *Global Journal of Emerging Market Economies* 3 (3) 281–89. doi:10.1177/097491011100300302.

Kiely, Ray. 1999. "The Last Refuge of the Noble Savage? A Critical Assessment of Post-Development Theory." *European Journal of Development Research* 11 (1): 30–55.

Kim, Sung Yun, and Yotam Margalit. 2021. "Tariffs as Electoral Weapons: The Political Geography of the US–China Trade War." *International Organization* 75 (Winter): 1–38.

Kingsbury, Paul, and Steve Pile. 2014. "Introduction: The Unconscious, Transference, Drives, Repetition and Other Things Tied to Geography." In *Psychoanalytic Geographies*, edited by Paul Kingsbury and Steve Pile, 1–40. Surrey, UK: Ashgate.

Kirchgaessner, Stephanie. 2021. "Israeli Spyware Company NSO Group Placed on US Blacklist." *Guardian*, November 3. https://www.theguardian.com/us-news/2021/nov/03/nso-group-pegasus-spyware-us-blacklist.

Klein, Naomi. 2020. "The Great Reset Conspiracy Smoothie." *Intercept*, December 8. https://theintercept.com/2020/12/08/great-reset-conspiracy/.

Knudsen, Ståle. 2014. "Is Escobar's 'Territories of Difference' Good Political Ecology? On Anthropological Engagements with Environmental Social Movements." *Social Analysis* 58 (2): 78–107.

Kohut, Heinz. 1973. *The Search for the Self-Selected Writings of Heinz Kohut: 1950-1978*. Vol. 2. New York: International Universities Press.

Krugman, Paul R., Maurice Obstfeld, and Marc J. Melitz. 2018. *International Trade: Theory and Policy*. 11th ed. Boston, MA: Pearson Education.

Kynge, James, and Martin Sandbu. 2021. "Will China Become the Centre of the World Economy?" Podcast. *Financial Times*, June 21. https://www.ft.com/video/4a0a55cd-b21d-4ae4-be4d-1cf92b50b6ba.

Lacan, Jacques. 1977. *Écrits: A Selection*. Translated by A. Sheridan. New York: Norton.

———. 1997. *The Ethics of Psychoanalysis: The Seminar of Jacques Lacan*. Book 7. Edited by Jacques-Alain Miller. New York: Norton.

———. 1998. *The Four Fundamental Concepts of Psychoanalysis: The Seminar of Jacques Lacan*. Book 11. Edited by Jacques-Alain Miller. New York: W. W. Norton.

———. 2006. *The Other Side of Psychoanalysis: The Seminar of Jacques Lacan*. Book 17. Edited by Jacques-Alain Miller. New York: Norton.

———. 2015. *Transference: The Seminar of Jacques Lacan*. Book 8. Edited by Jacques-Alain Miller. Translated by Bruce Fink. Cambridge: Polity.

Lambe, Brendan John, and Tomasz Piotr Wisniewski. 2018. "Stock Market Crashes Linked to Higher Rates of Suicide—New Research." *Conversation*, September 18. http://theconversation.com/stock-market-crashes-linked-to-higher-rates-of-suicide-new-research-101917.

Lapavitsas, Costas. 2013. "The Financialization of Capitalism: 'Profiting without Producing.'" *City* 17 (6): 792–805.

LaRosa, Michael J., and Germán R. Mejía. 2017. *Colombia: A Concise Contemporary History*. London: Rowman & Littlefield.

Latour, Bruno. 1987. *Science in Action: How to Follow Scientists and Engineers through Society*. Cambridge, MA: Harvard University Press.

Lau, Lawrence. 2019. *The China-US Trade War and Future Economic Relations*. Hong Kong: The Chinese University Press.

———. 2020a. "The China-U.S. Trade War and Future Economic Relations." OUHK—Great Speakers Series (podcast), March 8. https://www.youtube.com/watch?v=QqjFAOTjrnI.

———. 2020b. "The Impacts of the Trade War and the COVID-19 Epidemic on China U.S. Economic Relations." *China Review* 20 (4): 1–37.

Lazzarato, Maurizio. 2012. *The Making of the Indebted Man: An Essay on the Neoliberal Condition*. Translated by Joshua David Jordan. Cambridge, MA: MIT Press.

LeBaron, Genevieve, and Jane Lister. 2015. "Benchmarking Global Supply Chains: The Power of the 'Ethical Audit' Regime." *Review of International Studies* 41 (5): 905–24. https://doi.org/10.1017/S0260210515000388.

———. 2020. "The Hidden Costs of Global Supply Chain Solutions." *Review of International Political Economy*. https://doi.org/doi.org/10.1080/09692290.2021.1956993.

Ledeneva, Alena, ed. 2018. *The Global Encyclopaedia of Informality*. Vol. 1, *Towards Understanding of Social and Cultural Complexity*. London: UCL Press.

Leesberg, Julie, and Emperatriz Valencia. 1987. *Los sistemas de producción en el Medio Atrato. Informe.* Quibdo, Colombia: Proyecto DIAR-CODECHOCHO.

Leff, Enrique. 2021. *Political Ecology: Deconstructing Capital and Territorializing Life.* Berlin: Springer Nature.

Levitt, Kari, and Lloyd Best. 1975. "The Character of Caribbean Economy." In *Caribbean Economy,* edited by George Beckford, 53–75. Kingston, Jamaica: Institute of Social and Economic Research.

Lewin, Arie Y., Martin Kenney, and Johann Peter Murmann, eds. 2016. *China's Innovation Challenge: Overcoming the Middle-Income Trap.* Cambridge: Cambridge University Press.

Leys, Ruth. 2000. *Trauma: A Genealogy.* Chicago, IL: University of Chicago Press.

Li, Minqi. 2008. "Socialism, Capitalism, and Class Struggle: The Political Economy of Modern China." *Economic and Political Weekly* 43 (52): 77–85.

Lin, Justin Yifu. 2012. *The Quest for Prosperity: How Developing Economies Can Take Off.* Princeton, NJ: Princeton University Press.

Liu, Kerry. 2020. "China's Policy Response to the China US Trade War: An Initial Assessment." *Chinese Economy* 53 (2): 158–76.

Locke, John. 2003. *Political Writings.* Indianapolis, IN: Hackett.

———. 2006. *Locke on Money.* Oxford: Clarendon Press.

Long, Norman, and Bryan R. Roberts, eds. 1978. *Peasant Cooperation and Capitalist Expansion in Central Peru.* Austin: University of Texas Press.

Lubin, David, Johanna Chua, David Cowan, Piotr Kalisz, Tracy Xian Liao, Edward L Morse, Michel Nies, Ernesto Revilla, Ivan Tchakarov, Wei Zheng Kit, and Artem Zaigrin. 2018. *China's Belt and Road at Five: A Progress Report.* Citi GPS: Global Perspectives & Solutions, CitiGroup. https://www.citibank.com/commercialbank/insights/assets/docs/2018/Chinas_Belt_and_road_at_five.pdf.

Lugones, Maria. 2016. "The Coloniality of Gender." In *The Palgrave Handbook of Gender and Development,* edited by Wendy Harcourt, 13–33. London: Palgrave Macmillan.

Lyon, Sarah. 2006. "Evaluating Fair Trade Consumption: Politics, Defetishization and Producer Participation." *International Journal of Consumer Studies* 30 (5): 452–64. https://doi.org/doi.org/10.1111/j.1470-6431.2006.00530.x.

———. 2010. *Coffee and Community: Maya Farmers and Fair-Trade Markets.* Boulder: University Press of Colorado.

Lyotard, Jean-François. 1993. *Libidinal Economy.* Bloomington: Indiana University Press.

Maçães, Bruno. 2018. *Belt and Road: A Chinese World Order.* London: C. Hurst US.

Macdonald, Laura, and Nadia Ibrahim. 2019. *Canada's Feminist Trade Policy: An Alternative to Austerity Trade Politics?* Austerity and Its Alternatives. https://altausterity.mcmaster.ca/documents/laura-berlin-2019-to-post.pdf.

Machado, Roberto 2014. "The Informal Economy in Peru: Magnitude and Determinants, 1980–2011." *Apuntes. Revista de ciencias sociales* 41 (74): 197–233.

Mandel, Ernest. 1986. "In Defense of Socialist Planning." *New Left Review* 159:5–37.

Maniates, Michael F. 2001. "Individualization: Plant a Tree, Buy a Bike, Save the World?" *Global Environmental Politics* 1 (3): 31–52. https://doi.org/10.1162/152638001316881395.

Mao, Zedong. 1949. *Proclamation of the Central People's Government of the PRC.* Wilson Center. https://digitalarchive.wilsoncenter.org/document/121557.pdf?v=d41d8cd98f00b204e9800998ecf8427e.

Marcuse, Herbert. 1955. *Eros and Civilization a Philosophical Inquiry into Freud.* Boston, MA: Beacon Press.

Martin, Neale, and Kyle Morich. 2011. "Unconscious Mental Processes in Consumer Choice: Toward a New Model of Consumer Behavior." *Journal of Brand Management* 18 (7): 483–505. https://doi.org/10.1057/bm.2011.10.

Martin, Peter. 2021. *China's Civilian Army: The Making of Wolf Warrior Diplomacy.* New York: Oxford University Press.

Martínez Alier, Joan. 2002. *The Environmentalism of the Poor: Study of Ecological Conflicts and Valuation.* London: Edward Elgar.

Marx, Karl. 1887. *Capital: A Critique of Political Economy.* Vol. 1. Edited by Friedrich Engels. Moscow: Progress. https://www.marxists.org/archive/marx/works/1867-c1/index.htm.

———. 1970. *A Contribution to the Critique of Political Economy.* Moscow: Progress.

———. 1978. "Capital, Volume One." In *The Marx-Engels Reader,* edited by Robert C. Tucker, 294–438. New York: W. W. Norton.

———. 1992. *Early Writings.* Harmondsworth, UK: Penguin.

———. 1993. *Grundrisse: Foundations of the Critique of Political Economy.* Translated by Martin Nicolaus. London: Penguin.

———. 2000. *Karl Marx: Selected Writings.* Edited by David McLellan. Oxford: Oxford University Press.

———. 2004. *Capital: A Critique of Political Economy.* London: Penguin.

Marx, Karl, and Friedrich Engels. 1970. *The Communist Manifesto.* Beijing: The Floating Press.

———. 2003. *Collected Works.* Vols. 1–50. Moscow: Institute of Marxism-Leninism.

McBride, James, and Andrew Chatzky. 2018. "Is Made in China a Threat to Global Trade?" *Council on Foreign Relations,* May 13. https://www.cfr.org/backgrounder/made-china-2025-threat-global-trade.

McBride, James, Andrew Chatzky, and Anshu Siripurapu. 2019. "What's Next for the Trans-Pacific Partnership (TPP)?" *Council on Foreign Relations,* September 20. https://www.cfr.org/backgrounder/what-trans-pacific-partnership-tpp.

McGowan, Todd. 2004. *The End of Dissatisfaction? Jacques Lacan and the Emerging Society of Enjoyment.* Albany, NY: State University of New York Press.

———. 2013. *Enjoying What We Don't Have: The Political Project of Psychoanalysis*. Lincoln: University of Nebraska Press.

———. 2020. *Universality and Identity Politics*. New York: Columbia University Press.

McGrath, Siobhan. 2018. "Dis/articulations and the Interrogation of Development in GPN Research." *Progress in Human Geography* 42 (4): 509–28.

McMichael, Philip, and Heloise Weber. 2021. *Development and Social Change: A Global Perspective*. Thousand Oaks, CA: Sage.

McNally, David. 1993. *Against the Market: Political Economy, Market Socialism and the Marxist Critique*. London: Verso.

Megill, Allan. 2002. *Karl Marx: The Burden of Reason (Why Marx Rejected Politics and the Market)*. Lanham, MD: Rowman & Littlefield.

Melo Maya, Nelson, and Joey Pittoello. 2021. "Putting Southern Farmers First: Journeys to Decolonization." In *The Fair Trade Handbook: Building a Better World, Together*, edited by Gavin Fridell, Zack Gross, and Sean McHugh, 63–71. Halifax: Fernwood.

Mercer, Kobena. 2107. *The Fateful Triangle: Race, Ethnicity, and Nation*. Cambridge, MA: Harvard University Press.

Miliband, Ralph. 1983. *Class Power and State Power*. London: Verso.

Mill, John Stuart. 2004. *Principles of Political Economy with Some of Their Applications to Social Philosophy*. Edited by Stephen Nathanson. Indianapolis, IN: Hackett.

Miller, Paul. 2011. *Poorly Made in China: An Insider's Account of the China Production Game*. Hoboken, NJ: John Wiley & Sons.

Milonakis, Dimitris, and Ben Fine. 2009. *From Political Economy to Economics: Method, the Social, and the Historical in the Evolution of Economic Theory*. London: Routledge.

Mises, Ludwig von. 1966. *Human Action: A Treatise on Economics*. Chicago, IL: H. Regnery.

Mishra, Pankaj. 2020. "Grand Illusions." *New York Review of Books*, November 20. https://www.nybooks.com/articles/2020/11/19/liberalism-grand-illusions.

Moisi, Dominique. 2010. *The Geopolitics of Emotion: How Cultures of Fear, Humiliation, and Hope are Reshaping the World*. New York: Anchor.

Mol, Arthur, David Sonnenfeld, and Gerrit Spaargaren, eds. 2010. *The Ecological Modernisation Reader: Environmental Reform in Theory and Practice*. London: Routledge.

Morgan, Glenn, Marcus Vinícius Peinado Gomes, and Paola Perez-Aleman. 2016. "Transnational Governance Regimes in the Global South: Multinationals, States and NGOs as Political Actors." *Revista de Administração de Empresas* 56 (August): 374–79.

Morozov, Evgeny. 2018. "Reasserting Cyber Sovereignty: How States are Taking Back Control." *Guardian*, October 7. https://www.theguardian.com/

technology/2018/oct/07/states-take-back-cyber-control-technological-sovereignty.

———. 2020. "The Huawei War." *Le Monde Diplomatique*, November 10. https://mondediplo.com/2020/11/10huawei.

Morrell, Robert, and Sandra Swart. 2004. "Men in the Third World: Postcolonial Perspectives on Masculinity." In *Handbook of Studies on Men and Masculinities*, edited by Michael Kimmell, Jeff Hearn, and R. W. Connell, 90–113. Thousand Oaks, CA: Sage.

Mou, Chunxiao. 2020. " 'Thucydides' Trap, an Ethnocentric Misunderstanding of China." *Educational Philosophy and Theory*, 3–4.

Mullen, Andrew. 2021. "Explainer: US-China Trade War Timeline: Key Dates and Events Since July 2018." *South China Morning Post*, August 29. https://www.scmp.com/economy/china-economy/article/3146489/us-china-trade-war-timeline-key-dates-and-events-july-2018.

Myers, Gordon. 2004. *Banana Wars: The Price of Free Trade*. London: Zed.

Nawrotkiewicz, Joanna. 2021. "Understanding Chinese 'Wolf Warrior Diplomacy': Interview with Peter Martin." *National Bureau of Asian Research*, October 22. https://www.nbr.org/publication/understanding-chinese-wolf-warrior-diplomacy/.

Naylor, Lindsay. 2018. "Fair Trade Coffee Exchanges and Community Economies." *Environment and Planning A: Economy and Space* 50 (5): 1027–46. https://doi.org/10.1177/0308518x18768287.

Nelson, Valerie, and Adrienne Martin. 2013. *Final Technical Report: Assessing the Poverty Impact of Sustainability Standards*. Natural Resources Institute, University of Greenwich (Greenwich, UK). https://www.gov.uk/research-for-development-outputs/final-technical-report-assessing-the-poverty-impact-of-sustainability-standards.

Neumann, Roderick. 2009. Political Ecology. In *International Encyclopedia of Human Geography*, edited by Rob Kitchin and Nigel Thrift, 228–33. Oxford: Elsevier.

Nicita, Allesandro. 2019. *Trade and Trade Diversion Effects of United States Tariffs on China*. UNCTAD Research Paper No. 37 UNCTAD/SER.RP/2019/9. Trade Analysis Branch Division on International Trade and Commodities UNCTAD.

Nuijten, Monique, Martijn Koster, and Pieter de Vries. 2012. "Regimes of Spatial Ordering in Brazil: Neoliberalism, Leftist Populism and Modernist Aesthetics in Slum Upgrading in Recife." *Singapore Journal of Tropical Geography* 33 (2): 157–70.

O'Brian, Matt. 2020. "Trump Administration Imposes New Huawei Restrictions." *Washington Post*, August 17. https://www.washingtonpost.com/business/technology/trump-administration-imposes-new-huawei-restrictions/2020/08/17/c12df298-e095-11ea-82d8-5e55d47e90ca_story.html.

O'Connor, Tom. 2021. "Biden Faces Tough Path to Building a Better Belt and Road Than China." *Newsweek*, June 24. https://www.newsweek.com/biden-tough-path-building-better-belt-road-china-1603929.

O'Dea, S. 2021. "Number of Smartphones Sold to End Users Worldwide from 2007 to 2021." *Statista*, December 16. https://www.statista.com/statistics/263437/global-smartphone-sales-to-end-users-since-2007/.

Oliveira, Gustavo de L. T., Juan Liu, and Ben M. McKay, eds. 2021. *Beyond the Global Land Grab: New Directions for Research on Land Struggles and Global Agrarian Change.* London: Routledge.

Ortiz, Isabel, Sara Burke, Mohamed Berrada, and Hernán Saenz Cortés. 2022. *An Analysis of World Protests, 2006–2020.* Basingstoke, UK: Palgrave-Macmillan.

Oxfam. 2018. "Brazil: Extreme Inequality in Numbers." Oxfam International, November 13. https://www.oxfam.org/en/even-it-brazil/brazil-extreme-inequality-numbers.

———. 2020a. "5 Shocking Facts about Extreme Global Inequality and How to Even It Up." Oxfam International, January 20. https://www.oxfam.org/en/5-shocking-facts-about-extreme-global-inequality-and-how-even-it.

———. 2020b. "World's Billionaires Have More Wealth Than 4.6 Billion People." Oxfam International, January 20. https://www.oxfam.org/en/press-releases/worlds-billionaires-have-more-wealth-46-billion-people.

Oxford Business Group. 2018. *The Report: Thailand 2018.* https://oxfordbusinessgroup.com/thailand-2018.

Oya, Carlos, Florian Schaefer, Skalidou Dafni, Catherine McCosker, and Laurenz Langer. 2017. "Effects of Certification Schemes for Agricultural Production on Socio-Economic Outcomes in Low- and Middle-Income Countries: A Systematic Review." *Campbell Systematic Reviews* 3. https://doi.org/10.4073/csr.2017.3.

Özselçuk, Ceren, and Yahya M. Madra. 2010. "Enjoyment as an Economic Factor: Reading Marx with Lacan." *Subjectivity* 3 (3): 323–47.

Pan, Che. 2022. "China to Pursue Major Standards-Setting Role in 6G Mobile Technology amid Chinese Lab's Recent Breakthrough." *South China Morning Post*, January 13. https://www.scmp.com/tech/tech-war/article/3163261/china-pursue-major-standards-setting-role-6g-mobile-technology-amid.

Pareto, Vilfredo. 2014. *Manual of Political Economy: A Critical and Variorum Edition.* Edited by Aldo Montesano. Oxford: Oxford University Press.

Parisi, Laura. 2020. "Canada's New Feminist International Assistance Policy: Business as Usual?" *Foreign Policy Analysis* 16 (2): 163–80. https://doi.org/10.1093/fpa/orz027. https://doi.org/10.1093/fpa/orz027.

Patent Progress. N.d. "Too Many Patents." Accessed February 12, 2022. https://www.patentprogress.org/systemic-problems/too-many-patents/.

Peace Cable. 2018. "PEACE Cable Project Enters into Cable and Material Manufacturing Stage." October 22. http://www.peacecable.net/News/Detail/16589.

Peet, Richard. 2013. *Geography of Power: Making Global Economic Policy.* Zed.

———. 2018. "Power/Knowledge/Geography: Speculation at the End of History." In *Geographies of Knowledge and Power*, edited by Peter Meusburger, Derek Gregory, and Laura Suarsana, 263–76. New York: Springer.

Pegg, David. 2017. "Paradise Papers: Who's Who in the Leak of Offshore Secrets." *Guardian*, November 11. https://www.theguardian.com/news/ng-interactive/2017/nov/11/paradise-papers-whos-who-leak-offshore-secrets.

Pegg, David, Kalyeena Makortoff, Martin Chulov, Paul Lewis, and Luke Harding. 2022. "Revealed: Credit Suisse Leak Unmasks Criminals, Fraudsters and Corrupt Politicians." *Guardian*, February 20. https://www.theguardian.com/news/2022/feb/20/credit-suisse-secrets-leak-unmasks-criminals-fraudsters-corrupt-politicians.

Perez, Bien. 2020. "Explainer: What Is 5G and How Will It Change the World?" *South China Morning Post*, November 3. https://www.scmp.com/tech/big-tech/article/3108011/what-5g-and-how-will-it-change-world.

Peters, Michael A. 2020. "US–China Rivalry and 'Thucydides' Trap': Why This Is a Misleading Account: Introduction." *Educational Philosophy and Theory*, 1–2. https://doi.org/10.1080/00131857.2020.1799739.

Pfaller, Robert. 2012. *Interpassivity and Misdemeanors: The Analysis of Ideology and the Zizekian Toolbox.* Revue internationale de philosophie (3): 421–38.

Pieterse, Jan Nederveen. 2000. "After Post-Development." *Third World Quarterly* 21 (2): 175–91.

Pietz, William. 1987. "The Problem of the Fetish, II: The Origin of the Fetish." *RES: Anthropology and Aesthetics* (13): 23–45. http://www.jstor.org/stable/20166762.

Ponte, Stefano, and Timothy Sturgeon. 2014. "Explaining Governance in Global Value Chains: A Modular Theory-Building Effort." *Review of International Political Economy* 21 (1): 195–223. https://doi.org/10.1080/09692290.2013.809596.

Portes, Alejandro. 1996. "The Informal Economy: Perspectives from Latin America." In *Exploring the Underground Economy*, edited by S. Pozo, 147–65. Kalamazoo, MI: W. E. Upjohn Institute for Employment Research.

Poulantzas, Nicos. 1975. *Political Power and Social Classes.* London: Humanities Press.

Prashad, Vijay. 2012. *The Poorer Nations: A Possible History of the Global South.* London: Verso.

Princen, Thomas, Michael Maniates, and Ken Conca, eds. 2002. *Confronting Consumption.* Boston, MA: MIT Press.

Pruijn, Jerónimo. 2021. "The Roots of Fair Trade and SPP: My Experiences Alongside Small Producers." In *The Fair Trade Handbook: Building a Better World, Together*, edited by Gavin Fridell, Zack Gross, and Sean McHugh, 86–96. Halifax, Nova Scotia: Fernwood.

Qualcomm. N.d. "Everything You Need to Know about 5G." Accessed February 12, 2022. https://www.qualcomm.com/5g/what-is-5g.

Qin, Julia Ya. 2019. "Forced Technology Transfer and the US-China Trade War: Implications for International Economic Law." *Journal of International Economic Law* 22 (4): 743–62.

Quijano, Anibal. 1970. "Redefinición de la dependencia y marginalización en América Latina." Santiago, Chile: CESO.

———. 2000. "Coloniality of Power and Eurocentrism in Latin America." *International Sociology* 15 (2): 215–32.

Radcliffe, Sarah. 2012. "Development for a Postneoliberal Era? Sumak Kawsay, living well and the Limits to Decolonisation in Ecuador." *Geoforum* 43 (2): 240–49.

Ramadori, Claudio. 2021. "Made in China 2025—Everything You Need to Know." *New Horizons*, September, 15. https://nhglobalpartners.com/made-in-china-2025/.

Rancière, Jacques. 1999. *Disagreement: Politics and Philosophy*. Minneapolis: University of Minnesota Press.

Raynolds, Laura T. 2002. "Consumer/Producer Links in Fair Trade Coffee Networks." *Sociologia Ruralis* 42 (4): 404–24. https://doi.org/10.1111/1467-9523.00224.

Raynolds, Laura T., and Elizabeth A. Bennett, eds. 2015. *Handbook of Research on Fair Trade*. Cheltenham, UK: Edward Elgar.

Raynolds, Laura T., and Nicholas Greenfield. 2015. "Fair Trade: Movements and Markets." In *Handbook of Research on Fair Trade*, edited by Laura T. Raynolds and Elizabeth A. Bennett, 24–44. Cheltenham, UK: Edward Elgar.

Read, John. 2007. "Politics as Subjectification: Rethinking the Figure of the Worker in the Thought of Badiou and Rancière." *Philosophy Today* 51:25–132.

Reed, Darryl. 2021. "A Brief History of Fair Trade: From Charity to Autonomy and Justice." In *The Fair Trade Handbook: Building a Better World, Together*, edited by Gavin Fridell, Zack Gross, and Sean McHugh, 74–85. Halifax, Nova Scotia: Fernwood.

Reich, Wilhelm. 1974. *The Sexual Revolution: Toward a Self-Regulating Character Structure*. New York: Simon and Schuster.

Research and Markets. 2021. "Financial Services Global Market Report 2021: COVID-19 Impact and Recovery to 2030." Dublin. https://www.researchand-markets.com/reports/5240250/financial-services-global-market-report-2021.

Restrepo, Eduardo. 2008. *Eventualizing Blackness in Colombia*. PhD diss., University of North Carolina at Chapel Hill.

———. 2010. "Genealogia e impactos (no-intencionados) de las intervenciones para el desarrollo en el Chocó: El Proyecto de Desarrollo Integral Agricola Rural (DIAR)." In *El DIAR: Un Fracaso o una promesa no cumplida?*, edited by Pieter de Vries and Emperatri Valencia, 10–139. Chocó, Colombia: Universidad Technológica del Chocó.

Ricardo, David. 1876. *The Works of David Ricardo*. Edited by J. R. McCulloch. London: John Murray.

Roberts, Jason. 2020. "Political Ecology." In *Cambridge Encyclopedia of Anthropology*. http://doi.org/10.29164/20polieco.

Robinson, Cedric J. 2019. *On Racial Capitalism, Black Internationalism, and Cultures of Resistance*. London: Pluto Press.

———. 2000. *Black Marxism: The Making of the Black Radical Tradition*. Chapel Hill: University of North Carolina Press.

Roman, Richard, and Edur Velasco Arregui. 2015. *Continental Crucible: Big Business, Workers, and Unions in the Transformation of North America*. 2nd ed. Halifax, Nova Scotia: Fernwood.

Roy, Ananya. 2005. "Urban Informality: Toward an Epistemology of Planning." *Journal of the American Planning Association* 71 (2): 147–58.

———. 2010. *Poverty Capital: Microfinance and the Making of Development*. Abingdon, UK: Routledge.

Ruta, Michele, Matias Herrera Dappe, Somik Lall, Chunlin Zhang, Cristina Constantinescu, Mathilde Lebrand, Alen Mulabdic, and Erik Churchill. 2019. *Belt and Road Economics: Opportunities and Risks of Transport Corridors*. Washington, DC: The World Bank.

Rycroft, Charles. 1995. *Critical Dictionary of Psychoanalysis*. London: Penguin.

Sachs, Jeffrey D. 2005. *The End of Poverty: Economic Possibilities of Our Time*. New York: Penguin.

Sacks, David. 2021. "Countries in China's Belt and Road Initiative: Who's In and Who's Out." *Foreign Affairs*. Council on Foreign Relations, March, 24. https://www.cfr.org/blog/countries-chinas-belt-and-road-initiative-whos-and-whos-out.

Salaam Abdel-Malek, Hana. 2019. "Birth of a Nation-State: A Battle for Boundaries or Dialogue?" *International Journal of Applied Psychoanalytic Studies* 17 (1): 49–64. doi:10.1002/aps.1628.

Samman, Amin. 2022. "Eternal Return on Capital: Nihilistic Repetition in the Asset Economy." *Distinktion: Journal of Social Theory* 23 (1): 165–81.

Samman, Amin, and Stefano Sgambati. 2022. "Financial Eschatology and the Libidinal Economy of Leverage." *Theory, Culture & Society* (March): 1–19.

Sanders, Ronald. 2011. "Commentary: 'Time Out' on the Promises of European Union Partnership." *Caribbean News Now!*, June 17. Accessed July 6, 2011. http://www.caribbeannewsnow.com/topstory-Commentary%3A-%27Time-out%27-on-the-promises-of-European-Union-Partnership-6669.html.

Sassatelli, Roberta. 2015. "Consumer Culture, Sustainability and a New Vision of Consumer Sovereignty." *Sociologia Ruralis* 55 (4): 483–96. https://doi.org/https://doi.org/10.1111/soru.12081.

Sassen, Saskia. 2008. *Territory, Authority, Rights: From Medieval to Global Assemblages*. Princeton, NJ: Princeton University Press.

Schell, Orville, and John Delury. 2013. *Wealth and Power: China's Long March to the Twenty-First Century*. New York: Random House.

SCMP Reporters. 2020. "Explainer: What Is the US-China Trade War?" *South China Morning Post*, April 13. https://www.scmp.com/economy/china-economy/article/3078745/what-us-china-trade-war-how-it-started-and-what-inside-phase.

Selwyn, Benjamin. 2016. *Global Value Chains or Global Poverty Chains? A New Research Agenda: Working Paper No. 10*. The Centre for Global Political Economy Working Paper Series (Brighton, United Kingdom).

———. 2017. *The Struggle for Development*. Cambridge, UK: Polity Press.

Selwyn, Benjamin, Bettina Musiolek, and Artemisa Ijarja. 2020. "Making a Global Poverty Chain: Export Footwear Production and Gendered Labor Exploitation in Eastern and Central Europe." *Review of International Political Economy* 27 (2): 377–403. https://doi.org/10.1080/09692290.2019.1640124.

Shakir, Omar, and Maya Wong. 2021. "Mass Surveillance Fuels Oppression of Uighurs and Palestinians." *Al Jazeera*, November 24. https://www.aljazeera.com/opinions/2021/11/24/mass-surveillance-fuels-oppression-of-uyghurs-and-palestinians.

Shang, Carrie, and Wei Shen. 2021. "Beyond Trade War: Reevaluating Intellectual Property Bilateralism in the US–China." *Journal of International Economic Law* 24 (1): 53–76.

Sheng, Andrew. 2021. "In War against Coronavirus or the Israeli-Palestinian Conflict, Technological Might Always Wins." *South China Morning Post*, May 22. https://www.scmp.com/comment/opinion/article/3134320/war-against-covid-19-or-israeli-palestinian-conflict-technological.

Shepard, Daniel, and Mittal Anuradha. 2011. "The Great Land Grab: Rush for World's Farmland Threatens Food Security for the Poor." Oakland, CA: Oakland Institute. https://www.oaklandinstitute.org/great-land-grab-rush-world%E2%80%99s-farmland-threatens-food-security-poor.

Shepard, Wade. 2020. "How China's Belt and Road Became a 'Global Trail of Trouble.'" *Forbes*. January 29. https://www.forbes.com/sites/wadeshepard/2020/01/29/how-chinas-belt-and-road-became-a-global-trail-of-trouble/?sh=1753c787443d.

Shepherd, Ben. 2016. *Trade Facilitation and Global Value Chains: Opportunities for Sustainable Development*. International Center for Trade and Sustainable Development (ICTSD) (Geneva, Switzerland). http://www.ictsd.org.

Sheppard, Eric, Phillip Porter, David Faust, and Richa Nagar. 2009. *A World of Difference: Encountering and Contesting Development*. New York: Guildford Press.

Simon, David, ed. 2006. *Fifty Key Thinkers on Development*. London: Routledge.

Simpson, Charles R., and Anita Rapone. 2000. "Community Development from the Ground Up: Social-Justice Coffee." *Human Ecology Review* 7 (1): 46–57.

Sin, Ben. 2020. "How Huawei Managed to Sell the Most Phones in 2020 So Far: Re-releases in Europe and Chinese Consumers." *Forbes*, July, 30. https://

www.forbes.com/sites/bensin/2020/07/30/how-huawei-managed-to-sell-the-most-phones-in-2020-so-far-re-releases-in-europe-and-chinese-consumers/?sh=336a251ab9a8.

Sioh, Maureen. 2010. "The Hollow Within: Anxiety and Performing Postcolonial Financial Policies." *Third World Quarterly* 31 (4): 581–98.

———. 2014a. "A Small Narrow Space: Postcolonial Terrorialization and the Libidinal Economy." In *Psychoanalytic Geographies*, edited by Paul Kingsbury and Steve Pile, 279–94. Surrey, UK: Ashgate.

———. 2014b. "Manicheism Delirium: Desire and Disavowal in the Libidinal Economy of an Emerging Economy." *Third World Quarterly* 35 (7): 1162–78. https://doi.org/10.1080/01436597.2014.926106.

———. 2018a. "The Wound of Whiteness: Conceptualizing Economic Convergence as Trauma in the 2016 United States Presidential Election." *Geoforum* 95:112–21. https://doi.org/10.1016/j.geoforum.2018.06.020.

———. 2018b. "The Logic of Humiliation in Financial Conquest." In *Psychoanalysis and the GlObal*, edited by Ilan Kapoor, 25–47. Lincoln: University of Nebraska Press.

Smith, Adam. 1997. *The Wealth of Nations*. Books 1–3. Harmondsworth, UK: Penguin.

Smith, Gavin. 1989. *Livelihood and Resistance*. Los Angeles: University of California Press.

Smith, Zhanna Malekos. 2021. "New Tail for China's 'Wolf Warrior' Diplomats." Center for Strategic and International Studies, October 13. https://www.csis.org/analysis/new-tail-chinas-wolf-warrior-diplomats.

Soper, Kate. 2020. *Post-Growth Living: For an Alternative Hedonism*. London: Verso.

Sotiropoulos, Dimitris, John Milios, and Spyros Lapatsioras. 2013. *A Political Economy of Contemporary Capitalism and Its Crisis: Demystifying Finance*. London: Routledge.

Spivak, Gayatri Chakravorty. 1988. "Can the Subaltern Speak?" In *Marxism and Interpretation of Culture*, edited by C. Nelson and L. Grossberg, 271–313. Chicago, IL: University of Illinois Press.

Staricco, Juan Ignacio. 2017. "Class Dynamics and Ideological Construction in the Struggle over Fairness: A Neo-Gramscian Examination of the Fairtrade Initiative." *Journal of Peasant Studies*. https://doi.org/10.1080/03066150.2017.1337003.

Staritz, Cornelia, and José Guilherme Reis, eds. 2013. *Global Value Chains, Economic Upgrading, and Gender: Case Studies of the Horticulture, Tourism, and Call Center Industries*. Washington, DC: The World Bank.

Starosta, Guido. 2010. "Global Commodity Chains and the Marxian Law of Value." *Antipode* 42 (2): 433–65. https://doi.org/10.1111/j.1467-8330.2009.00753.x.

State Council of the People's Republic of China. 2022. "Made in China 2025." February 10. https://english.www.gov.cn/2016special/madeinchina2025.

Stolle, Dietlind, and Michele Micheletti. 2013. *Political Consumerism: Global Responsiblity in Action*. Cambridge: Cambridge University Press.

Storey, Andy. 2000. "Post-Development Theory: Romanticism and Pontius Pilate Politics." *Development* 43 (4): 40–46.

Studwell, Joe. 2013. *How Asia Works: Success and Failure in the World's Most Dynamic Region*. New York: Grove Press.

Sturgeon, Timothy. 2009. "From Commodity Chains to Value Chains: Inter-disciplinary Theory Building in an Age of Globalization." In *Frontiers of Commodity Chain Research*, edited by Jennifer Bair, 110–35. Stanford, CA: Stanford University Press.

Suwandi, Intan. 2019. *Value Chains: The New Economic Imperialism*. New York: Monthly Review Press.

Swyngedouw, Erik. 2016. "Trouble with Nature: 'Ecology as the New Opium for the Masses.'" In *The Ashgate Research Companion to Planning Theory*, edited by Jean Hillier and Patsy Healey, 317–36. Abingdon, UK: Routledge.

Takagi, Yusuke, Veerayooth Kanchoochat, and Tetsushi Sonobe, eds. 2019. *Developmental State Building: The Politics of Emerging Economies*. Springer e-book. https://link.springer.com/book/10.1007%2F978-981-13-2904-3.

Tallontire, Anne, Catherine Dolan, Sally Smith, and Stephanie Barrientos. 2005. "Reaching the Marginalised? Gender Value Chains and Ethical Trade in African Horticulture." *Development in Practice* 15 (3/4): 559–71. https://doi.org/10.1080/09614520500075771.

Tang, Frank. 2021. "China Plots Economic Recovery Path, Technological Innovation a 'Matter of Survival' for Beijing." *South China Morning Post,* November 24. https://www.scmp.com/economy/china-economy/article/3157205/china-plots-economic-recovery-path-technological-innovation?module=lead_hero_story&pgtype=homepage.

Taylor, Adam, and Emily Rauhala. 2021."The Biden Administration Gets a Taste of China's 'Wolf Warrior' Diplomacy." *Washington Post,* March 19. https://www.washingtonpost.com/world/2021/03/19/biden-blinken-china-wolf-warrior.

Taylor, Marcus. 2011. "Race You to the Bottom . . . and Back Again? The Uneven Development of Labour Codes of Conduct." *New Political Economy* 16 (4): 445–62. https://doi.org/10.1080/13563467.2011.519023.

Thomas, Clive. 1974. *Dependence and Transformation: The Economics of the Transition to Socialism*. New York: Monthly Review Press.

Tiessen, Rebecca. 2019. "What's New about Canada's Feminist International Assistance Policy and Why 'More of the Same' Matters." *School of Public Policy Publications*. https://papers.ssrn.com/abstract=3506896.

Tomšič, Samo. 2015. *The Capitalist Unconscious: Marx and Lacan*. London: Verso.

Townsend, Will. 2019. "Who Is 'Really' Leading in Mobile 5G, Part 4: Infrastructure Equipment Providers." *Forbes*, July 19. https://www.forbes.com/sites/moor

insights/2019/07/19/who-is-really-leading-in-mobile-5g-part-4-infrastructure-equipment-providers/?sh=2acab6269130.

UNDP (United Nations Development Programme). 2012. *Gender and Economic Policy Management Initiative—Asia and the Pacific: Gender and Trade.* Asia-Pacific Regional Centre, United Nations Development Programme (Bangkok, Thailand). http://www.asia-pacific.undp.org/content/dam/rbap/docs/Research%20&%20Publications/womens_empowerment/gepmi/RBAP-Gender-2012-GEPMI-Module-9.pdf.

US Trade Representative. N.d. Undated. "The People's Republic of China." Accessed February 16, 2022. https://ustr.gov/countries-regions/china-mongolia-taiwan/peoples-republic-china.

Veblen, Thorstein. 1904. *The Theory of Business Enterprise.* New York: C. Scribner's.

———. 1953. *The Theory of the Leisure Class.* New York: Mentor.

———. 1965. *The Engineers and the Price System.* New York: A. M. Kelley.

———. 2006. *Conspicuous Consumption.* New York: Penguin.

Von Neumann, John, and Oskar Morgenstern. 1953. *Theory of Games and Economic Behavior.* Princeton, NJ: Princeton University Press.

Wabgou, Maguematic. 2012. *Movimiento social Afrocolombiano, negro, raizal y palenquero: El largo camino hacia la construccion de espacios comunes y alianzas estrategicas para la incidencia politica en Colombia.* Bogotá: Universidad Nacional de Colombia.

Wade, Robert. 2017. "The Developmental State: Dead or Alive." *Development and Change* 49 (2): 518–46. doi:10.1111/dech.12381.

Walker, Carl. 2007. *Depression and Globalization: The Politics of Mental Health in the 21st Century.* New York: Springer.

Wallerstein, Immanuel Maurice. 2004. *World-Systems Analysis: An Introduction.* Durham, NC: Duke University Press.

Wang, Orange. 2022. "US-China Reach Trade Talk 'Stalemate' Despite Expiry of Phase-One Deal as Beijing, Washington Remain Silent." *South China Morning Post*, January 5. https://www.scmp.com/economy/china-economy/article/3162111/us-china-relations-beijing-washington-reach-trade-talk?-module=lead_hero_story&pgtype=homepage.

Wang, Zichen. 2021. "Xi Jinping's Speech on Science & Tech on May 28, 2021." *Pekingnology*, June 8. https://pekingnology.substack.com/p/xi-jinpings-speech-on-science-and.

Warburton, Moira, and Sarah Berman. 2021. "Defense Tells Canada Court That Huawei CFO's Arrest Was Legal, but Not Her Detainment." *Reuters*, March 31. https://www.reuters.com/article/us-usa-huawei-tech-canada-idINKBN2BN3MD.

Watts, Michael. 1983. *Silent Violence: Food, Famine, and Peasantry in Northern Nigeria.* Athens: University of Georgia Press. Reprinted 2013.

———. 2015. "Now and Then: The Origins of Political Ecology and the Rebirth of Adaptation as a Form of Thought." In *The Routledge Handbook of Polit-*

ical Ecology, edited by Tom Perreault, Gavin Bridge, and James McCarthy, 19–50. London: Routledge.

Weber, Isabella M. 2021. *How China Escaped Shock Therapy: The Market Reform Debate*. London: Routledge.

Wells, Callista. 2021. "China's Civilian Army: The Making of Wolf Warrior Diplomacy." *Shorenstein APARC News*, November 30. https://aparc.fsi.stanford.edu/news/chinas-civilian-army-making-wolf-warrior-diplomacy.

West, Paige. 2012. *From Modern Production to Imagined Primitive: The Social World of Coffee from Papua New Guinea*. Durham, NC: Duke University Press.

Wilderson, Frank B., Saidiya Hartman, Steve Martinot, Jared Sexton, and Hortense J. Spillers. 2017. *Afro-Pessimism: An Introduction*. Minneapolis, MN: Racked & Dispatched. https://rackedanddispatched.noblogs.org/files/2017/01/Afro-pessimism2_imposed.pdf.

Williams, Eric Eustace. 2021. *Capitalism and Slavery*. 3rd ed. Chapel Hill: University of North Carolina Press.

Wilson, Japhy. 2014. *Jeffrey Sachs: The Strange Case of Dr. Shock and Mr. Aid*. London: Verso.

Wintour, Patrick. 2021a. "Canada, China and US Were All Doomed to Lose in Meng Wanzhou's Case." *Guardian*, September 24. https://www.theguardian.com/technology/2021/sep/24/meng-wanzhou-canada-china-us-settlement-analysis.

———. 2021b. "G7 Backs Biden Infrastructure Plan to Rival China's Belt and Road Initiative." *Guardian*, June 12. https://www.theguardian.com/world/2021/jun/12/g7-global-infrastructure-plan-to-rival-chinas-belt-and-road-initiative.

Wolf, Eric. 1972. "Ownership and Political Ecology." *Anthropological Quarterly* 45 (3): 201–5.

Wolff, Jonas. 2019. "The Political Economy of Post-Neoliberalism in Bolivia: Policies, Elites, and the MAS Government." *European Review of Latin American and Caribbean Studies*, no. 108 (December): 109–29.

World Bank. 1993. *The East Asian Miracle: Economic Growth and Public Policy*. New York: Oxford University Press.

———. 2020. *Gross Domestic Product 2020*. https://databank.worldbank.org/data/download/GDP.pdf.

———. N.d. *The World Bank in China*. October 12, 2021. https://www.worldbank.org/en/country/china/overview#1.

World Bank, World Trade Organization. 2020. *The Role of Trade in Promoting Gender Equality*. Libro. Washington, DC: World Bank.

Worldwatch. 2013. "The State of Consumption Today." Washington, DC: Worldwatch Institute. http://www.adorngeo.com/uploads/2/7/3/5/27350967/the_state_of_consumption_today.pdf.

Wright, Melissa. 2013. *Disposable Women and Other Myths of Global Capitalism*. London: Routledge.

WTO (World Trade Organization). 2011. *World Trade Report 2011: The WTO and Preferential Trade Agreements: From Co-existence to Coherence*. World Trade Organization (Geneva). http://www.wto.org.

———. 2017. *World Trade Report 2017: Trade, Technology, and Jobs*. World Trade Organization (Geneva). http://www.wto.org.

———. 2018. *World Trade Report 2018: The Future of World Trade: How Digital Technologies are Transforming Global Commerce*. World Trade Organization (Geneva). http://www.wto.org.

Xi, Jinping. 2021a. "Full Text of Xi Jinping's Speech on the CCP's 100th Anniversary." *Nikkei Asia*, July 1. https://asia.nikkei.com/Politics/Full-text-of-Xi-Jinping-s-speech-on-the-CCP-s-100th-anniversary.

———. 2021b. "Xi Jinping's Full Speech at the U.N.'s 76th General Assembly." September 22. https://asia.nikkei.com/Politics/International-relations/Xi-Jinping-s-full-speech-at-the-U.N.-s-76th-General-Assembly2.

Yahoo Finance. 2022. "US-China Tech War: Beijing Unveils Grand Plan to Grow Digital Economy as US Moves Forward with Competition Bill." January 13. https://finance.yahoo.com/news/us-china-tech-war-beijing-093000693.html.

Yang, Yao. 2020. "China's Bold New Five-Year Plan." *East Asia Forum*, December 13. https://www.eastasiaforum.org/2020/12/13/chinas-bold-new-five-year-plan/.

Yang, Ziman, and Yu Zhang. 2016. "Experts Welcome Hesteel's Serbian Steel Buy." *China Daily*, April 20. http://www.chinadaily.com.cn/business/2016-04/20/content_24685288.htm.

Zhang, Kevin, ed. 2006. *China as the World Factory*. London: Routledge. https://doi.org/10.4324/9780203799529.

Zhu, Zhiqun. 2020. "Interpreting China's 'Wolf-Warrior Diplomacy.'" *Diplomat*, May 15. https://thediplomat.com/2020/05/interpreting-chinas-wolf-warrior-diplomacy/.

Žižek, Slavoj. 1989. *The Sublime Object of Ideology*. London: Verso.

———. 1997. "Multiculturalism, or, the Cultural Logic of Multinational Capitalism." *New Left Review* 225 (1): 28–51.

———. 2006. *The Parallax View*. Cambridge, MA: MIT Press.

———. 2008. *In Defense of Lost Causes*. London: Verso.

———. 2009. *First as Tragedy, Then as Farce*. London: Verso.

———. 2011. *Living in the End Times*. London: Verso.

———. 2012. *Less Than Nothing: Hegel and the Shadow of Dialectical Materialism*. London: Verso.

———. 2014. *Absolute Recoil: Towards a New Foundation of Dialectical Materialism*. London: Verso.

———. 2015. "The Need to Traverse the Fantasy." *In These Times*, December 28.

———. 2016. *Refugees, Terror and Other Troubles with the Neighbors: Against the Double Blackmail*. London: Penguin.

———. 2019. "Morales Proved in Bolivia that Democratic Socialism Can Work—but the People Cannot Be Ignored." *Independent*, November 19. https://www.independent.co.uk/voices/bolivia-protests-coup-evo-morales-socialism-election-religion-a9208871.html.

———. 2020. *Sex and the Failed Absolute*. London: Bloomsbury Academic.

———. 2021. "Corruption for Everybody! What the Wallstreetbets Story Tells Us." *Spectator*, February 1. https://spectatorworld.com/topic/corruption-for-everybody-slavoj-zizek-wallstreetbets/.

Zupančič, Alenka. 2017. *What Is Sex?* Cambridge, MA: MIT Press.

Zvogbo, Kelebogile, and Meredith Loken. 2020. "Why Race Matters in International Relations." *Foreign Policy*, June 19. https://foreignpolicy.com/2020/06/19/why-race-matters-international-relations-ir.

Index

www.ingramcontent.com/pod-product-compliance
Lightning Source LLC
Chambersburg PA
CBHW020351270326
41926CB00007B/382